GENDER PERSPECTIVES IN COMPUTING

GENDER PERSPECTIVES IN COMPUTING
An Anthology

M. Suriya, S. Balakrishnan

KALPAZ

Gender Perspectives in Computing : An Anthology

ISBN: 978-81-7835-925-0

Published in 2012 in India by
Kalpaz Publications
C-30, Satyawati Nagar,
Delhi-110052
E-mail: kalpaz@hotmail.com
Phone : 9212729499

Laser Typesetting : Quick Media, Delhi
Printed at : G. Print Process,Delhi

Contents

Preface

The book entitled "Gender Perspectives in Computing: An Anthology" is compilation of research papers contributed by Dr. Suriya and her associates from India, Germany, Australia and UK. Dr. Suriya, during the last three decades, has been engaging to analyse the gender and ICT as well as explaining the causes and consequences of under representation of women in IT. In addition, her contribution on the Bibliometric analysis of the research publications of women gives greater insights in understanding not only the research issues but also the structure of the discipline on gender in informatics.

The book contains twenty three research papers in the field of Gender in Information Technology which have been classified into three sections. The first section contains seven papers which deals with "women in IT education." The specific issues discussed in these papers are Participation of Women in IT around the various countries at global level, Status of Women's Representation in Computing Work, Women's Participation in Computer Science Education and IT Related Professions, Factors Influencing Women's Participation in Computing and so on.

The first two papers given in Section II deal with integration and application of ICT in various sectors that have gained momentum in India in the last two decades. The issues related to the demand and increasing job opportunities for women in IT and ITES sectors, government departments, and in the community information centres are also discussed in some of the research papers. The pieces of research work come with the conclution that India has witnessed a shift from depending upon the so-called male-centric formal employment to women-centric informal employment. Further, Employment and Career Prospects of Gender Groups, Educational Attainment Needs for the BPO Sectors, Web Design and Call Centres have also been assessed in a paper included in the second section. The most significant features relating to the women empowerment viz., Gender Democracy, Gender-Based Differences in Information Technology are also the focused area in research papers contributed by Dr. Suriya.

The six papers contained in section III deal with the assessment of the evolutionary perspective of 'Gender in IT', Knowledge management system. The analytical works relating to mapping of the publications using Bibliometric analysis and Co-word analysis is expected to add knowledge in the field of Information sciences.

Thus, the works have focused on greater articulation of the theory and empirical testing of women in IT professions both at the national and international levels. The findings on the causes of under representation of women in IT fields, the gender issues prevailing in the career development of the IT professionals, obstacles on the involvement of women in IT sector will be of policy relevance. Further attempts to identify increasing job opportunities in BPO Industry, Software-Export Service, Web Design and Call Centres, Medical Transcription Service, Back-Office Functions gives insights from the perspective of women empowerment.

Dr. B. Mathavan
Associate Professor in Economics
Annamalai University
Chidambaram, Tamil Nadu

SECTION I

GENDER ISSUES IN COMPUTING: INTERNATIONAL PERSPECTIVE

1
Career Development of IT Professionals

Equal opportunity recommendations, moreover, ask women to exchange major aspects of their gender identity for a masculine version without prescribing a similar de-gender process for men.

Each period of technological change carries with it high expectations of societal and organisational restructuring that favours the disadvantaged. This holds true for information and communication technologies too. Embedded in the post-Fordist mode of production organisation, it is presumed that IT will create new windows of opportunities and accelerate social mobility for new entrants like women, in an institutional framework that is not as, yet, shaped by traditional power relations. Reforms in the social and economic sector have so propitiated that, IT is one of the best-equal opportunity areas 'that provide wider opportunities for women to enter and succeed in this industry'. Nevertheless, the validity of these claims is yet to be established through empirical analysis. For such a transition in attitudes towards gender to take place, certain prerequisites have to be met. First, there should be an adequate proportion of technically trained female labour force. Second, for the permeation of an alternate gender culture, there needs to be a process of de-learning and re-learning from the new work environment for both men and women (Haraway, 1997; Cockburn and Ormond, 1993). In essence, the family life of a woman and her professional commitments adapt to one another. Even as early as the 1980's, research that centred on the effect of new technologies on women's jobs spawned a whole body of literature developing which explores the relationship between women and technology. Of all the approaches, the following two are widely followed and revered (Henwood, 1993).

Women in technology approach focuses on the 'exclusion of females from computer work, with change expected to come about via equal access to education and employment.

Women and technology approach explore 'the nature of technological work, its development over time and its articulation with changing gender relations'.

Women in technology approach simply tries to involve more women. Whereas the second approach has a broader focus on the nature of technological work. These different approaches have also been identified in the literature on women and science (Wajcman 1993). Wajcman and others, (Fox-Kellar 1986, Grundy 1994) suggested that women in technology approach have limited potential; assuming, as it does, that given the right encouragement and opportunities girls will gladly become scientists, computing professionals or engineers and engage in the present work practices in these fields. This approach locates the problem in women (their socialisation, their aspirations and values), but does not ask the broader questions of whether and in what way science and its institutions could be reshaped to accommodate women. The equal opportunity recommendations, moreover, ask women to exchange major aspects of their gender identity for a masculine version without prescribing a similar 'de-gender' process for men (Wajcman 1993).

Henwood (1993) also advocates a wariness of the 'add women and stir' approach and argues for frameworks, which address the many ways in which technology and gender interact. Henwood suggests that access to skills is not enough to secure a permanent place for women in the technological workplace and that the source of the inequality needs to be addressed (1993). Battel (1994), on the other hand, does not deny the relevance of this argument but adopts a more pragmatic view point; the difficulties surrounding women and technology involve wider social questions than computer courses alone can hope to solve. Therefore, the means, the know-how to 'break through the barriers which make the computer as a machine meaningless' to women, must be made available to them. Grundy (1994) acknowledges that despite the superficiality of the add-more-women approach, it must nevertheless, be implemented, as it is a precondition to the 'emasculation' of computing.

Women and technology looks into the gender segregation of skills and jobs and the gender sensitivity of the organisation in particular. It aims to alter the masculine practices of these occupations so that women could enter into such work without any loss of identity or integrity (Grundy, 1994). Women should not be required to 'play the game' or accept working conditions such as ten hour days, frequent weekend work or travel, in order to fit into the computer culture (Dain 1991). Wajcman (1990) advocates that what is needed is a transformation in the nature of paid and unpaid work, as well as looking at the impact women can have on technology and technology on women. Drawing from this approach, the following parameters have been used to analyse the gender regime in the IT sector of the sample nations-proportion of women across the various IT occupations/sectors, working conditions, practical gender needs of women, learning and career paths. The actual situation can be evaluated from the published literature available on this theme from some American, Asian-Pacific and European countries.

GLOBAL PARTICIPATION OF WOMEN IN IT: 'ADD WOMEN AND STIR'

North and Latin American Countries

United States

A chronological analysis of gender dimension in IT industries in the USA can be broadly grouped into three different phases: viz., first (1970-1989); second (1990-1998) and third periods (1999-2002). This classification of the time period is derived on the basis of the rate of publications on women issues in computing in the last three decades.

During the initial period less than 20% of women participated in the IT labour force and out of these, a high majority of them were clustered in the lower hierarchy of the IT occupations. According to a Computer-world survey (1974), women represented 99% of key-punchers and between 13 to 20% of business system analysts and programmers. A decade later, this position had changed marginally. The representation of women across different specialities during the 80's was in the order of 92% data-entry operators and 59% computer operators, which clearly indicated that the trend towards women's status in the IT-based jobs had not improved but remained identical to that of the situation in 1970's (Strober and Arnold, 1987).

The Task Force on Recruiting Under-represented Groups (1998) reported that women constituted only 25% of the IT work force during the second period (1990-1998) and that women remained under-represented in most IT occupations. In spite of the encouragement from the government and the various computer-based organisations, women made up only 30% of computer scientists, 32% of system analysts, 35% of computer programmers, 10% of IS directors, 18% of project leaders and 14% of application development managers (Frenkal, 1990). Though it was a significant improvement over earlier periods, still women's position in the higher echelons of the professions appeared limited (Donato, 1990; Wright & Jacob, 1995; Computer-world Salary Survey, 1995).

This situation correlates closely with the gender situation in computing education in the US during the last three decades. It is reported that the number of men earning degrees in computer and information sciences far outstripped those earned by women throughout the 1970's, 1980's and early 1990's. Men gained 86.5% of American BA degrees in computing in the period 1971-72, giving them a near monopolistic hold over the field of work. By 1981-82, women were contesting this strong-hold by increasing their share of computer science BA's to 35%. However, expectations that this 20% growth signalled that the tide was irrevocably turning against male domination was floundered soon. By 1991-92, the proportion of women earning degrees in this field had once again fallen to 28.7%; and this figure was still falling into 1992-93 (US Department of Education, 1994; Woodfield, R, 2000).

Despite many initiatives by organisations, women have not yet achieved parity, especially in senior level positions (Candee, 1997). It is observed that the following have contributed for women's lower representation in the IT industry, namely, (i) masculine and technical connotations attached with computing, (ii) gender socialisation with technology; (iii) male dominated structure and culture of employment within the industry; (iv) employer's hiring strategies; (v) women's reluctance to participate in IT education, and many others.

However, one could notice a trend towards closing down of gender segregation in IT occupations in the second phase (Table 1). It is interesting to note that women's representation in positions of power and responsibility are also increasing though slowly, their presence in the lower-level positions are shrinking over the years. Wright and Jacob (1995) also have pointed out that the degree of sex segregation across computer specialities, as measured by the index of dissimilarity declined over the periods. This is calculated for four specialities (such as computer programmers, operation system researchers and analysts, computer systems analysts and other specialities and electrical and electronic engineers) by using the data obtained from U.S. Bureau of Labour Statistics. The gheottisation thesis is not found to be relevant in the case of women's position in the IT labour market in the US and there seems to be closing down of gender gap in the occupational hierarchy.

Table 1 : Representation of Women in the organisational hierachy in IT Sector

Job Categories	*1970*	*1980*	*1990*	*1995*
Computer Scientists & Systems Analsis	15%	22%	34%	39%
Programmers	23%	31%	36%	39.7%
Computer Operators	29%	59%	66%	40.9%
Data Entry Clerks	90%	92%	87%	60.4%

Source: (i) Computerworld 1974, 1995 Survey , Bureau of Labour Studies U.S. Dept. of Labour (ii) Honwood File (1993)

As for the end of the period between 1999-2002, 1999 saw women represented 28 percent of the total IT work force (Steinbach, 2002) and then subsequently, in 2001, 20% of computer programmers and computer specialists (US Dept. of Labour, Women's Bureau, 2002), 27.4% of computer systems analysts and scientists and 10.4% of engineers were women. Clearly, women have not yet been equally recruited nor have they found gender equity among the top IT occupations. In order to improve the IT labour market potential of the country, the US government has made various recommendations, including encouraging the participation of under represented groups (Engineering Workforce Committee, IEEE-USA, 2000). It is estimated that computer and data processing services will be the fastest growing industry in the US economy, with employment expected to increase 86 percent between 2000 and 2010. Computer specialists account for almost half of all employees in this industry. Therefore, several national projects have been developed by the Women's Bureau to address the high technology initiative for women.

As far as the roadblocks to women's entry into the IT related fields are concerned, women's preference for non-scientific and non-technical subjects is cited as one of the major reasons. It is said that many of the women who have made their in-roads into high-tech industries studied computers, mathematics, engineering, or other science and technology disciplines as undergraduate students. For example, in 1996, men were three times more likely to choose computer science as a field of study than women.

Table 2 : Educational Requirements and numbers of operational, development and computing staff

Job Category	*Education*	*Total*	*Female*	*Female%*	*Male*
Firm Alpha					
Data entry	I	780	447	57	533
Data preparation	I	904	492	54	412
Production control technician	II	115	61	53	54
Teleprocessor Operator	II	19	6	32	13
Computer operator	II	238	69	37	149
Production analyst	III	59	15	25	44
Computer programmer	II/III	148	47	32	101
Application analyst	III	375	100	27	275
System analyst	III	65	10	15	55
Sub-total		2,703	1,267	47	1,436
Firm Beta					
Data entry	I	6	2	33	4
Computer operator	II	38	1	3	37
Computer programmer	II	92	11	12	81
EDP analyst	III	358	67	19	291
Sub-total		494	81	15	413
Firm Gamma					
Data entry	I	307	193	63	114
Data preparation	I	271	126	46	145
Production control technician	II	75	31	41	45
Computer operator	II	105	19	18	85
Production analyst	III	26	2	8	24
Prodution analyst	III	26	2	8	24
EDP documents	II	28	17	61	11
Computer programmer	II	55	19	35	36
O & M organizations and methods analyst	III	165	54	33	111
EDP analyst	III	133	30	23	103
Sub-total		1,166	491	42	675
Total		4,303	1,792	42	2,511

Source: Elaborated from data supplied in 1982 by firms ALPHA, BETA and GAMMA NB Level I Represents the first 8 years of general education (ages 7-15). Level II In the next 3 years of education (ages16-18). Level III Refers to tertary graduates In the case of the firm Gamma, the composition of computing staff in the total labour force is about 69% and they undertake electronic data processing and data preparation work.Out of these, women account for 47% of the EDP jobs and 53% of the operational jobs.

This parallels women's participation in other technology-related disciplines. Overall, women earn about 1 of every 6 bachelor level degrees awarded in engineering- the gateway to many technical careers in the United States economy. The information technology work force convocation has highlighted some of the barriers, that blocked women, which include (i) less encouragement to enter technical education and careers due to a lack of role models in the technical professions in school, at home, in post-secondary education, in the work force, and among high-tech business owners and executives; (ii) image of the IT profession; (iii) learning styles; (iv) lack of networks among peer groups; (v) glass ceiling; (vi) employers bias in hiring policies, etc. (Carens, 1998).

A study conducted by the Carnegie Mellon University in the United States indicates that early exposure to science and technology could change women's perceptions of IT programmes.

Brazil

Brazil is one of the few countries in the developing economies where the growth in the software sector has boosted the IT labour market. Contrary to the expectations that this sector, due to its dynamic and multidimensional development, would open up new possibilities for women to move across the various occupational hierarchies, it has resulted in constructing and maintaining gender differences and in creating male hierarchies. For instance, case studies conducted by Soares (1989) showed that women accounted for a major share of employment only in jobs related to data entry. In the largest firm studied, around 60 per cent of the data entry and data preparation staff were women. In another firm, women were responsible for 40 per cent of total computing jobs, but while 87 per cent of data entry employees were females, only 37 per cent of programmers and analysts were women. These findings appear to support the broad scenario outlined by Cockburn (1985), that the generation and diffusion of information technologies has not substantially altered the traditional pattern of work. Another case study (Fatima Janine Gaio, 1990) has been conducted to examine the employment pattern of women in software firms (Table 2) in the mid 1990's. This study has tried to find the concentration of women in two major work activities; operational work and developmental work. It is observed that both the firms taken for analysis (Alpha & Gamma) seemed to have employed large numbers of workers at the operational level of data processing, and women account for a significant share of these jobs. The Alpha firm employed around 54% (N=2703) of computing staff in its total workforce.

Out of these 78% (N=2115) are employed at the operational level. About 52% of these jobs (N=1100) at this level are held by women, representing around 79% of the total computing staff. In other words, women's share in firm Alpha is found to be higher at the base of the operational pyramid, viz. data entry and data preparation and production control technicians. The same firm employed 148 programmers, 375 application analysts and 65 system analysts to carry out the software development work.

Women accounted for 32% in the development work and they are distributed in the order of 27% in the categories of application analysts and 15% in system analysts. Table 2 illustrates the work pattern of male and female computer workers in the firm Alpha, Gamma and Beta.

Europe

An examination of women's position in the IT labour market in the European countries would be more meaningful, if they are analysed on the light of women's status in IT education at the tertiary level. Figure 1 presents the proportion of women students in mathematics and computer science courses in the European Union (EU) member states. It is observed that there exists a marked difference among the member countries with respect to women's education in IT oriented disciplines. While the Netherlands, Belgium and Finland have less than 20% of female students in these academic disciplines, in Portugal, Italy and Sweden more than 30% of the students are female.

Nevertheless, this picture cannot give a clear idea of the enrolment of women in computer science, since in some countries, like in Germany the proportion of women studying mathematics is much larger than those studying computer science, (Statistisches Bundesamt - Hochschulstatistik 2001). In Germany, several initiatives, both from the state as well as from private companies like IBM, encourage girls to study computer science and retain them during their study years in this still predominantly masculine field. Though, there is an increase in the enrolment of women in computer science studies in the last years, it has reached only up to 15% of the total computer science students in German universities. In polytechnics, this percentage is down to 13% (Statistisches Bundesamt 2001).

According to a recent study in Sweden (Swedish Ministry of Industry, Employment and Communications, 2000) 28% of the graduates from IT courses are female. The Norwegian University of Science and Technology has introduced a special quota system for women in computer science studies in 1997. The results of this project have been very positive: in the first two years, the percentage of female students increased to more than 30% (OECD 2002).

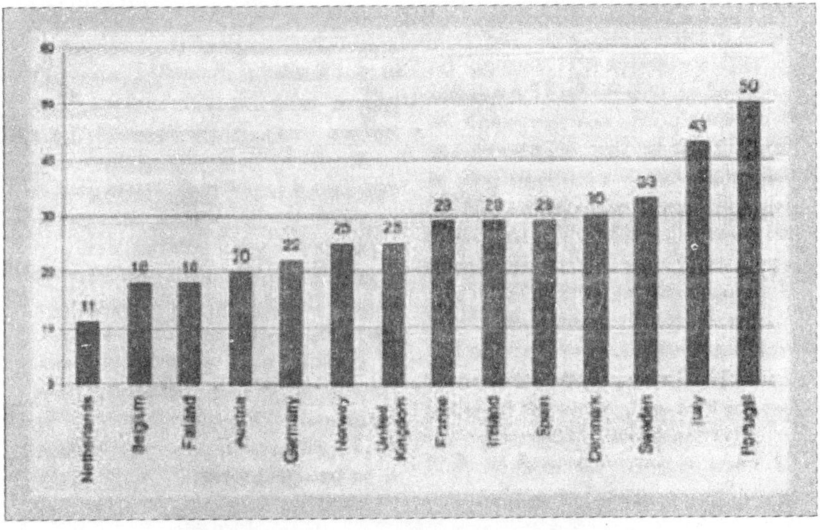

Fig. 1. Proportion of European female students in Mathematics and Computer Science

United Kingdom

The software industry is the fastest growing sector in the UK (Panteli 1997), nevertheless, women remain starkly under represented in all sectors of the computing industry. Though there has been an increase in the number of women entering IT occupations since the seventies, gender equity has not been achieved in this industry in the whole of the EU. To gain a broad idea of the IT labour force in its complexity, we have to consider two important aspects. Not every worker in this sector is performing IT related tasks, since marketing, sales or other service tasks are related to this field. On the other hand, many IT workers are occupied in sectors that are not strictly related to IT production, like business or financial service sectors (OECD 2002). This difficulty to cope with the IT sector as a whole is an added obstruct to the lack of data available about women joining the IT labour force. An analysis of national statistics (IDPM Report, 1996) reveals that the proportion of women has fallen since the 1980's from 25 per cent to 19 per cent in 1993 and in 1996 it is between 21 to 22 per cent. Fig. 2 illustrates the status of women in the various IT related occupations in the UK during 1995 (Panteli, 97). The proportion of women is higher in consumer services (27%), followed by programming (22%) and system analysts (21%) whereas they represent a very low proportion in the management positions of the IT labour force (10% or less). Regarding the changing trends from 1994 to 1995, it was observed (see Fig. 3) that the proportion of women employed as IT operators and programmers and customer services showed a decreasing trend while their position in IT management, system analysis and technical support showed an increasing trend during the study period. The possible reasons for the fluctuations in the trend of women's participation in the IT labour market may be traced to their numbers in computing education over the last three decades. It is noted that women's entrance to the computer courses fell from 24% in 1978 to 22 % in 1981 and then to 10% in 1985.

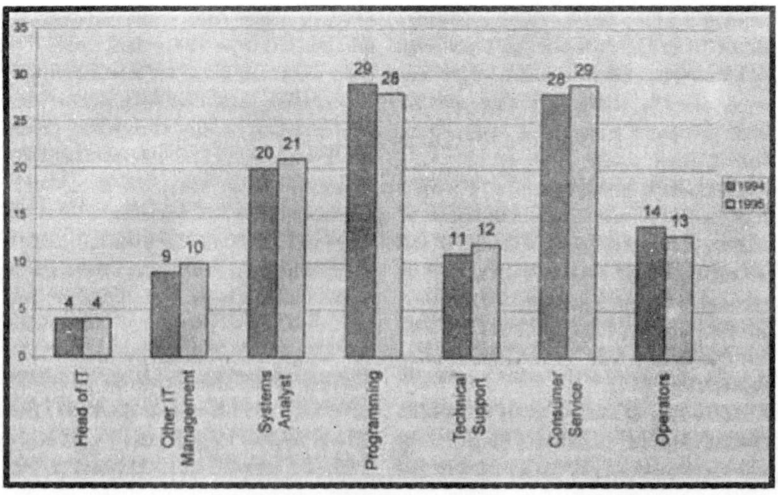

Fig. 2. UK Women in IT

Since the mid-eighties, the proportion of women started stabilising and in the year 2000, it is ranging between 20% to 25% of the total enrolment in computing, both in the universities and polytechnics (Ruth, 2000). Connor et al (2001), also has cited the fluctuating trend in the percentage of female computer science graduates –21 percent in 1998/1999 as compared with 22 percent in 1994-1997 (Millar and Jagger, 2001).

Women's substantial under representation in the core ICT science and engineering curricula in education systems, means that they are excluded from core ICT occupations. To increase the number of women in the IT education and training tracks, computers and the Internet should be integrated early into school curricula to encourage girls to pursue science and mathematics courses. Greater awareness of how ICT skills could lead to a wider range of careers for women will attract them into the ICT field. It is to be noted that gender digital divide is not consistent across Europe. While the UK has one of the lowest proportions of female university students in maths and computer science courses, female enrolment in Italy and Spain at university-level in these subjects is far greater, and women comprise around 50% of their ICT workforces.

The Netherlands

The studies by Tijdens (1991, 1994, 1997), and Hoek et al (1989) explained that women occupied a very low proportion in the EDP jobs, and this occurred when there has been a strong demand for the IT professionals. A chronological analysis also reveals that women's share in the IT labour market has decreased constantly over the period of time from 9.4% in 1976 to 6.1% in 1986, a decrease of no less than 35%. In addition to their quantitative under-representation, they occupy predominantly the lower segmentation of the job categories (table 3). In majority of the organisations, men occupy back end technical jobs while women occupy the processing and administrative jobs. Moreover, women end up in the so-called 'dead-end' functions and men in what is called the 'growth' functions. The authors have identified that employer's preference for male employees is the primary cause for the lower proportion of women apart from the gender socialisation practices. In addition to this, the percentage of women attending computer courses at a university or polytechnic level is very low (about 10-11%). The disparity or occupational inequality between men and women could be identified from the national statistics. However, in 1993, the percentage of females had grown to 8.9% among systems analysts and to 13.0% among programmers. Because of the fast changes in the IT labour markets, it is presumed that the gender segregation in the IT occupation will also change slowly.

Table 3 : Gender segregation in computing occupations in the Netherlands

Job category	*Men (%)*	*Women (%)*
Systems Analysis	94.8	5.2
Programmers	91.7	8.3
Data Typists	5.7	94.3
Operators	85.7	14.1

Source: National Bureau of Statistics. The Hague 1963.

Asia and Pacific Region

Australia

Very few desegregated data are available in Australia to show the number of men and women in decision-making positions in computing. From the 1992-93 statistic it is noted that the proportion of men-working at the higher-paid end of the computer services industry (as proprietors or directors and computing technical staff), is considerably higher than that for women. In contrast, the proportion of women engaged in lower-paid, non-technical work was considerably higher than the proportion of men. For instance, the proportion of men working in computer maintenance services (75%), computer consultancy service (67%) is higher than that of women, whereas women are predominantly higher in the data processing services and information storage and retrieval services (80%). The proportion of women are considerably higher in the part-time jobs also (28% women and 6% men in cc mputer service industry and over 56% in data processing services). It is reported that the existence of a 'glass ceiling' in the IT firms is limiting women's career progression (http://www.osw.dpmc.gov.au/content/publications/stimulat.html).

India

The technology revolution is changing the gender calculus in India, one of the world's most traditional societies (Chen, May

Yee, 2000). Women find new independence. Women play a larger part in the expansion of software market in India and they constitute 45% of the high tech work force. Women account for 50% in the engineering colleges as well as in the software training sectors. In the organisational hierarchy, more women have occupied the responsible and high-profile positions but a few have climbed all the way up. The number of women executives has multiplied in the last few years (Kishori Gopal Krishnan, 2000).

The Indian software industry is growing in three different directions viz: (i) industries involved in product development; (ii) offshore software services ; and (iii) on-site maintenance and implementation services. Based on the size of the employees, the IT companies are classified as high, middle, low-end companies.

The software sector in India has created a tremendous amount of new forms of work of different qualities. It is estimated that the future prospects of employment in the software sector amounts to 2 million jobs in software production and another 2.2 million jobs in IT-enabled services by the year 2008 (NASSCOM, 2000).

Though IT sector has offered equal employment opportunities to the gender groups, differences are noticed in the types of activity that men and women software professionals specialise in (table 4). Surveys among the software professionals showed that a high concentration of men exists in export software firms, while women are present in higher proportion in domestic low-end and IT-enabled services. This implies that at the entry level itself there is a marked gender differential in access to employment in this sector.

In addition, during personal discussions, both men and women indicated that due to domestic responsibilities, a few women were unable to cope with the work intensity in high-end activities. The interviews reported that IT-enabled services provide shift-based work, which women prefer. An age-wise distribution of the gender groups reveals that IT industry is dominated by men and women in their twenties. Especially, the middle-end, domestic low-end and IT enabled firms seem to be more dependent on persons in their early twenties.

The high-end firms deviate slightly from this norm, indicating a possible greater presence of experienced professionals.

The sex-wise distribution of professionals across age also substantiates the above observation that the distribution is clustered in the first two-age cohorts, i.e. below 25 and 26-30. Among the sampled women professionals, a majority is below 30 category. And, if we exclude the women employees in IT enabled services (ITES), we could find a greater reduction in the number of women employees in the upper age groups. A possible inference is that women are less represented in middle and upper positions.

Table 4 : Distribution of IT professionals (per cent)

Sex-wise distribution of professionals in different firm types						
Gender	*High End*	*Middle End*	*Export End*	*Domestic Low-end*	*IT-Enabled*	*Total*
Male	39.6	9.4	35.4	8.3	7.3	100
Female	21.3	17.0	27.7	12.8	21.3	100
Age distribution of professionals by firm types						
Firm Types	*–25*	*26-30*	*31-35*	*36-40*	*41+*	*Total*
High-End	20.8	39.6	25.0	10.4	4.2	100
Middle-End	58.8	35.3	5.9	0	0	100
Export-Low End	44.7	38.3	8.5	0		100
Domestic Low End	57.1	42.9	0	0	6.4	100
IT enabled	53.0	23.5	17.6	0	0	100
Total	41.6	37.1	14	3.5	5.9	100
Sex-wise distribution of professionals across age-groups						
Gender	*–25*	*26-30*	*31-35*	*36-40*	*41+*	*Total*
Male	36.5	35.4	19.8	3.1	5.2	100
Female	48.9	40.4	2.1	4.3	4.3	100
Total	41.6	37.1	14	3.5	4.2	100

Sex-wise distribution of professionals by locality				
Gender	*Metropolitan*	*Urban*	*Semi-urban*	*Rural*
Male	40.6	44.8	8.3	6.3
Female	51.1	40.4	8.5	0.0
Total	44.1	43.4	8.4	

The locational origins of employees reveals the absence of 'rural brains' in the industry. Survey reports indicated that the IT industry is urban-based and it favours socially and economically favoured groups. The 'ruralities' have the least access to this upcoming industry. Moreover, the English-speaking criterion applicable across the range of activities is an immediate disadvantage for rural aspirant. This exclusiveness becomes even more evident in the case of women professionals wherein a majority of them belong to metropolitan cities and none came from the rural districts.

The IT Taskforce survey (Suriya, 1998) reported that both men and women in the software sector have shared equal qualification and experience and there seems to be equality of opportunities for women in the IT labour market. Most of the companies believe that women are intellectually on par with men and they are sincere and loyal.

The leading multinational companies, such as, the IBM, tries to bring in more women into IT and encourages them with creches for their small ones, flexible working hours, part-time jobs and at times working from home facility. The economic independence and new social status offered by this profession attracts majority of the women to take up carriers in computing. In a country where arranged marriages are standard and brides are occasionally even killed for insufficient dowries, the software boom is offering new liberties to a small but influential group of women. These women from programmers to project managers at top companies are deciding if and when they want to marry and whether they want to have children. And they are commanding unusual respect from family members, who grant them 'male' privileges from household and a say in household finances. There is a greater awareness amongst the families to give the equal education and career opportunities to both sons and daughters. Though there are arguments in favour of women in the IT sector, the survey reports indicated that women professionals are still a minority in this sector in India with a clear trend towards clustering at the lower ends of the job hierarchy leading to feminisation of certain service activities. Issues related to mobility and growth of women professionals are caught up in the gender trap as in other service sectors or in traditional sectors. The trade off for women who opt for a career vis-à-vis the gender roles ascribed to them as care givers in the absence of adequate social security measures and other support mechanisms leaves women professionals with an 'either-or' situation.

It is observed that the IT industry's attitude is one of benign statistical discrimination of women by accepting the gender constraints of women. Sectors wherein women's work participation is relatively high, there is a provision for crèches. Hence, if the IT policy claims of a gender-neutral sector are to come true, it is imperative to first address the practical needs of women professionals (ILO, 2001).

Malaysia

It is interesting to note that almost 60% of the women are employed in the software industries of Malaysia. Women's share in the direct high-skilled jobs increased from 42% in 1985 to 45% in 1990, reflecting healthy inroads made by women in the professional category. On the other hand, their share of the low-skilled data processing operators declined from 75% to 62% in 1990 (Cecilia Ng, 2000). However, the number of women holding top positions in the IT industry is smaller compared to their male counter parts which again may be due to the fact that IT is engineering- and technical-focused, which is traditionally a male domain. The growing participation of women in computer education is one of the factors for their higher level of entry into the IT labour market. A 1992 survey of seven of the principal private schools and colleges showed an increasing number of students enrolling in computer courses or related subjects. Between 1987 and 1992, 957 males and 1,207 females graduated in computer packages and software programmes, and 2,234 males and 1,637 females in computer courses or subjects. At the tertiary level, there are almost equal numbers of female and male students.

Academic programmes offered by tertiary institutions in the area of computing, informatics, information technology and related fields have grown largely because of national policies that have encouraged their development. A number of universities offer degree courses in computer science programmes. The University Uttara Malaysia has started a School of Information Technology, and the Kolej Tunku Abdul Rahman offers a diploma in computer science. There were 4,215 students in computer related courses in tertiary institutions for the 1990-1991 academic year. Female students comprised 51.4 per cent of total intake, 47.6 per cent at the degree level, 55.5 per cent at the diploma level and 29 per cent at the certificate level.

Women are becoming numerically almost as visible as men in the software sector in Malaysia. However, they are generally clustered in the low-skilled end of the hierarchy with little prospect of career progression, while male workers dominate the technical and managerial occupations.

The question is why there is such an uneven distribution of male and female employees across ICT-related occupations and what could be done to address this? The training policies in developing countries are in theory gender-neutral. In practice, however, they are less often geared to the life cycle and aspirations of men. The reasons for this paradoxical situation are plenty. One of the reasons include the lower participation of women in technical and science subjects which is reflected in their placement in low-skilled and low-status jobs in high-tech sector.

The following table (5) illustrates women's domination in the non-science and non-technical subjects in their course of studies. Sex based socialisation and stereotyping of women's education and skills training is declining, but it is still a reality today. However, it is to be noted that young women in developing countries are not as affected as U.S. women by attitudes that computer science is not an attractive field to enter. For example, women comprise between 30 and 50% of students in computer science and other natural sciences in a number of developing countries like Malaysia. The other impeding factor for women's active participation in IT sector is their family commitments.

Table 5 : Opportunities for Men and Women in CSE in Malaysia between 1987 and 1992 (private institutions)

Coureses	*Male*	*Female*
Degrees in computer package and computer programme	957	1207*
Degrees in computer courses/studies	2234	1637
Degrees in electronic courses	476	9

Source: Despite the opportunities for women in CSE in the private sector, women prefer software programs rather than competing for higher qualifications in computer studies and electronics/electrical courses.

Women, particularly of child bearing age, find it difficult to cope with the training given either by employers or by private sector institutions. The drop-out rate for women even in the high-skilled software services sector has been alarming, including areas where there is a need for trained personnel (Ng, 2001). Studies reported that women themselves settle for a less demanding position in order to have more time for their family and to maintain the overall quality of life (Arun and Arun, 2002).

CONCLUSION

A closer look at the status of women in different occupational specialties shows that despite their increased representation, women do not have equal access to thedifferent levels of occupational hierarchies. They are over-represented in some types of lower-level jobs (e.g. programmers and operators) and under-represented in higher-level jobs (i.e. project leaders and IS managers). Computing, therefore, has remained a gender segregated, male-dominated occupation.

It can be said that the high-tech industries which are looked upon as 'great equalisers' do not give adequate berth for women's occupational development nor do they necessarily produce an integrated workforce and equality of opportunities for men and women (Strober & Arnold, 1987). It is high time now to look beyond the 'add more women' approach towards the fundamental nature of technological work.

REFERENCES

- Arun, Shoba; Arun, Thankom, (2001). "ICTs, gender and development: women in software production in Kerala". *Journal of international development*, pp. 39-50.
- Battel, Roisin (1994). 'Women and Technology: A place for hardware'. Adam, Alison & Owen, Jenny (eds), Proceedings of the 5th IFIP International Conference on Women, Work and Computerisation,Breaking Old Boundaries : Building New Forms, Manchester, pp. 397-404.
- Bundesanstalt fur Arbeit, (2001). *Frauen und IT*. Zukunftsorientierte Arbeitsmarktpolitik.
- Candee, Wilde, (1997). "Women Cut through IT's Glass ceiling." Information Week, Jan 20, 1997.
- Carens, Kelly, H. (1998). "Expanding Women's Role in Science and Technology", U.S. Department of Commerce, March 26, 1998. URL: www.ta.doc.gov/speeches/techwomn. htm

- Cecilia Ng Choon Sim and Carol Yong (2000). "A case study of the telecommunications industry in Malaysia". In *Information technology, gender and employment*. www.unu.edu/unupress/unupbooks/uu37we/uu37we0k.htm
- Chen May Yee,(2000). "India's Other Tech Revolution: Women Find New Independence". *Technology Journal Asia*, October 30, 2000, http://www.calbaptist.edu/dskubik/india.htm
- Cockburn. C and Ormond. S (1993). *Gender and Technolosing in the Making*. Sage, London.
- Dain, Julia 1991. 'Women and computing: Some responses to falling numbers in higher education', *Women's Studies International Forum*, 14(3), pp. 217-225.
- Donoto, Katharine M, (1990. *Programming for Change*? The Growing Demand for Women Systems Analysts. Philadelphia, Temple University Press.
- Famulla, M.A. et al. (1992) *Personlichkeit und Computer*, Oplanden, Westdetscher, Verlag.
- Fox-Keller, Evelyn (1986). "How Gender Matters: Or, Why is it so hard for us to count past two?" Harding, Jan. *Persectives on gender and science*, Falmer Press, Sussex, pp. 168-83.
- Garcia de Cortazar, (1996). M & Garcia de Leon, M.A.., "Las Mujeres Ingenieras on Espana Sociologia de las Mujeres espanolas" Editorial Complutense, Madrid, pp. 243-65.
- Grundy, Frances, (1994). "What is to be done? A Feminist Critique of Science", *Technology and Computing*. Gates. 1(1), pp. 21-32.
- Harway, Donna, (1997). *Feminism and Techno Science*. New York / London
- Hoek, Saskia van; Rienstra, Els, (1989). Women's training centres: Alida de Jongschool, Utrecht, The Netherlands, *Strategies and Education*. Tijdens, K; Jennings, M; Wagner, I; Weggelaar.
- M,Women. "Work and Computerization: Forming New Alliances". The Netherlands, Elsevier Science Publishers B.V., Part: 3." Chap. 24.
- Henwood, Flis 1993. "Establishing Gender Perspectives on Information Technology: Problems, Issues and Opportunities." *Gendered by Design? Information Technology and Office Systems*, Green, Eileen; Owen, Jenny; Pain, Den (eds), Taylor & Francis, London, pp. 31-52.
- IDPM Report, (1996). "The End is Nigh – 1996 IT Skills Trend Report", The Institute for the Management of Information Systems, U.K.

- ILO, (2001). Labour in the New Economy: The Case of the Indian Software Labour Market, New Delhi pp. 1-70.
- Kishori Gopalkrishnan, (2000). *Women in India: Breaking the Stereotype*, www.siliconindia.com/women/career women/womeninindia.html
- *Kreinenbaum M.A. & Metz*-Gockel. S, (1992). "Koedukation und Technikkompetenz". Don Madchen, Weinneim, Juventa, Chap. 2. NORTH AMERICA. USA.
- Nasscom (2000). "NASSCOM'S IT Enabled Services 2000". September 19-20, 2000 http://www.gate4india.com/event/event_nasscomIES2000.htm
- Ng, Cecilia (ed.) (2001). *Teleworking and Development in Malaysia*, UNDP, UNU/INTECH and Southbound: Kuala Lumpur and Penang.
- Oechtering, Veronika; Behnke, Roswitha, (1995). "Situations and Advancement Measures in Germany." Communications of the ACM, Jan, 1995.
- Panteli, Androniki; Stack, Janet; Ramsay, Harvie (1997). "Gender and Professional Ethics in the IT industry", *Journal of Business Ethics*.
- Sonnentag, S, (1994). Team Leading Software Development ; a comparison between Women and Men". In Adam et al(Eds), Women, "Old boundaries building new forms. Amsterdam, Elsevier, pp : 379 – 91.
- Soares. A. Dos .S, (1989). "A Organizacao do Trabalho Informatico", MBA dissertation, Sao Paulo, PUC-S.P, Ruth Wood Field, *Women work and computing*, Cambridge University Press, London.
- Steinbach, Theresa .A Eta., (2002). "Encouraging Minority Enrolment in IT Degree programs through participatory, organization". DePaul University, Chicago, Illinois , USA.
- Strober, Myra H; Arnold, Carolyn L. (1987). *Integrated Circuits/ Segregated Labour: Women in Computer-Related Occupations and High-Tech Industries*. Publications Washington, D.C. National Academy Press,
- Suriya, (1998). "Gender Development in Information Technology with special reference to the National Informatics Centre in India (NIC)", Taskforce Survey Report
- Tijdens, Kea G, (1991). *Women in EDP Departments*. Eriksson, Inger V. ; Kitchenham, Barbara A; Tijdens, KeaG. Women, Work, Computerisation: Understanding and Overcoming Bias in Work and Proceedings of the IFIP TC9/WG 9.1 Conference, North-Holland, Amsterdam,.
- Vehvilainen, Marja, (1997). *Genders and Expertise in Retrospect: Pioneers of Computing in Finland*, Grundy, A.F; Kohler, D; Oechtering,

V; Petersen, U. Women, Work and Computerization: Spinning a Web from Past to Future". London, Springer, Topic: 6, Chap. 6.2.

- Wajcman, Judy 1990. "Women, Technology and Work', *Refractory Girl*, 35, pp. 7-10.
- Wajcman, Judy, (1993). "The masculine mystique: A feminist analysis of science and technology". Probert, Belinda & Wilson, Bruce. Pink Collar Blues - *Work, Gender and Technology*. Melbourne: Melbourne University Press, pp. 20-40.

NOTES

- Management includes directors, managers, consulting managers and assistant managers.
- Executive includes systems analysts, analyst programmers, executives, network specialists, consultants, internet technicians, engineers, project leaders, project team leaders, finance personnel and accountants.
- Non-executive is divided into two categories.
- Technical – technical writers, computer operators and conversion operators.
- Administration – administrators/ Supervisors, support co-ordinates, executive assistants, secretaries and receptionists; clerical (data entry clerks and clerical staff); and dispatch. Company A has a total of 92 full-time employees and 163 contract staffs (11 supervisors and 152 clerks).

2

Gender Issues in the Career Development of the IT Professionals : A Global Perspective

INTRODUCTION

The gender issues prevailing in the career development of the IT professionals have received wider attention in the recent years and they have been analysed from three different angles viz: (i) masculine organisational culture (Calas and Smircich 1992); (ii) inequalities in external and internal labour markets (Reskin and Roos 1990; Gallie 1996); and gendered restructuring and regeneration of the labour process in women's work. Among these issues, the masculine culture of the organisation has been viewed from two different perspectives: one is the 'organisational environment' representing (i) masculine dominance and the exercise of male power in the IT workplace; (ii) the informal organisational practices, and networks favouring male professionals; and (iii) the sex harassment and humilations. The other one is the 'occupational culture' representing (i) the symbolic significance of the technology being attached with representations of masculine power (McNeil, 1987; Linn, 1987); (ii) the structure and culture of computing work; and (iii) the career path attached with men and women's work. Similarly, the issue of gender inequality in the IT labour market has been analysed on the basis of (i) the career goals of men and women in computing industry; (ii) the rate of mobility of men and women across organisations and functional areas; (iii) the specialty required for career progression; (iv) the promotion criteria and procedures; (v) the work-home conflict and (vi) the access to training. The influence of these factors on the career advancement of women IT professionals has become the key research question during the last two decades at the global context. The third issue has been looked at from the point of view of how far the fast changing situation in the IT industry and IT labour market has affected the advancement of women during the last decade. A closer examination of these issues at the global context will reveal not only the factors that have shaped or impeded women's development in the IT career, but also the nations that have paved the way for the development of women in the IT career.

MALE DOMINANCE IN THE IT WORK ENVIRONMENT

The masculine dominance and the exercise of male power in the IT workplace have been highlighted in some of the UK-based studies . They have described about stereotyping of female and male roles, the existing ideologies relating to their respective styles and competencies. Grundy (1994) has explained the prevalence of sexism in the computing department of a District Health Authority (DHA) in the UK. She has brought to light the ways in which men dominated the work environment viz: (i) volume of speech, (ii) topics of conversation-computing and non-computing, (iii) seeking advice from colleagues, (iv) non-acceptance of women's abilities, (v) constant competitive behaviour etc. She has further highlighted the inequalities prevailing in the workplace which would discourage women to take full participation in the organisation. Bloomfield (1989) and Woodfield (1994) have remarked about the system of language that the male members in the computing work adopted to bond members (males) together and to exclude the non-members (females). This language is embedded with jargons, aggressive imageries, and terminology which are meaningful only to members. These attitudes make women feel alienated in the workspot and forced them to leave the organisation in the long run. For instance, a female system developer in Vehvlaninen's study, described herself as a 'non-entity' (literally nothing) within this world, and revealed her helplessness in defining her work in the dominant computer systems jargon adopted in the organisation (1994b: 111). Some researchers, notably Panteli et al (1997) and Ramsay et al (1997) have documented how the women subjects of their studies were not been treated properly and how they were undermined by their male supervisors. Further evidence to this male domination is noticed from the account of Webster (1996) who has reported that women found it difficult to get into the senior ranks in Silicon Valley and the very few women who achieved vice-presidential status in Microsoft were not well-received by their male colleagues. They resented deeply the incursion of women into senior posts in Microsoft. Webster has commented that throughout the computing hierarchy, women are on the alien territory, and the culture and practice of computing profession is redolent with a myriad of forms of masculinity.

Several studies have reported the inexplicable damage that this 'male culture' brought on the women's progression in the IT profession. For instance as early as 1989, Cockburn has observed that this 'culture' may sound soft and malleable but it provides a powerful mechanism for marginalising and alienating women, for forcing them to 'fail' and to withdraw from competition with men for the more skilled, interesting and well-paid occupations. Hacker (1989), for example, has hinted that women's decision to drop themselves from technical fields in their mid-career might be due to in part to a dislike of the field's culture. If this trend continues, women would further suffer from reduced opportunities within the IT industries. The study of Ramsay et al has also illustrated how the 'power' and 'authority' exerted by the male computer workers in a computing division of a college have affected the women employees. In the case study presented, the male member (Don) has sought to establish his superiority in the organisation by intervening the work of the women professionals (Maureen and Mary), proclaiming his prowess and by taking the credit (reputation and reward) for the work done by them. In another organisation, the male member (Graham) has exerted his authority as a system manager in forcing his female colleague (Maria) to change her long-booked holidays to suit him, complaining about the chatter and loud radio played by her to relive stress and tedium in the various phases of work; and freeze her out of the inter-college network project. These incidences have been shown as evidences of a strong gendering of IS work environment acting against women's career advancement. The studies of Ramsay et al (1997) and Shapiro (1994) have established that organisational culture of computing is the root cause for both the lower representation of women in positions of power and authority and also for leaving the computing environment before their tenure of service. It is thus clear that not only the computing occupation but also the nature of the computing environment that is hostile to women's development in the profession.

To meet out this problem, it is recommended that the IT industry has to provide better career opportunities in addition to establish a healthier and supportive work environment for its staff especially to women (Stacks et al 1998). Pearson et al (1997) have, therefore, concluded that the participation of the staff in the success of the IT organisation is a matter of strategic importance and as such it becomes obligatory on the part of the employers to protect the professional and non-professional requirements of their staff both men and women in order to safeguard the organisational progress.

A few US-based studies also have examined how the predominance of male-culture in the IT organisations curtail the professional activities of women and force them to leave the organisation before they complete their tenure. For instance, Candee (1997) has presented the (i) different forms in which male domination is getting expressed in an organisation and the (ii) adverse effect that it has brought on women's career development. Robin Jeffries, a senior staff engineer at Sun Microsytems and moderator of the Sun Senior Technical Women's Forum has reported that the organisational culture at Sun makes it difficult for women to excel: "Sun is a place where everybody is very vocal and the loudest is the opinion that is heard. If you're quiet in one room, you might not be heard. Women are the more likey to be the quite ones in the room." This kind of male culture forbids women from having equal participation in the organisational activities and ultimately it hampers their progress. In the same manner, Judy Bamberger, a computer consultant in Oregon has reported that many women in the industry have faced hard time in getting their voices heard and in most of the brainstorming sessions, their voices are ignored (DeBare, 1996). Especially in board meetings and discussions, men ignore those women who speak softly or politely. To make them being heard, women have to adopt the styles of communication of their male colleagues. A senior staff engineer at Sun Microsystem has admitted that she used to adopt the male culture of pounding her fist on the table to make her voice being heard and accepted the fact that it would not be practically possible for all women at the senior position to adopt this aggressive style of communication. Thus, the existing organisational climate does not allow women to behave in their own way and they are forced to get into the male-culture to make themselves visible in the organisation.

In some organisations, both in formal and informal meetings women engineers and programmers have been isolated and they never have been treated as part of the system. This kind of explicit discouragement has forced many active and intelligent young women to drop out of high-tech pipeline (DeBare, 1996). The incongenial work environment prevailing in IT can also be inferred from the statement of Emma Morris when she says: "the culture sometimes makes it harder for women to get ahead if she doesn't have her ducks in a row" (Fillon, 1997).

The other forms of male culture that alienated women from the industry have been pictured by Hemenway (1995) and Steinem (1992). They have explained that some of the masculine behaviours such as (i) remarks that devalue women; (ii) bullying; (iii) sexist jokes; (iv) locker-room-calibre-conversation; (v) a focus on male-oriented activities and widespread use of metaphors from these activities; (vi) display of images, either on walls or computer monitors, that portray women as sex objects have made women feel left out and unwelcome in the profession. The Catalyst report (1992) has further added that this sort of behaviours cause unnecessary burden for women who are already struggling to cope with the delicate process of balancing career and family, and with managing their self-images as competent females in a male-dominated culture. To avoid these struggles and pressures, many women retreated to the safer, less challenging support functions—the "female ghettos".

The studies from the USA have reported that even in organisations where male and female are treated equally, there are parts of high-tech culture that pose extra challenge for women. The study by Debare (1996) has narrated an incident in which the office party at Microsoft has turned into a 'big food fight'. Me Curdy, the software engineer and the organiser of the party felt offended when the male members have 'started shaking up the champagne and shooting at each other' and created a kind of 'frat-house' atmosphere which is found to be less comfortable for many women. The purpose of celebrating the release of the world renowned software product 'Windows 95' after working thousands of hours in the lab is defeated by these so-called 'male-culture' in the organisation.

An analysis of the organisational culture and the working conditions of the European countries also have shown the same trend. For instance, Olde (1990) has surveyed the (i) working culture and the (ii) labour conditions prevailing in four IT companies in the Netherlands and identified that these organisational factors have not contributed positively to women's

Table 2.1 : Opinions of female information technologists concerning working in IT (N=614)

Sl. No.	*Working Conditions*	*Agree*	*Neutral*	*Disagree*
1.	Working Culture			
	(i) It is a pity that so few women work in information technology	51%	37%	12%
	(ii) The culture within IT to 'work all the time' sometimes irritates me	31%	29%	40%
	(iii) The continuous pressure to 'keep up with the developments in the field' puts a heavy pressure upon this work	50%	26%	24%
2.	Labour Conditions:			
	(i) I think that the limited possibilities to work part-time restrict the possibilities of combining work and having children	55%	32%	13%
	(ii) According to me work in IT (e.g. labour conditions, working procedures and workclimate) is especially geared to the wishes of male colleagues	30%	30%	40%
	(iii) If you would interrupt working in IT for some years, e.g. to take care of your children, it will be very difficult to re-enter the profession	80%	15%	5%

career development. Majority of the female information technologists have stated that these companies have (i) shown preference for men in some vital positions (ii) generated less promotional chances for women (iii) exhibited scepticism about women's qualities and on the whole (iv) have not implemented the equal opportunities for women in this industry. The following table has illustrated the opinion of the female information technologists regarding their working environment in this organisation, while women leave their jobs quite often. The following table illustrates the entry and exit rates of the men and women working in the IS department.

Table 2.2 : Proportion of Women and Men Entering and Leaving the Female and Male Workforce at the EDP Department

Employee Changes at the EDP Dept.	*81-83*	*83-85*	*85-87*
Perc. of women entering the LF	47%	8%	70%
Perc. of women leaving the LF	0%	35%	75%
Perc. of men entering the LF	19%	27%	22%
Perc. of men leaving the LF	7%	6%	23%

This study further reveals that in terms of staff strength and average working hours, the women stand lower than that of their male colleagues. A clear picture of the representation of women in the IS department could be noticed from the following table.

Table 2.3: The strength of women and their average working hours in the EDP department

EDP DEPARTMENT	*1981*	*1983*	*1985*	*1987*	*GR*
No of employees at the department	51	65	68	65	27%
No of women at the department	9	17	12	10	11%
Women's average hours at the dept.	78%	47%	75%	90%	
Men's average hours at the dept.	98%	100%	100%	100%	

The study by Machinnon has portrayed the organisational culture of the IT industries in Australia. For many women the organisation mirrors 'male culture' and they consider it is 'a site of power struggle in which women are bound to lose'. Furthermore, sexual harassment is an ever present reality for most women in some form or another, from overt propositioning to the prevalence of sexist jokes. For many, this creates an atmosphere of acute discomfort, a feeling of being out of place. For others it means consciously denying their femininity if they are to be seen as serious workers.

Similarly, the study by Oechtering (1995) has reported the impressions of the women computer employees regarding the working conditions in the IT organisations. For instance, Heike Hengstenberg has conducted a survey among the women computer scientists and gathered their opinions on the designing of the workplace. He identified that there was a great demand for reduced and more flexible working hours but without having any negative implications on their career prospects. [9] Christine Roloff also found similar results in her investigation about the female computer scientists and chemists. He has also highlighted the extent to which the absence of support facilities like the childcare system affected the career of women. The effect of child-care system on the working life of women professionals has been emphasised by comparing the working conditions before and after the reunification of Germany. Before reunification, in the German Democratic Republic, 90% of all women (and 90% of women with children) had been employed, predominantly with full-time jobs. This was one of the highest employment rates of women in the world (the West German figure was 63% in 1990) and it was mainly the result of an extensive childcare system funded by the state. Here are some examples: 12 months parental leave (five at full pay and seven months at 80%) was granted and usually taken by women. In 1987, for children over 12 months, the childcare system guaranteed a nursery place for 81% of children aged 1-2 years and for 94% of children over the age of 3. This was available free of charge [10]. This structure is destroyed after the reunification; most of the childcare offers had been tied to enterprises and fell victim to the reunification process.

In West Germany, provisions for women with children look far poorer: there is a maximum statutory parental leave of three years with guaranteed return to work. That may sound good, but only the first few months are subsidised with 600 DM (half the German subsistence level). Creches and day-care nurseries hardly exist at all. Most of the kindergartens (for children aged 3-7) provides care only in the morning. In a few companies some measures for employees with children have been introduced, but normally these voluntary offers can be withdrawn by the employers, such as during uncertain economic times.

INFORMAL ORGANISATIONAL PRACTICES AND NETWORKS IN IT ENVIRONMENT

The work place culture also privileges men than women in professional development. Tierney (1995) has identified a range of informal practices and relationships in software companies that are helpful to career progression and from which women are largely excluded-the lunch time drinks in the pub to which only men are invited, and the networking amongst the 'lads'—critical parts of getting on and going up in the IT world. In addition, male bonding, conversations, swearing and sexual jokes serve to exclude women from social interactions between IT staff and thus from important sources of information about career progression and opportunities (Cockburn, 1985a). Grundy (1994) has described how men in the computer industry have also formed exclusive clubs playing commando-type games in local woodlands at weekends. In the IT world, therefore, men are groomed and ready for a career which depends less upon formal IT skills and knowledge but more strongly upon adherence to a set of informal 'rules of the game'. It is no exaggeration to find that men are much more strongly represented in senior IT jobs than women. This is borne out by an insider's account of the industry in Silicon Valley, in which it is stated that women have found it difficult to get into the senior ranks (Cringely, 1992).

The male culture prevailing in the IT organisations which undermine women is attributed to a number of factors (Adam et al 1993). For example, long hours are common in the computing industries. If all the important decisions are made in the pub after 5pm, then the women who picks up her child from the nursery at that time has to miss out the real business of the day. Deliberations on women's exclusion from dining clubs, the golf courses and changing room types of interaction in tightly structured organisations also add to this problem (Edgar-Nevill 1991). But there has been only a limited discussions on how to bring women into these informal organisational forums. Since women find it difficult to penetrate into the political and communication networks, the organisations can bring the informal communications to the workplace, making it much easier for the perceptive women to keep in tune both with corporate objectives and the organisation politics. Providing entry for women in less formal debate and negotiations would perhaps enable them to keep in touch with the industry as a whole and makes it much easier for them to compete on equal terms with her male counterparts.

Since career progression depends to a larger extent on the informal process within organisations viz: (i) the informal promotion procedures such as networking (Tierney) and (ii) informal promotion criteria such as 'fitting in' (Shapiro, 1994), it becomes curious to know the ways in which men and women learn of these informal process. Gender differences in gaining access to informal networks or grapevines has gained momentum because those who are marginal to this dominant information network may be disadvantaged in gradually trading up their careers in the external and internal labour markets (Preston 1986; Winstanley 1986; Anderson 1982; Hall et al 1985; Oakey 1984). For instance, Tierney has examined the variations in exploiting this informal career resources by the male and female software engineers working in a multinational company at Dublin. The 'lads' in this organisation have constituted the most dominant grapevine through which they have gained access to work-related information (viz: Performance Bonus, Employee Appraisal etc) and thereby they are in the best position to capitalise on the firm's semi-formal structuring of work. Hence, the absence of an extensive, standardised promotion ladder in this form does not constitute a barrier for the lads. They have been able to 'flit lucratively through an upwardingly spiralling series of seemingly secondary peripheral jobs' with the help of their network, while their female colleagues find themselves 'stuck' in their primary jobs due to their lack of access to network. Men have exploited the career resources and 'just naturally' progress higher and faster through the skill hierarchy. Similarly, the other lads in the organisation have achieved occupational and organisational mobility while their female counterparts have found themselves thwarted in their preferred career path. The lad's informal networks in addition to their designing skills, business flair and client contacts have helped them to emerge as independent mobile professionals in the external labour market. The key position that they have occupied within the internal labour market, and their ability to achieve the shift from 'being managed' to being manager' over the course of their organisational career within the company indicate the strength of their network. On the contrary, their female collegues have not been able to translate their competencies into professional achievement. In short, this study has demonstrated that the lads have the necessary drive and ability to achieve their target (informal promotion) by getting the sponsporship from their colleagues as managers. In contrast, the 'non-lads' in the organisation have suffered either from an absence of sponsorship or sponsorship of a detrimental kind. In this informally-organised and collegiate workplace, it is the lads who emerge as the occupational winners and women find it difficult to penetrate into this culture. This could be attributed to their lack of access to these networks.

Some of the US-based studies (Baroudi et al 1995) also have indicated that women have been excluded from the formal and informal networks of the corporation's primary operations. This lack of opportunities for extra and intra organisational interaction has seriously handicapped women in their career advancement. Since women have often settled into the lower-paying and lower-productivity positions, their opportunities to interact with peers and other members within and outside the organisations have been limited than their male colleagues; this has caused women being ignorant of most of the career related information. Moreover, the poor representation of women in IT managerial sector is attributed to their lack of participation in 'boundary-spanning' activities as aggressively as men. All these suggest that women must take the initiative to expand their networking in order to increase their visibility in the orgnaisation and to enhance their career opportunities.

3

Gender and Computing Work: An International Comparative Study

ABSTRACT

In the context of the current state of women in Information Technology (IT) this paper seeks to extend our understanding of the impact of occupational culture on gender relations in selected countries namely USA, UK, The Netherlands and Finland. The perspective adopted is one which takes account of the gender dimension of national cultures, notably masculinity and femininity. The evidence shows that gender segregation and under-representation seem to exist in both feminine and masculine national cultures suggesting that at least some elements of computing occupational culture transcend national boundaries.

INTRODUCTION

The low representation of women, in the field of computing, has received increasing attention during the past few years. Studies on this topic have been carried out in various countries and geographical regions in an attempt to highlight the trends in women's participation in this industry. In general, there is a consensus in the literature that the occupational culture of the computing environment has been a constraint for women's recruitment, retention and promotion in computing work and a factor that alienates women causing many to decide not to enter this occupation (Wright, 1997a). Computing is an occupation that has been predominantly white, middle-class and male-dominated; in other words, it is a sector that is seen to be 'female-unfriendly'. In this paper, we carry out a cross-national study on this issue. We suggest that the national culture, which has so-far been neglected from this literature, coexists with the occupational culture and, therefore, its influence should be considered when assessing differences in the state of women in computing between countries. In particular, the paper examines and compares the level of gender representation and segregation in computing work across various countries with both feminine and masculine cultures by detailing the most recent statistics in this area. The paper then develops a discussion on the potential influence of the national culture and the occupational culture on gender representation and segregation in computing work. Our findings help to unravel some of the reasons for similarities and differences between feminine and masculine societies with regard to this issue.

In the following sections, we review the existing literature as an investigation of the occupational culture of computing, whilst in the section that follows we examine the reflection of the national gender culture on the occupational culture of computing.

THE OCCUPATIONAL CULTURE OF COMPUTING

Trice (1993) who studied occupational cultures across various work-places defined 'occupational cultures' as collectives which consist of ideologies (emotionally charged and taken for granted beliefs) and cultural forms (mechanisms such as stories, rituals and myths which affirm and express these beliefs). Occupational cultures structure social relations, encourage ethnocentrism and could be dysfunctional as well as functional (Wright, 1996:82). As Wright puts it: "...viewing computer work, through the lenses of occupational culture, suggests a way to unify seemingly disparate factors [on women's absence from this occupation] into a cohesive whole" (1996, p. 81). In her study, Wright (1996) provides an interesting account of the computing occupational culture by reviewing the cultural history of computing, its masculine nature and its engineering basis. Her main arguments are presented and complemented by the work of other researchers in this section.

In many occupations, the pattern of gender segregation has been established through historical sedimentation of role allocation, such as, for example, the clerical (female-dominated) sector and the engineering (male dominated) sector. Computing, which has only come into existence during World War II, might be seen as potentially less bound by traditions e.g. as men's or women's work, and therefore as a gender-neutral occupation offering opportunities to both men and women to enter and progress.

Contrary to this general assumption, however, the values and norms of engineering have been found to be especially prominent in computing and, therefore despite its newness, there has been evidence of gender segregation and ghettoization in this sector as much as in other longer-established technically-oriented and male-dominated professions. As it is noted in Wright (1997), the first computers were physically constructed by electrical engineers and, therefore, computing from its early years became a subordinate to electrical engineering.

According to Trice (1993), because subordinate occupational cultures take on the ideologies and cultural forms of their dominant culture, the computing culture took on the occupational culture of electrical engineering. The latter comprises a style of calculation and a pattern of working that is predominantly mathematical and structured in nature. Turkle (1984, 1995) argues that men are more likely to be comfortable with a 'hard' computing style that emphasises mathematical calculation, while women are more comfortable working through interfaces that permit a 'soft', flexible style, allowing experimentation, a non-sequential and a non-hierarchical approach. Based on the results of her study which involved interviews and observations with 1000 participants of all ages during the 1980s and 1990s, Turkle distinguishes between two different computing cultures: one is the culture of calculation and the other is the culture of simulation. The culture of calculation corresponds to the hard programming style which emphasizes a mathematical-driven structure with rigorous guidelines and procedures. By contrast, the culture of simulation adopts the soft programming style which allows for interaction, flexibility, trial and error and experimentation. Wright finds (1997) that in computing workplaces, both of these cultures could be evident, although the culture of simulation is more evident among users who are, not-surprisingly, female dominated. Groups of computer professionals on the other are characterised by the culture of calculation and are male-dominated

Other accounts develop an image of masculinity in computing and its effect on women (Grundy, 1996. Henwood, 1993; Kiesler et al, 1985; Wajcman, 1991; Wright, 1996). Wright reports research which shows how stereotypes about computing jobs as 'male' are held by both men and women at work (1996). Hemenway (1995) describes four 'forces' which make for discrimination and pressure for women in industries like computing. First, women with traditional feminine work- styles, seeking consensus and team effort, are seen as less confident and capable than men; while those women who emulate masculine behaviour are seen as aggressive and are rejected by men for not conforming to feminine stereotypes. A second force is the tendency for employees to cluster with others like themselves. This can work to the disadvantage of women and the advantage of men, because males associate with, take advice from and establish trust relations with each other creating a network more likely to supply key information and contacts relevant to promotion opportunities. Similarly, Tierney (1995) reports networking advantages for 'the lads' specifically in the computing sector. Hemenway's third force is the reproduction of 'mental roles' of success in the image of senior males. This will also tend to lead to the potential of female candidates to be devalued through such comparison. Fourth, male behaviours (such as 'harmless' joking, 'laddish' conversation, discussion of male interests, and in extreme form harassment) are proved stressful and over time can erode women's self-confidence and ability to present themselves successfully.

In the same vein, Henwood (1993) also argues that the reasons for women's exclusion from the IT industry is primarily due to the masculine culture of technology and the pattern of sex-segregation practices in this sector. Even today, women continue to perceive computing as a field for men. An interesting explanation of this trend has been advanced by McIllwee and Robinson (1992). They feel that the 'masculine culture' of the profession discourages women from entering it, because it requires aggressive displays of technical self-confidence and hands-on ability for success. Women in this culture are particularly affected by the obsession with technology and hands-on activities, because the gender socialisation experienced by most women yields a distinct lack of experience in 'tinkering' with electronics. Even when they acquire the necessary skills, women do not seem to become as comfortable or as obsessed as their male counterparts. The display required is that of masculinity, playing a role with which women are uncomfortable, even when they are capable of its performance. The work by Kiesler et al (1985), Turkle (1984) and Wright (1996) also reiterates the fact that the exclusion of women from the IT industry is due to the alienation of women to this kind of technical culture.

What emerges from this literature is that computing carries 'progenetic' engineering and masculine characteristics. Even though other computing styles have been identified (e.g. the soft style of simulation), the engineering—masculine computing culture seems to be particularly predominant in organisations where computing work is the primary activity, such as software organisations (Wright, 1996).

THE POTENTIAL INFLUENCE OF NATIONAL CULTURE ON GENDER ISSUES IN COMPUTING WORK

The relevant literature has paid little attention to the potential influence of national culture and practices on gender integration or segregation in the labour force. As we have shown in the previous section, computing is not a gender neutral occupation; rather evidence exists of gender segregation. In this section, we examine the potential influence of national culture on gendered patterns in computing work. This perspective embodies the idea that national culture as a social aggregate may develop sets of common assumptions and values about work and organisational patterns which are shared by its members. An important implication following from this view is that national culture and not only the occupational culture will exert influence on the values, styles and career orientation of computing staff in different countries.

National cultures comprise of beliefs and values which normally unconsciously govern people's perceptions and behaviour (Hostede, 1980). Individuals with different national backgrounds have beliefs and underpinning values which hold different assumptions and expectations about relationships among people. Hofstede (1980), who studied organisational cultures and individual behaviour in 53 countries, found that some societies are characterised by masculine features and others by feminine features. According to Hofstede (1990:82):

"Masculinity pertains to the societies in which social gender roles are clearly distinct (i.e. men are supposed to be assertive, tough, and focused on material success whereas women are supposed to be more modest, tender and concerned with the quality of life); femininity pertains to societies in which social gender roles overlap (i.e. both men and women are supposed to be modest, tender, and concerned with the quality of life)."

Based on the above description, Hofstede found that among the masculine countries are the Anglo-American societies such as Ireland, UK, US, Australia, New Zealand, but also Japan (which was found as being the most masculine society), India, Greece and the Arab-speaking countries. Among the most feminine countries were found to be Sweden, Norway, the Netherlands, Denmark and Finland. People from different national cultures are, therefore, expected to behave and act differently, as mentioned above. In this paper, we aim to explore the potential influence of feminine and masculine national cultures on gender relations in computing work. Though subject to some criticism (Tayeb, 1988; Whitley, 1992), Hofstede's research provides the most widely used basis for standardised examination of national values and has received substantial corroboration (e.g. Sondergaard, 1994). Based on Hofstede's work, therefore, we develop the specific objectives of this present study.

In feminine societies, boys and girls at school study the same subjects. Furthermore, collaboration is encouraged whilst fighting and competition are discouraged. This is in contrast to what's going on in masculine societies where boys and girls study different subjects and where students tend to be as visible as possible in classrooms and tend to compete with each other. When taking into account these characteristics, the representation of women in computing education is expected to be different in feminine and masculine cultures. Therefore, the first objective of the study is to explore any similarities and differences regarding the representation of women in computing science education across the national cultures.

Management and work practices were also found to be different in feminine and masculine cultures. The former tends to promote equality, solidarity and quality of work life whilst the latter emphasizes equity, competition among colleagues and performance. Hofstede's earlier work (1980, pp. 292,306) identified that the participation of women in senior level technical and professional jobs is higher in feminine countries, as a percentage of all working women in the labour force of the country. Therefore, the second objective of the study is to explore whether a) gender representation in IT and b) gender segregation differ between masculine and feminine societies. The third objective of the study will be to discuss how national cultures may influence the state of women in computing work.

RESEARCH APPROACH

For the purpose of our research, we selected four countries to participate in this international comparative study. These are: UK, US, the Netherlands and Finland and they were chosen due to their masculine and feminine cultural characteristics. In terms of national cultures, the Netherlands and Finland ranked low (with 14 and 26 respectively) on Hofstede's masculinity index, while UK and the US scored higher (66 and 62 respectively). Therefore, the two latter countries, UK and US have clearly been identified as masculine and the other two, the Netherlands and Finland, have been identified as feminine. Nation-wide statistics and other studies carried out in these different countries are presented and compared.

For comparative purposes, however, and for the purpose of this paper, we decided to restrict our analysis to the main computing related jobs identified by the Labour Force Survey (1992) in the UK as being: computer managers, system analysts, programmers and computer operators (e.g. data-entry clerks). All these jobs comply with Wright's definition (1997, p. 2) of 'computer work' as 'support for other people's usage of computer systems.

WOMEN IN COMPUTING EDUCATION

Unesco (1995) has provided the most comprehensive cross-national statistics on the percentages of female graduates from mathematic and computer science programmes in 71 countries (in Wright, 1997a, b). Data were roughly available in 1990. For the purpose of this study we compiled Table 3.1 which provides the representation of women in maths and computer science degrees at different periods of time. The Unesco statistics were used to compile this information for US, Finland and the Netherlands. Since the Unesco report did not compile statistics about the UK, the Social Europe Supplement 3/93, which reports on the share of women among students on university computing science courses, was used to complement the table. Even though the Unesco and the Social Europe Supplement statistics do not correspond to the same periods of time, they do provide an indication of the trends in these countries.

Table 3.1: Cross National Comparison of Women's Representation of Graduates in Mathematics and Computer Science, 1975, 1985, 1990 (UNESCO, 1995)

	1975 *% Women*	*1985* *%Women*	*1990* *% Women*
US	32.3	39.4	36.4
UK (*)	25 (1970)	23 (1980)	13 (1989)
Netherlands	9.9	14.0	12.9
Finland	32.3	25.6	20.9

(*) Share of women among students on university computer science courses, Social Europe S3/93.

In the US there has been an increasing share of women in computing science education from 32.3 % in 1975 to 39.4% in 1985. This, however, dropped to 36.4 % in 1990. The Netherlands experienced similar rising and then declining trends, although the share of female students remains low overall. In contrast to these trends, Finland and the UK present a gradual fall since the seventies. However, a recent European report claims that the intake of women, onto IT courses in 1998 at some of the higher educational institutes in Finland, was around half the total students (IDS Employment Europe, 1998). This presents a significant increase in the proportion of female students graduating with computing qualifications in this country. The declining representation of female graduates in computing during the 80s and early 90s has been explained by Vehvilainen (1997) as being due to the male dominated technical universities and colleges which discouraged female entrants. During the 1980s, there were only 8-10% of females IT students in technical universities in Finland. Whilst this was happening, women have started gaining an increasing share of graduates with formal education in systems analysis and development. The availability of courses on systems design in Finnish universities, since the 1970s, has opened the doors for females to study computing degrees (Vehvilainen, 1997).

Despite the Finnish situation, UK has experienced the steepest and long lasting decline of women taking computer science qualifications; this is evident in table-1. More recent statistics report that in 1995 women's participation in undergraduate courses with computer science as a major, dropped to 11.9% (Siann, 1997), reinforces these declining trends.

The above statistics do not show the degree of collaboration and competition between boys and girls at school which are characteristics found respectively in feminine and masculine societies. They do suggest, however, that boys and girls, in masculine as well as feminine countries, do not study the same subjects. Instead, the representation of female students in computing science courses is lower in all the four countries with the US having the highest proportion, the Netherlands the lowest, and the UK the longest-lasting decline.

WOMEN'S REPRESENTATION IN COMPUTING WORK

There has been an increase in the number of women entering IT occupations since the seventies. However, women are under-represented in this industry in all member-states of the European Union and other countries. For instance, statistics available report that, in the early 1990s, no member state of the European Union had a percentage above 30% and in most cases it was nearer 20% (Social Europe, S3/93). International comparisons reveal a widespread tendency for the proportion of the female IT workforce to rise until mid 1980s and then fall (Wright 1997a). Table 3.2 presents the representation of women in the selected countries over three decades: 1970s, 1980s and 1990s.

This chronological analysis of gender has revealed that there has been little progress in the degree of representation of women in IT in the last three decades. Women have remained overall under-represented in this sector. The Netherlands has retained the lowest representation of women in IT since 1970s. Even though the statistics available in the late 1980s were promising, forecasting an increasing trend, these have decreased again in the latest available figures of 1993. In 1993 in particular, the percentage of females had grown to 8.9% among systems analysts and to 13.5% among programmers (Tijdens, 1994). In brief, the Netherlands show trends that are increasing in the 80s and then decreasing again in the 90s.

Table 3.2: Trends in female shares of IT occupations

	1970s	*1980s*	*1990s*
United States (1)			
- System Analysts	15% (1970)	23% (1980), 28% (1984)	32% (1990)
- Programmers	23% (1970)	31% (1980), 34% (1984)	41% (1990)
United Kingdom (2)			
- Analysts/Programmers		21 % (1984)	16.45% (1994)
The Netherlands (3)			
- System Analysts	5% (1979)	10% (1989)	8.9% (1993)
- Programmers	8% (1979)	10 % (1989)	13% (1993)
Finland (4)			
- Systems Developers	-	26% (1980)	35 % (1998)

Sources: (1) Frenkel, 1990 (2) Social Europe S3/93; Labour Force Statistics, Summer 1994 (3) Social Europe S3/93; Tijdens, 1994 (4): Vehvilaninen, 1997; IDS, Employment Europe, No. 438, June 1998.

The most detailed statistics on women in IT present the US situation. This is not surprising since the majority of the literature on this topic is based in the US. It is only in the last few years that researchers have begun examining gender issues in computing in other countries. US reports indicate increasing trends throughout the last three decades. The share of female systems analysts rose from 15% in 1970 to 32% in 1990 whilst the share of female programmers rose from 23% in 1970 to 41% in 1990. More recent statistics (Computerworld, 1995) report that in the US, women account for 37% of the IT professionals which although higher than the representation of women in any European country, it is 7% below the national average of women in the total workforce of the country. Finland also shows a significant increase in female systems developers from 26% in 1980 to 35% in 1998 (IDS, Employment Europe, 1998).

In contrast to the trends of the US, the Netherlands and Finland, the UK presents a very gloomy picture with the shares of women declining not only in specific specialties, such as, the one of analysts/programmers (table 2), but also overall. At present, the UK experiences a declining trend in the representation of women in computing work, for example, from a high of 25% women in the IT workforce in the UK in the 1980s, the proportion has fallen to a low of 19% in 1996, with only 12% of the British Computer Society membership being women. In 1984, the female share of IT professional occupations was 21% but this dropped to 19.5 % by 1989 (Social Europe S3/93). In 1991, there were reports that identified an even lower representation of women at 18% (LFS, 1992). Whilst this implied that fewer than two in ten professional jobs in computing (i.e. systems and data processing managers, analysts, programmers) were held by women, seven out of ten lower status computing jobs (e.g. data entry clerks, help-desk etc) were held by women (Grundy, 1996). Compared, therefore, to the Dutch experience, the UK reports a higher representation of women but also the most long lasting decline, evident in the 80s and throughout the 90s.

ANALYSIS: UNDER-REPRESENTATION BUT ALSO SEGREGATION

We begin this section by correlating the proportion of women receiving degrees in computing-related disciplines and the proportion of women actually employed in IT occupations. It is observed that for the UK and the Netherlands these two factors show a parallel trend. For instance, since 80s, in the UK there seems to be a downward trend in both the proportion of women awarded with computing qualifications and the proportion of women entering IT occupations. Furthermore, the increasing and then declining trend in the participation of women in computing education is replicated in the IT labour force. Following from these parallel trends, a possible explanation, for low representation of women in IT occupations, is the decreasing number of female students who graduate with a computer science degree. According to researchers in this field, it is the image of computing as technical and male-dominated, the perception that computing work is a field for antisocial individuals, and the socialisation and identification of women themselves away from maths and science and thus not suited for such work which prevent the majority of females from pursuing computing as a career (Grundy, 1996; Siann, 1997; Wilson, 1997). Drawing on such findings, a number of organisations and associations target the promotion of countervailing views as the chosen means to change the status quo for the better (e.g. in the UK, some of these are:'Women in Science and Engineering', 'Women into Computing' etc.).

Although the declining number of female students who graduate with computing science degrees should be given serious attention, this should not be seen as the sole reason for the degree of female representation in IT occupations. This is reinforced by comparing the trends above for the US. For this country, the trend of female participation in computing education is not parallel to the female participation in the IT workforce of the country. Although the statistics available present an increasing representation of women in the IT workforce throughout three decades under consideration, the educational statistics show a declining representation as we move from the 80s to the 90s. Panteli et al (1999b) have argued that due to the diverse nature of IT occupations, there are in fact increasing opportunities for women to enter the industry from a wide range of backgrounds. During the late 40s and 50s, programming was the major type of computing work, but in the 90s, IT also includes jobs in the areas of systems management, communications and networks, systems development, technical support, operations, user support and help-desk operations (NCC 1992, 1997). The diversification of specialties and skills in this industry offers prospects not only for computing qualifications but also for those with business-like qualifications (Tijdens, 1991) or post-graduate IT degrees to enter IT occupations. Furthermore, a study by Carey (1991/2) shows that 47 % of all new entrants to computing work in the US were from other occupations within their employing organisations.

Participation in computing education is a key factor which affects women's representation in the IT workforce. This, however, has been reported to have both positive and negative effects in different countries. According to Kirkup (1992) and Oost (1991) the Finnish women entered systems design through formal education whereas in the Netherlands and the UK the start of formal education has not necessarily promoted; in fact, it has lowered women's representation in IT occupations. It is, therefore, believed that in addition to educational reasons, other factors have exerted an influence on the representation of women and their significance should not be neglected. Further, to this continuous under-representation of women in IT in the selected countries, several researchers reported that gender segregation is very much predominant in this industry and it has absorbed the patriarchal power structure of the traditional engineering industries. The focus and direction of these studies are multi-dimensional with some studies using large, nation-wide data and statistics, and other studies using micro-level data in an attempt to find out the distributional pattern of women across the individual organisations and their level of penetration across the occupational hierarchy. Below, we present a sample of these studies.

The gender hierarchy, in the IT profession, is not new and its history can be traced back to the 70s. The increasing trends in the representation of women in IT, such as in the US case, have not prevented gender hierarchy and inequality. The 1974 Computerworld survey has reported that 99% of the women held the position of key punchers while 13% to 20% of them worked as business system analysts and programmers. Strober and Arnold (1985) carried out an exhaustive research relating to women in the high-tech occupations in the US in the 70s and 80s. Their research has reiterated the fact that women remain far away from the most vulnerable and crucial occupations in the sector. They argued that various other environmental factors such as the emergence of the women's movement, the growing technical education, the initiatives from the government and computing organisations, and above all, the implementation of equal opportunities in employment have not brought out a change in the occupational status of women in high-tech industries, such as IT.

A study by Kraft and Dubnoff (1983) has also probed the extent of gender segregation in computing. According to this study, women have been better represented in software jobs compared to hardware jobs. However, even within software workplaces, they have not assumed significant role and status. Most of them have been concentrated in the lower status jobs such as business programming, documentation and maintenance. Women in the upper level managerial and supervisory levels are in a minority. The study has identified that while 22% of women in the sample are managers of some kind, men are three times more likely to be in upper level managerial posts than women. This study has also brought to light the secondary status attached to women in IT management: women are often seen to supervise more women than men. Other studies (Donato, 1990, Frenkel, 1990) confirm that women are over-represented in some types of lower-level jobs (e.g. programmers and operators) and under-represented in higher level positions (e.g. project leaders and managers).

Studies on gender-based patterns of employment and work experience in IT have presented similar outcomes in the UK and the Netherlands. For example, in the UK, it was found (IDPM IT report 1996 in Panteli, et al, 1999b) that the presence of women declines on moving up the hierarchy. For instance, although in 1996 women constitute 11.7% of management in all areas, only 7.3 % of heads of IT departments are women. Women are not only under-represented at the supervisory and managerial level, but also in the higher ranks of the technical track. For example, although they constitute 26.9% of the total number of trainee programmers, only 8.3% of principal programmers are females. Similarly, although there are 25.5% female assistant technical analysts, only 6.2% of the senior technical consultants are female. The proportion of women reaches 40% and above only for those specialties that are related to administrative and support functions: e.g. help desk assistant 62.4%, help desk analyst 47.3%, help desk supervisor 47.1%, assistant user support analyst 44.2% etc. The proportion of women in the programming and the more technical-related occupations, reaches 25% or more in mainly junior positions (e.g. junior analyst programmer 26.2%), traineeships (e.g. trainee analyst programmer 29.4%), or assistantship posts (assistant technical analyst 25%).

A Dutch study (Hoek and Rienstra, 1989) shows similar findings: further to their quantitative under-representation, women occupy predominantly the lower segmentation of the job categories. In the majority of the organisations that participated in the study, the managerial, technical and designing jobs are occupied by men while the processing and administrative jobs are occupied by women. Moreover, women end up in the so-called 'dead-end' functions and men in what it is called the 'growth' functions. Grundy (1996) in the UK gave similar descriptions of such job segregation: 'messy' jobs for the women and 'pure' jobs for the men.

Even in Finland where there is a large female participation in professional computing education and development work, there has been evidence of barriers caused by male-domination in the computing environment. According to Vehvilainen (1997), women not only avoid entering technical universities as was reported earlier, but they are also in a minority in professional publications and executive committees, and whilst there are only few women at managerial IT positions. Even though the Finnish computing association is no longer the so-called 'brothers' club' with a male membership only, it still remains as 'the world without women' where despite its female members, women are not encouraged to take an active role in its activities.

Overall, women are found to be under-represented and disadvantaged at the high-status and prestigious IT jobs in all four countries. The implications of this are discussed below.

DISCUSSION AND CONCLUSION

The chronological and geographical analysis, presented above, of the gender dimension during the last three decades in the four selected countries has marked the predominance of male culture in computing and across its different occupational specialties. A closer look at the status of women in different occupational specialties shows that despite their increased representation, women do not have equal access to the different levels of occupational hierarchies. They are over-represented in some types of lower-level jobs (e.g. programmers and operators) and underrepresented in higher level jobs (i.e. project leaders and IS managers) . Computing, therefore, has remained a gender segregated, male-dominated occupation.

Following from this finding, it can be said that the high-tech industries which are looked upon as the 'great equalisers' do not give adequate berth for women's occupational development nor do they necessarily produce an integrated work force and equality of opportunities for men and women (Strober & Arnold, 1987). As was discussed in Section 1 of this paper, the occupational culture of computing has been particularly vulnerable to influences from various sources and factors. Its links to traditional masculine environments such as electrical engineering, the competitive and fast changing nature of work which exist and pervade across various countries and continents, all contribute to building and sustaining a masculine, male-dominated work environment. What we are finding in this comparative study is that the image of computing can override national values. In both feminine and masculine societies, women are not only under-represented but also experience similar barriers to their retention and career development in the field. This identification leads us to conclude that since similar patterns of under-representation and segregation are occurring in a number of countries, at least some elements of the computing occupational culture transcend national boundaries.

We are, therefore, finding that the computing culture has a role to play with regard to the state of women in this occupation, regardless of national characteristics. This masculine-engineering driven occupational culture of computing is reinforced by the way work is done. The increasing number of structured tools and methodologies in software development, the competitive nature of work, the frequent tight deadlines and the project-based nature of work all contribute to a tremendous amount of pressure on requiring developers to work longer and unsociable hours. And it is often those who are able to cope with these demands and succeed that are promoted into the managerial positions (Knights and Murray, 1994). Moreover, the speed of technological change makes it difficult to catch up with technological advancements for those who take a career break, notably women who take maternity leave, and for those who can only work on a part-time basis, again mainly women with family responsibilities.

The above characteristics have been identified in various countries reinforcing our finding that the occupational culture of computing transcends national boundaries. Such argument supports the findings of a study by Gerpott, Domsch and Kettler (1988). These researchers stated that in high-tech companies the sense of technological excellence overrides other considerations, engineers across national boundaries being more likely to share the culture of other engineers than their fellow countrymen. As they put it: "R&D professionals may form a special occupational subculture across countries; because scientific methods and standards are generally valid independently of country boundaries" (p.456). In the case of IT, offshore programming and globalisation contribute to the spread of the occupational methods and standards across the globe. From various reports, we understand that multinational IT organisations have transferred their North American culture to other parts of the world. To quote Vehvilainen (1997:438): " ...there was a belief that the US training and testing could be applied in Finland as easily as the computer machines, IBM is known as an especially male-dominated company, the organisational of which ... has remained very male also in Finland" even when women are gaining increasing access in the labour force of the country. Similar accounts have been provided by researchers in other countries (e.g. Rafferty, 1997, Tierney, 1993). Some suggestions, such as the increased availability of special training and career development programmes have been made in Panteli et al (1999a), but these and others require action. We, therefore, think that multinational and transnational IT organisations have a responsibility and are in a better position to innovate in the way they do business and exert an influence with regard to the gender-patterns of work in various countries.

Last but not the least, it is significant to note that all the four selected countries have been found by Hofstede to carry individualist values, the tendency to look after one's self (and the immediate family) and not to look in collectivist terms. This similarity may partially explain the continuation of the competitive, technology-driven culture of computing which adversely affects women's representation in this sector. This though should be treated with caution (due to lack of empirical data). We do believe, however, that similar studies in the future should incorporate additional countries. It would be particularly interesting to incorporate countries such as India and other Asian countries which have been experiencing a dramatic boom in their software development industries and also because they support collectivism and the integration of people into cohesive groups. Some researchers (Greenhill, et al, 1996) have indicated that women of Asian origin constitute between 30% to 40% of the women studying IT at Universities in Australia. This, therefore, represents a significant area of further research.

REFERENCES

- Carey M.L. (1991/92). "Occupational Advancement from Within". Occupational Outlook, Quarterly, Winter, pp. 9-13.
- *Computerworld*, 9th Annual Salary & Survey:"/Unequal Opportunities", September 4, 1, pp. 70-72, 74, 78.
- Donato, K.M. (1990). "Programming for Change? The Growing Demand for Women Systems Analysts". In Reskin B.F. and Roos, P.A. (Eds), *Job Queues, Gender Queues: Explaining Women's Inroads into Male Occupations*, Philadelphia: Temple University Press.
- Frenkel, K.A. (1990). Women and Computing, Communications of the ACM, 33, 11, pp. 34-36.
- Gerpott, T.J., Domsch, M. and Keller, R.T. (1988), Career Orientations in Different Countries and Companies: An Empirical investigation of West German, British and US Industrial R&D Professionals, *Journal of Management Studies*, 25:5, September, pp. 439-462.
- Greenbaum, J.M. (1979). *In the Name of Efficiency*, Philadelphia: Temple University Press.
- Greenhill, A., von Hellens, L.A., Nielsen, S.H. and Pringle, R. (1996). "Asian Women in IT Education – An Australian Examination." Proceedings of the First Australian Conference on Computer Science Education (ACSE_96), Sydney, July.
- Grundy, F. (1996). *Women and Computers*, Exeter: Intellect Books.
- Hacker, S. (1989). *Pleasure, Power and Technology*, London: Unwin Hyman.
- Hemenway, K. (1995) "Human nature and the glass ceiling in industry". *Communications of the ACM* 38. 1. pp. 55-62.
- Henwood, F. (1993). "Establishing gender perspectives on information technology: problems, issues and opportunities." *In Gendered By design: Information Technology and Office Systems* (E Green et al, eds) London: Taylor & Francis.
- Hofstede G. (1980). *Culture's Consequences: International Differences in Work-Related Values*, Beverly Hills. CA. Sage Publications.
- Hofstede, G. (1990). *Cultures and Organizations: Intercultural Cooperation and its Importance for Survival*. London: HarperCollins Publishers.
- Hoek, S. and Riestra E. (1989). *Strategies and Education*. In Tijdens K., Jennings, M., Wagner, I. and Weggelaar, M (eds), "Women, Work and Computerization: Forming New Alliances". Elsevier, Amsterdam.
- IDPM Report (1996). "The End is Nigh - 1996 IT Skills Trend Report". The Institute for the Management of Information Systems, UK.

- IDS (Incomes Data Services). "Employment Europe (1998), Finland: IT Sector in search of more talent." No. 438, June, 21-22.
- Kiesler, S., Sproull, L. and Eccles J S (1985)." Pool halls, chips and war games: women in the culture of computing." *Psychology of Women Quarterly*, 9.
- Kirkup, G (1992), The Social Constrution of Computers: Hammers or Harpsichords? Kirkup, T.G. and Keller, L.S. (eds), Inventing Women, Science, Technology and Gender, Cambridge: Polity Press.
- Knights, D. and Murray, F. (1994). "Managers Divided - Organisational Policies and Information Technology Management." *Wiley Series in Information Systems*, London: Wiley.
- Kraft, P. and Dubnoff, S. (1983), "Software Workers Survey. *Computerworld*, November 14. pp. 1-13.
- *Labour Force Statistics*, UK (1992, 1994).
- McIlwee, J. S. & Robinson, J. G. (1992) "Women In Engineering: Gender, Power & Workplace Culture, *SUNY*. Albany.
- National Computing Centre (1992). "Salaries and Staff Issues in Computing, 1992.
- National Computing Centre (1997). "Salaries and Staff Issues in Computing, 1997".
- Oost, E.van (1991). "The Process of Sex-typing of Computer Occupations". In Eriksson, I.V. Kitchenham, B.A. and Tijdens, K.G. (Eds). *Women, Work and Computerisation*, Amsterdam: Elsevier Science Publishers B.V. (North-Holland).
- Panteli, A., Stack, J. and Ramsay, H. (1999a). "Gender and Professional Ethics in the IT Industry". *Journal of Business* Ethics, forthcoming.
- Panteli, A., Stack, J., Atkinson, M. and Ramsay, J. (1999b). "Women in the UK IT Industry: An Empirical Study." *European Journal of Information Systems*, Forthcoming
- Rafferty T (1997). "Factors that Attract Women to Careers in Information Technology - A Case Study in Ireland". In Grundy, A.F. Kohler, D., Oechtering, V. and Petersen, U. (Eds), *Women, Work and Computerisation - Spinning a Web from Past to Future*, "Berlin. Springer.
- Siann, G. (1997). We can, we don't want to: factors influencing women's participation in computing." In Lander, R. and Adams, A. (eds,) op. cit.
- *Social Europe - Occupational Segregation of Women and Men in the European Community* - Supplement 3/93, 70-76
- Sondergaard, M. (1994). "Research Note:Hofstede's Consequences: a study of reviews, citations and replications, *Organisation Studies*. 15.3, pp. 447-456

- Strober, M. H. and Arnold, C. L. (1987) "Integrated Circuits/ Segregated Labour: Women in Computer Related Occupations and High-Tech Industries". In National Research Council (Ed), *Computer Chips and Paper Clips: Technology and women's Employment*, Washington DC: National Academy Press.
- Tayeb, M. (1982). "Contingency Theory and Culture: A study of matched English and the Indian Manufacturing Firms". *Organisation Studies*, 8. pp. 241-261.
- Tierney, M. (1993). "Negotiating a Software Career: Informal Work Practices and 'The Lads' in a Software Installation". In Grint, K. and Gill, R. (Eds) The Gender-Technology Relation: Contemporary Theory and Research. London: Taylor & Francis.
- Tijdens K (1991). "Women in EDP Departments". In Eriksson, I.V. Kitchenham, B. A. and Tijdens, K.G. (Eds), *Women, Work and Computerization*. Amsterdam: Elsevier Science Publishers B.V. (North-Holland).
- Tijdens, K. (1994). "Behind the Screens: The Foreseen and Unforeseen Impact of Computerization on Female Office Worker's Job". In Eberhart, T. And Wachter, C. (eds) Proceedings of the 2nd European Feminist Research Conference, Austria
- Trice H. (1993). *Occupational Subcultures in the Workplace*, Ithaca, NY: ILR Press.
- Turkle, S. (1984). *The Second Self: Computers and the Human Spirit*. NY. Simon & Schuster.
- Turkle, S. (1995). *Life on the Screen: Identity in the Age of the Internet*, NY. Simon & Schuster.
- Vehvilainen, M. (1997), Gender and Expertise in Retrospect: Pioneers of Computing in Finland. In Lander, R. and Adam, A. (eds). *op. cit.*
- Wajcman, J. (1991). *Feminism Confronts Technology*. London. Polity Press
- Wilson, F. (1997). "Computing, computer science and computer scientists: how they are perceived". In Lander & Adams, 1997 *op. cit.*
- Wright, R. (1996). "The Occupational Masculinity of Computing". In Cheng, C. (Ed). *Masculinities in Organisations*, London. Sage.
- Wright, R. (1997a). *Women Computer Professionals: Progress and Resistance*. Lewiston: Edwin Mellen Press
- Wright, R. (1997b). "Women in Computing: A Cross National Analysis". In Lander R. and Adams, A. (eds). *Intellect, Exeter*

4

Gender Based Digital Divide in the Web Related Occupations in the Universities: A Cross Country Study

ABSTRACT

This study makes an evaluation of the extent to which the escalation of the labour demand, the transformation of work culture and the diversification of the professional characteristics of the web profession have attracted women to enter into this new branch of IT occupation. It examines the role being played by the male and female workers in the creative, technical and management areas of web designing. It analyses the gender differences and similarities in the pattern of knowledge and skill acquisition in the web related technologies.

INTRODUCTION

The situation for women in computing has both improved and worsened with a wake of new technologies. The rise of internet and web technologies have created a great difference in the patterns of women's work and achievement in computing[1],[2]. Studies reported that ever since internet explosion began, women have risen from scant minority to great majority in the web based occupations and gained prominence both as developers of internet content and as users[3]. The talent-starved, non-hierarchical and the gender-blind meritocracy of the internet and web-based industries recruit increasingly a larger number of women [4] and the digital divide along gender lines seemed to be diminishing in this sector [5, 6]. The hybrid nature (technical & creative culture) of the work[7], the autonomous and flexible work environment[8] and the escalating demand for the web workers[9],[10] acted favourably for wide spread participation of women in the entire production process of the web sector. The purpose of our study to examine how far the general image of the web sector as a 'gender-blind' one stands true and the extent to which the gender-based digital divide has been bridged in the web environment of the universities.

RESEARCH BACKGROUND

The status of women in the web-based occupations has received greater attention in the recent years and the discussions are directed towards both the upsides and the downsides of women working in this new profession. The focus of most of the existing literature has been centring around the following thematic categories: (i) changing labour market conditions, (ii) women friendly organisational culture (iii) changing role of women in the field of technology and (iv) the closing gender based digital divide in the web occupation.

As regards the labour market condition is concerned, unlike other IT branches of work, web profession is based on diverse skills and it generates a demand for employees having solid foundation in the technical and creative skills. This professional demand is an added advantage for women to gain access into this profession. Due to their innate sense for creativity and artistic talents, women are making a difference in the web world and break the myth that it is a man's world[11],[12],[13]. The spring 2000 issue of Equity illustrates that women are the key players in the web based occupations and through their performance, women have placed themselves in the vital positions in the labour market. The reason for this optimistic trend is that this new profession opens its gateway for a wide range of professionals with new skills, not just computer scientists. Women with degrees in mathematics, business administration and even medieval history also can also enter and progress in this profession[14].

As far as the organisational factors are concerned, research has shown that workplace culture plays a substantial role in shaping women's involvement in the labour market[15]. The individual autonomy, equal opportunities, 'comfortable, causal, friendly and professional atmosphere', 'family-like collaborative community characteristic of the workplace', the 'avenues for constant learning' and above all 'the fewer gender-related issues' are considered as the motivating factors for women to enter into the web profession in large numbers.

Regarding women's role in technology, studies have pointed out that it is not only in the production of content, but also in the sphere of production of technology that women's presence is noticed in the knowledge based industries[16]. It is also cited that women's overwhelming participation in the web work may be largely due to the fast paced, dynamic and challenging nature of the work and the equal opportunities to participate in the design and implementation of web technology. The survey reports also have confirmed that women have experienced 'an exhilarating sense of achievement, impact, satisfaction and opportunity for creative freedom' in the web based work. This is because in the other branches of IT, the works are crafted around men whereas in this profession, the works are crafted around both and men and women. It is also believed that web work liberated women from the old stereotypes and gender-related obstacles in the work place and thereby unleashed great energy and talent into workplace[17]. Some of the studies have reported that the web occupation is 'gender blind' at this point and allow women to play a significant role in the web development[18,19,20].

Contrary to the above discussion, there are a few studies which focused on the downsides of the women's position in the web profession. They highlight on the issues, such as: (i) lower representation of women in critical areas of work (ii) polarisation of gender roles in web occupation (iii) women's lack of necessary skills in technology, (iv) and lack of opportunities for updating skills in web occupation. With regard to women's presence in different areas of work, it is stated that though women constitute a larger proportion in the web work, the top slot always go to men. It is felt that a very general polarisation of roles take place in the web environment where men are much more proactive in pursuing careers in the technical areas and women in the 'people'-oriented areas. 'Women's share of programming and implementation part of the web work is particularly low, and their presence is relatively high in content production and administration'. Women's lack of acquaintance with a wide range of skills, and their inability to update their knowledge in the state-of-the-art technologies are cited as the cause for their lower representation in the vital areas of work' ".

The foregoing studies brought to focus two important aspects: one is about the existence of mixed career opportunities for women in the web profession and the other one is about the lack of studies on the status of women in the web activities in the public sector especially in the educational sector where web designing is carried out in a large scale. However, it is to be noted that there are distinct differences between the business and university web development processes in terms of their (i) work environment , (ii) nature of work, (iii) demand for skill sets, (iv) recruitment; and (v) training process etc. Web work gains momentum in the universities only in the recent years and it is primarily considered as a communication and marketing tool now and there are efforts to make it an integral part of the academic system in the future. There has been a great pressure from the university administration and from the user community for the development of a dynamic and integrated web environment. As building a web site for a university is a complex process, involving a huge volume of hyper media information from dozens of departments, the demand for professionals specialising in different areas of web work are acute. It is interesting to know how these mounting demand for web workers in the universities has been responded by the men and women workers in the university. Though the quantum of trade literature predicting the expanding opportunities for women in the web field are larger, the empirical research on women's position in the web related profession is very much limited. Further more, there is absolutely no study available on the gender dimension of web work in the public organisations like the universities that are actively involved in the web projects at a large scale in the recent times.

STATEMENT OF THE PROBLEM

The universities are at a cross roads of transformation from the traditional to the virtual organisations and there is a great pressure on the institutions to go online for marketing their courses and for projecting their research and academic achievements. This process of development generated an acute demand for web professionals to create and implement a dynamic web environment for the entire organisational units of the universities. The question is how far the mounting demand for the web workers has motivated the gender groups in the university to take up this new area of work. What is the contribution of men and women in the evolution and the development process of the university web sites? Where do men and women place themselves in the content production, management and technical implementation part of the web work being carried out in the various organisational units of the universities? Do men and women equip themselves adequately to take up an active role in the various production process of the web site development? What is their level of acquaintance with the web related infrastructure, hardware & software tools and techniques?. On the whole, this study aims at investigating how far universities are gender-blind in accommodating men and women in performing the web related jobs which is considered as the most important agenda of the universities in the present context and how far men and women are professionally qualified to cope with the demand of the institutions.

OBJECTIVES

The specific objectives of this study are listed below:

(i) To identify the organisational and demographic profile of the participants in the web environment in the sample universities

(ii) To assess the situation of men and women in the working practices (web development, database management, graphic designing, server support, coding and programming, creation and maintenance of web pages, content development etc) and working environment (computer centre, administration, library, and academic departments/ faculties)

(iii) To explore whether there exists gender differences in educational attainment, skill equipment, and acquaintance with technological infrastructure (multimedia workstations, hardware and software).

(iv) To identify the variation in the motivation, career experiences, and perception of the work environment among the men and women involved in the web design project of the sample institution.

(v) To map the prospects and barriers that women face in this area work in the university selected for this study.

METHODOLOGY

Our study does focus its attention on the web professionals in the Albert Ludwigs University of Freiburg, Germany (ALU-FR) and University of Western Ontario, Canada (UWO-CA). An inventory of these workers have been collected both from the Internet and also from personnel lists maintained in the computer sections of the respective universities. Among the total of 156 members (M=128, F=28) involved in web designing in the ALU-FR, a sample of 58 (M=45, F=13) has been selected. In the same way out the total of 190 members (M=90, F=100) engaged in web development in UWO-CA. a sample of 90 (M=45, F=45) members has been selected for the present study. The entire web designers were contacted with a request for participation in our survey but only 58 members from the ALU-FR and 90 from the UWO-CA expressed their willingness to take up our survey. Thus the participation rate of the respondents is 37 percent in the ALU-FR and 47 percent in the UWO-CA. The period of our survey is between March to May, 2001. The data have been collected by circulating a questionnaire and also by interviewing the respondents involved in the web team of the various academic departments, administrative sections, library and the computer centre in the sample universities. The questionnaire covers aspects related to the demographic, educational and the skill profile of the male and female web professionals. It also includes career-related aspects such as motivation for the choice of this work, mode of work, assignment of tasks, nature of training, organisational environment, acquaintance with the technological infrastructure, career prospectus and the problems encountered. Data analysis has been carried out using SPSS6.

DISCUSSION AND INTERPRETATION OF THE FINDINGS

Questions related to the active players in the web team of the sample universities could be answered from the organisational and gender profile of our study. It is noted that web site development project has been undertaken as a shared responsibility of the major organisational units in the universities. Although it is a collaborative effort of the professionals from the academic, administrative, library and computing units, the dominance of the academic unit in the web development process is noted which might be due to the fact that the academic units are under great pressure to integrate the internet and web technologies into the teaching and research programmes. As far as the role of gender in the web work is concerned, there is a striking contrast in the representation of men and women in the web related occupations in the sample institutions. Women are underrepresented in the web team of ALU-FR and they are marginalised in most of the organisational units reflecting the lack of institutional and individual initiatives and support to get in more women to this work. On the contrary, one could notice gender equity in the representation of men and women in the web team of UWO-CA and they have gained access to the web team of the various organisational units. Surprisingly, women's representation outnumber men in the web team of the computing unit in the UWO-CA (which is generally considered as the male domain) indicating that women are edging over their male counterparts in the technical jobs. On the whole, the opportunities for women in the web work seems to be mixed depending upon the organisation where they work. It also shows the impact of the organisational and occupational factors on women's work life in this new technology.

The research questions related to the professional requirements of the web work and the opportunities opened up for male and female members are illustrated in the demographic profile (age, education and subject background of the respondents) of our study. The age pattern of the respondents from ALU-FR and UWO-CA shows that age is not a barrier for the men and women professionals to take up assignments in web designing in the universities. As web designing is a recent phenomena, it is expected that only the youngsters, who are exposed to the new technologies, could participate in the web designing work. On the contrary, it is observed that men and women belonged to all age categories could find equal opportunities in this new area of work[4]. The educational pattern of the web team of the sample universities shows that members with diverse educational background could find placement in the work. The flexibility in the requirement of educational qualifications has allowed women with both basic and advanced level educational qualifications to gain access to the web work in the sample universities. Though women are not on par with men with respect to their qualifications at the advance level (ALU-FR: M=66%, F=20%, UWO-CA: M=27%,

F=19%) , that has not hindered them from participating on equal line with men in the web profession. The knowledge base or subject background of the respondents shows that members with both computing and non computing base are receptive to the web related work in the universities. This aspect of the profession facilitated more women from non-computing also to get into the web work in the sample institutions. The representation of gender groups with computing base (ALU-FR:M=44%, F=18%, UWO-CA: M=26%, F=19%), and non-computing base (ALU-FR: M=33%, F=5%; M=24%, F=31%) indicates the domination of men in the computing and women in the non-computing field. However, one could see the narrowing down of the gender gap in the case of web professionals in UWO-CA where the proportion of women with computing background are almost closer to men. The foregoing factors indicate the flexibility existing at the access point in the web profession which is an encouragement for larger participation of men and women with heterogeneous professional characteristics. Questions related to which occupational groups of the university population are more attracted to web profession are discussed at length in the work profile of our study. It is observed that participants of the web project of the universities are a large band of people from professors to students. Realising the futuristic and the communicative value of the web, members from all cadres and ranks volunteered to work in the web project and considered it as an 'add on' for their professional development. This trend has marked the emergence of the new working culture in the university that necessitates the close collaboration of diverse professionals, all working within a highly co-ordinated and structured development process in order to achieve the common cause of creation of the university web sites. However, it is to be noted that the involvement of the technical staff is higher (ALU-FR=50%; UWO-CA=53%) than the professional and managerial staff in both the universities selected for study. The indispensability of the technical staff for web designing is noted from their representation in the web team of each and every one of the organisational units in the universities. There is no single web team in the universities without adequate representation of technical staff. The representation of women with technical background varies with institutions. There is an equal representation of men and women with technical job background in the web team of UWO-CA (M=28%, F=25%), while women with technical job background is very much negligible (M=45%, F=5%) in the web team of ALU-FR. Gender difference is also seen in the representation of male and female members from the professional (ALU-FR: M=24%, F=5%, UWO-CA: M=10%, 3%) and managerial (M=8%, F=13%, M=12%, F=22%) job categories. Majority of the men from the professional job categories and women from the managerial job categories take part in the web work.

How far women are succeeded in getting into the critical areas of web work can be seen from the discussions in Table. The placement of women across the content production, programming and implementation part of web work shows a heterogeneous trend. In the case of ALU-FR, men dominate the entire range of tasks right from content designing (M=41%, F=12%), programming and implementation (M=37%, F=10%). In the case of UWO-CA, men dominate the programming and implementation part of the web work (M=34%. F=15%), while women dominate the content designing area of work (M=17%, F=34%). Although there is an equal sharing of work among the gender groups in the UWO-CA, the critical areas of work are predominated by men.

The skill based and multitasking nature of the web occupation demands a wide range of skills from the professionals and those who equip themselves to play the multiple roles could survive successfully in this profession. The question is where are women in these skill areas and what role women play in the web work. The findings of our survey reflects the skill level of the respondents from the various organisational units and the gender groups. Regarding creativity, our study shows that a vast majority of the respondents have developed skills in the core areas of creativity namely, web designing and (ALU-FR=75%, UWO-CA=80) content designing (ALU-FR=62%, UWO-CA=67%). In the other peripheral regions (skill regions where demand is not so high at the moment) only a moderate or low percentage of respondents have acquired skills. As universities prefer to develop simple web pages as against those flashy ones of the commercial sites, (so as to reach students working in different levels of hardware infrastructure) there is no heavy demands on the complex skills relating to animation, illustration etc.

With regard to creative areas of web work, the extent of skill gap between the male and female members in the UWO-CA is almost absent in the core regions (web designing and content designing) and exists only at a minimum level in the peripheral regions. On the other hand, the skill gap in creativity is vast among the gender groups in ALU-FR which again is due to the overall under representation of women in the web work. As far as skills in the areas of web management is concerned, the overall percentage of respondents proficient in this field is not so high as in the case of creative skills. Web planning is the most critical area among the managerial skills where a moderate percentage of the respondents have gained experience. There is no skill gap among the gender groups with respect to web planning in UWO-CA though the differences are negligible in the other regions. In the case of ALU-FR, the skill gap is high among the gender groups in web planning and copy right information management, while it is moderate in other regions. The magnitude of skill gap in the technical regions are high among the gender groups in ALU-FR and moderate in UWO-CA, reconfirming the predominance of male in the technical areas of work in the digital media[25]. It also confirms with the early survey results which identified that women's share of technical job is particularly low, and their presence in content production and in administration is relatively high[26]. To reach an effective gender balance, it is necessary that women have a much more important role in technology design and management rather than content production or administrative occupation. This situation calls for some conscious effort on the part of the institution to offer more training and placement for women in the technical areas of web work.

CONCLUSION

The entire discussion of this study centred around two major issues viz: gender technology relation in the context of web media and gender relation in public organisations especially in the university environment. As far as the gender technology relation is concerned, it is identified that web media seems to be gender neutral at the entry point by allowing both men and women of all age groups, educational and subject background to gain access to the web related occupations in the sample institutions. With respect to women's participation in the web work, there seems to be a paradoxical situation in the sample institutions which needs further explorations. The lower participation of women in the web occupation in the ALU-FR may be the reflection of the gender based digital divide that exists in the IT sector of the sample country. The equal participation of women in the web occupation in general and their predominance in the computing unit in the case of UWO-CA indicate the gender -neutrality of the organisational environment. The relation between the professional equipment (subject and occupational background) and the areas of work (content / technical production) assignment is established. Since the proportion of women with computing qualification and technical occupational background are higher in UWO-CA than in ALU-FR, their role in the critical areas of work (web implementation) is also significant. It is argued that to achieve gender balance in the web work, it is necessary that majority of women should turn to the technical rather than the content production work[27].

REFERENCES

1. Spender, Dale. (2000). "The digital life style for women". *CPSR Newsletter*. Vol.18. No. 1. pp. 1-6.
2. Spertus, Ellen and Pine, Evelyn. (2000). "Gender in the internet age." *CPSR Newsletter*. Vol. 18. No. l. pp. 1-2.
3. "Women on the Internet: Fact or Fiction?" *Web Review 1996* www.msnbc.com/news/539322.aspeaglewoman.simracing. dk/ women/web4women. htmWeaver, Jane. (2001).
4. "Cracking the glass ceiling." MSNBC's Summit in Silicon Valley, 2000. http://www.msnbc.com/news/539322.asp
5. Chu, Show Wie. (2001). "Digital gender divide" *Globe and Mail*. February 19.2001.pp. 1-2. http: //www, globeandmai S .com/ ganv'ROB/20010 219/RPOLL.html
6. Silicon Valley Partnership (2000). "Definition of Digital divide" http://www.siliconvalleypartnership.org/digidiv. htm
7. December, John and Ginsburg, Mark (2000). "Introduction to Web Systems and Applications". http://doc.rinet.ru:8083/cG13.2/ ch7.html
8. Information Technology Association of Canada. (2000). "Women in Infɔrmation Technology (Win IT) Learn about IT Trends". http://www.wittnn.com/english/winit/learnabout/ trends.html

9. Regan & Associates. (1997). "A labour market analysis of the interactive digital media industry: opportunities in multimedia". North valley private industry council (NOVA), CA. p. 2.

10. Scruggs, Patricia C, Cortright, Joseph and Douglas, Marcia. (1999). "Designing Portland's future: The role of the Creative Services Industry: A report written for the Portland Development Commission and the Industry and professional organisation of the Creative Services Cluster". June.

11. Partridge, Thea. (1996). "Techbabes: Women and the Internet"-Seminar. Feb. 15th, 1996, Vancouver, BC. http://www.techbabes.eom/Rants/seminarfeb96.h tml

12. Spender, Dale (2000). "The Digital Life Style for Women". *The CPSR Newsletter*, Vol. 18. Number 1. pp. 1-6.

13. Melymuka, Kathleen (2000). "Bridging a gap for women in IT". *Computer World*, July 17. pp. 1- 4.

14. Erbe, Bonne. (2000). "Women and Technology". http://www.listproc, bucknell.edu/archives/femecon- 1/200007/msg00025.html

15. Gill, Rosalind (2000). "New Media: Working Practices in the Electronic Arts". *European Commission and London School of Economics.* July.

16. Mitter, Swasti (2000). "Women in knowledge societies". http://www.womenaction.org/gkii/swasti.html

17. Gewirtz, Mindy L, Lindsey, Ann. (2000). "Women in the New Economy: Insights and Realities". GLS Consulting Inc., 2000. pp. 1-22.

18. Napier, JoAnn etal (2000). "Technology with curves: Women reshaping the digital landscape".Chapters.ca

19. WOW (2001). "Women on the Web Conference", held on March 8-10, 2001, Hamberg, Germany.

20. Weaver, Jane. (2000). "Cracking the glass ceiling". Silicon Summit II.hltp:/'ww\\.msnbc.com/news/539322.asp

21. Crawford, Noel and Troute, Derek. (1995). "IT & Women- Life in 2020-Heaven or Hell?" http://www.es.ted.ie/courses/ism/smis/resource/discuss/itmwd95b.html

22. Forcella, Mariagrazia. (2000). "Women professionals in the media in the context of new technological developments: Final Study". European Parliament, Director General for Research, Directorate A, *The STOA Programme*, Luxembourg, PE 168.380/Fin.St. pp. 1-70.

23. Taggart, Nancy and O'Gara, Chloe. (2000). "Training women for leadership and success in IT." http://www.wroldbank. org/ edinvest/genderLp.pdf

24. Hansen, Steve and Deshpande, Yogesh (1999). "Identifying a skills hierarchy for participants in the web environment". http:// ausweb.scu.edu.au/aw99_archive/aw99/pro ceedings/hansen/ paper.html

25. Gill, Rosalind and Dodd Diane. (1999). "New Media: Working practices in the electronic arts". Paper presented at the conference held at LSE, London, November 12th-14th, 1999.

26. Forcella, Mariagrazia (2000). "Women professionals in the media in the context of new technological developments". European Parliament, Directorate General for Research, Directorate A, *The STOA Programme.*

27. Taggart, Nancy and O'Gara, Chloe. (2000). "Training women for leadership and success in IT." Academy for Educational Development. *World Bank Report.*

5

Participation of Women in The Web Development in The Universities: A Case Study

ABSTRACT

This study makes an evaluation of the extent to which the escalation of the labour demand, the transformation of work culture and the diversification of the professional characteristics of the web profession have attracted women to enter into this new branch of IT occupation. It examines the role being played by the male and female workers in the creative, technical and management areas of web designing. It analyses the gender differences and similarities in the pattern of knowledge and skill acquisition in the web related technologies. Further, it investigates the trends in the preconceived ideas of gender roles in the web based occupations.

INTRODUCTION

Web design as a profession is marked by rapid commercialisation and technical changes since 1995 and the demand for the web professionals is getting accelerated in the recent years both in the commercial and institutional sectors. This new unexplored expansion of web work in the universities demands an evaluation of members participating in the web team of the university; the role and responsibilities of male and female participants in the web development; their professional and academic background; their training and exposure in the area of web designing; their motivation to entry into this new area of work, the nature of tasks they undertake in their respective departments and their overall contribution to the web project of the university. The aim of our study is to explore the situation of men and women in web designing in a public institution and to examine the extent to which this new technology breaks or reinforces the gender division of labour. It attempts to analyse the preparedness of men and wcmen to take up technological route by taking into consideration of their educational, skill and training background. Further, it tries to see the role of women as the designers or creators of this new technology rather than disempowered users of this technology for business, entertainment, and educational purposes. It also examines how far universities as public organisations foster equal opportunities for men and women in the field of web related works. In short, our study focuses its attention on women's participation in the web media from the gender technology and organisational perspectives on the basis of a case study.

OBJECTIVES

The specific objectives of this study are listed below.

I. To identify the demographic and the organisational profile of the participants in the web environment in the sample university.

II. To assess the situation of men and women in the working practices (web development, database management, graphic designing, server support, coding & programming, creation & maintenance of web pages, content development etc) and working environment (computer centre, administration, library, & academic departments/ faculties).

III. To explore whether there exists gender differences in educational attainment, skill equipment, and acquaintance with technological infrastructure (multimedia workstations, hardware and software).

METHODOLOGY

Our study focus its attention on the web designers in the University of Freiburg, Germany. An inventory of these workers were collected both from the Internet and also from personnel list maintained in the computer section of the university. The total population of the web designers is 156 among which male members are 128 and female members are 28. The entire web designers were contacted with a request for participation in our survey but only 58 of them expressed their willingness to take up our survey. Thus, the participation rate of the respondents is 37 percent.

Among those accepted to take up the survey, 45 are men and 13 are women. The period of the survey is April-May, 2001. The data are collected by contacting each one of the respondents in the various academic departments, administrative sections, library and the computer centre during their leisure time . A questionnaire covering aspects related to the demographic, educational and the skill profile of the male and female web professionals was used in the face to face interviews. It also included career related aspects such as motivation for the choice of this work, mode of work, assignment of tasks, nature of training, organisational environment, acquaintance with the technological infrastructure, career prospectus and the problems encountered. Data analysis was then carried out using SPSS6.

DATA ANALYSIS

In order to examine the various issues raised in the objectives, we have conducted a descriptive analysis of the data collected. As the size of the population of the male and female respondents of our study is unequal, both the groups are treated as a separate population in the analysis. The following section illustrates the status of men and women in the web environment of the sample university.

DEMOGRAPHIC PROFILE OF THE WEB DESIGNERS IN THE SAMPLE UNIVERSITY

The demographic pattern of our sample reflects that web team of the university comprises of largely male, young and highly qualified members. Despite the fact that web profession accommodates more women than the other IT professions[3], we could notice from our sample that the representation of women in this area of work is limited. This might probably reflect the general trend prevailing in the university where the women population is relatively lower than their male counterparts in IT occupations. As far as age and academic qualifications are concerned, both men and women are on the equal levels. This again reinstates the fact that the web team of the sample institution consists mostly of the youngsters with high academic background. It is generally argued that academic qualification is not essential for taking up web-related jobs, but in the context of producing web content, the importance of the academic training as an 'add on' is realised.

ORGANISATIONAL PROFILE OF THE WEB DESIGNERS

The organisational pattern of the respondents reflects the web team composition of the major units (faculties, computer centre, administration, library and other centres) in the university. The size of the web team varies significantly among the different organisational units (faculteis = 57% , computer centre=12%, administration^ 2%, the library =10%) which gives rise to the argument that those units that engage more people, register greater progress than those that engage less people towards web based activities. The web team of the faculty of informatics and applied sciences is larger than the other faculties which is to some extent reflective of the availability of local expertise/human resources in these faculties. There are distinct differences in the distribution of men and women web professionals across the various units and faculties. There is no representation of women in the web team of the computer centre, while the participation of men are higher in this unit. Also, in units which are commonly considered as women's area of work like the administration and library, the web team members are mostly men. Within the faculties, men web professionals are seen largely in informatics while women are seen in applied sciences. The distribution pattern of men and women among the various units and faculties to some extent coincide wth their subject background.

OCCUPATIONAL PROFILE OF THE WEB DESIGNERS

The occupational pattern of the web team (Table 1) consists of members from diverse areas of organisational (units/faculties)and occupational categories (job positions). Overwhelming involvement of professionals from all cadres and ranks may be due to the fact that to acquire skills in web designing is considered as an 'add on' for their professional development. This trend has marked the emergence of the new working culture in the university that necessitates the close collaboration of diverse professionals all working within a highly co-ordinated and structured development process in order to achieve the common cause of creation of the university web sites. Gender analysis reveals a distinct difference in the occupational background of the male and female members taking part in the web team of the university. Our sample shows that the web team composed of a larger percentage of men from the computing and the teaching occupaions and women from the administrative occupations. The above result seems to support the assumption that web designing is receptive to men and women from both high-tech and non-high tech background.

Table 5.1 : Occupational Profile of the Respondents

(A) ACADEMIC	[M=14 (31%)	I F=2 (15%)	IIC. LIBRARY	I M=4 (8%)	I F=l (8%)
Professors	6 (13%)	1 (8%)	Section Heads	3(7%)	1 (8%)
Associate Professors	6(13%)	0(0%)	7. Assistenl Heads	1(2%)	0(0%)
Assistent Professors/ Scientific Assistent	2 (4%)				1 (8%)
(B) ADMINISTRATIVE	M=l (2%)	F=7 (54%)	D. COMPUTING	M=26 (57%)	F=3 (23%)
			8. Team Leader	3 (7%)	0(0%)
Associate Head	1 (2%)	4 (30%)	9. Manager-IS	1 (2%)	0 (0%)
Assistent Heads	0 (0%)	3 (23%)	10 Coordinator IS	1 (2%)	0 (0%)
			11. System Administrators	7 (16%)	0(0%)
			12.Web Professionals	7 (16%)	1(8%)
			13. Student Consultants	7 (16%)	2(15%)

KNOWLEDGE/SUBJECT BASE OF THE WEB-DESIGNERS

Regarding the knowledge/subject base of the respondents, our analysis shows that in majority of the cases, women represent the nontechnical group of the web team. The indispensability of the non-computer professionals in this occupation has been invariably noted from the studies. As web profession is both an art and a science, it involves both the creative (design) and the constructive (navigation, performance and administration) activities and, therefore, the need for specialists combining these two areas are required. It is noted from our sample that woman have a strong knowledge base in various arts, information science, social science and science subject background, while men have background in the computing and allied subject fields indicating that the web team of the university has the necessary input for the creative and constructive areas of work.

Table 5.2 : Subject Background of the Respondents

Sl.No.	*Subject Background*	*Male*	*Female*	*Total*
1.	Liberal Arts and Languages	2(4%)	0 (0%)	2 (3%)
2.	Library & Information Science	2(4%)	0(0%)	2 (3%)
3.	Social Sciences	13(28%)	8 (62%)	21(35%)
4.	Biological & Medical Sciences	2(4%)	4 (30%)	6110%)
5.	Computer Sciences	18(40%)	1 (8%)	19(33%)
6.	Physical Sciences	9 (20%).	0 (0%)	9(16%)
	Total	45(100%)	13(100%)	58(100%)

TASK PROFILE OF THE WEB DESIGNERS

With respect to the work pattern of the participant in the web environment, gender equity is maintained. The representation of women is noticed in some of the traditional (technical) male areas of work, like web implementation, creation of web based databases, web server support, and coding & programming (see Table 5). The representation of men in some of the women's area of work, namely, web page creation and content development is also seen. Though the male and female domains of work were well documented, the present study shows a slight deviation from the traditional role playing by men and women in their area of

Table: 5.3 : Types of Tasks Undertaken by the Respondents

Sl.No.	*Tasks*	*Male*	*Female*	*Total*
1.	Web applications/ implementation	4(9%)	1 (8%)	5 (9%)
2.	Creation of web based databases	5(11%)	2 (15%)	7(12%)
3.	Designing graphics, animation and flash	3(7%)	0	3 (5%)
4.	Web server support	6(13%)	2(15%)	8 (14%)
5.	Coding and programming	3 (7%)	1 (8%)	4 (7%)
6.	Web page development and maintenance	18(40%)	3 (23%)	21(36%)
7.	Content development	6(13%)	4(31%)	10(17%)
	Total	45 (100%)	13(100%)	58(100%)

work. The presence of men and women are noticed in both areas of work and the gender differences with respect to the work domains are marginal (see Table 5). The roles or assignments of tasks taken by the gender groups give the impression that web development is neither a male's or a female's domain but it is a genderless area of work where both men and women with creative and technical knowledge could work.

SKILL PROFILE OF THE WEB DESIGNERS IN THE AREAS OF CREATIVITY, MANAGEMENT AND TECHNICAL WORK

An overview of the skill patterns of the respondents in the area of creativity shows that the concentration of majority of them seemed to be on a few areas of skills like creation of web pages and content designing. This convergence of attention on developing skills proficiency in certain areas, can be viewed from two different perspectives; one is from the nature of the work (demand for work) and the other one is from the people involved in this work. As far as the nature of work is concerned, the universities are going in for a simple web sites that contain information in the form of texts and graphics (not flashy and highly technical). All those who know how to create and edit hypertext along with a basic knowledge of scripting (e.g. CGI, Java, perl, c and unix shell scripts) graphics application techniques (e.g photoshop, fractal painter and 3D modelling) and TCP/IP networking could perform the job of a web page designer efficiently5. Similarly, content creation requires both creative as well as technical and operational skills and it is stated that such skills could be acquired on the job. With respect to skills like animation, interface designing and illustration which requires a long training and practice, most of the respondents have remarked that they cannot afford to invest their time on these areas, since they are neither rewarding nor being considered as essential for performing their main job. In this context, it is worth considering the nature of the web development process in the university atmosphere. It is undertaken not as an exclusive profession of the staff and students, but it is taken as part of their other regular assignments. Probably, that might be the reasons why the proportion of respondents having proficiency in certain skill areas which are on the high demand in the industry labour market like, animation, illustration and graphic designing are only moderate in the university. The lower proportion of participants on the transferable skills (art directing, directing and video film production) suggests the diminishing demand for those skills in web designing, since these roles have been taken up by the web designer. Considerations for the lay-out, texts, images and graphics, determinations of the volume of digital information on a single page, the layers and sub-layers, and the links etc governed by the web page designer. Therefore, specialised skills in art direction and direction is not considered as important by the participants. Among the female respondents, invariably the percentage of women possessing some of the emergent (web designing-92%)and convergent (content designing- 85%) creative skills are higher than their male colleagues. Therefore, one could argue that women's expertise in wider access to the web development. Certain creative skills in web designing help them to gain With respect to the level of application of creative skills on current work by men and women, the latter seemed to score a higher level which coincide with the theoretical assumption that women are competent in the creative skills[6] and the artistic element required for web related works. It also seems to support the statement that 'the intellectual/creative arenas which forms the core of the web profession is 'becoming more of a level playing field'[7] and the web is considered as an equaliser and ideal medium for women to make progress.

Regarding women's proficiency in the managerial skills, especially in the area of planning web sites, confirm the general assumption that women score well as managers in the decentralised organisations where team work and delegations are considered as the key.[9] The lower application of the managerial skills in the areas of financial, advertising and copyright by the respondents could be justified on the ground that universities are still in the initial stage of the web development activities, and therefore, the need for holistic and strategic web production management skills may not be required at this juncture. As the skill requirement goes with the stage of web development, the need for people with specialised management skills may be required in the future. Gender difference is noticed in the pattern of skill development in the different managerial areas. Women seemed to show proficiency in the web planning and product management, while the male seemed to show efficiency in the areas of web promotion activities, copyright information management and financial management.

The higher score of male respondents, in all the technical skill areas of web designing, reconfirm the predominance of male in the technical areas of work, especially in the digital media work.[10] Studies also have reported the lower visibility of women in the technical areas of multimedia and web industries. It is suggested that women's lower representation in technical areas is a result of the gendered nature of the prior industry practices in information technology and media production.[11] In the present context, the lower representation of women in the technical areas may be attributed to the fact that majority of the female participants of this study are from the social science background (60%) and, therefore, their proficiency in the technical areas are relatively lower. However, programming skills alone is not the be all and end all of this profession. It needs a proper blend of programming skills with sufficient proficiency in content development and production techniques. In that respect, women have the necessary skill base to participate as active agents in the web designing process. The general trend prevailing among the web industry is that technical skills can be acquired whereas the creative skills are rare and it is considered as a scarcest resource. In summary, the skill profile of the respondents reveals that a fairly high proportion of men and women possess the skills needed to perform the work. The skill profile of the female respondents are higher in the creative (M=40%, F=49%) and management areas (M=28%, F=40%), while the male respondents are higher in technical areas (M=49%, F=34%) of work. The skill acquisition status of women in all the major areas of work gives the impression that they possess the necessary input to be an active agent in the web development in the university environment. The dominance of women in certain skill regions, like creativity and management, which are considered as the core areas of web designing, makes one to assume that the scope of women to be the designer rather than just the user of this new technology are large. It is also reported that women seemed to have acquired a large share of the skills and characteristics relevant for the digital age[12].

Table 5.4 : Proficiency of the respondents in three major skills domains

Sl.No.	*Skill Domains*	*Male (%)*	*Female (%)*
1.	Creative Skills	40%	49%
2.	Management Skills	28%	40%
3.	Technical Skills	49%	34%

GENDER DIFFERENCE IN THE PERCEIVED AND THE ACTUAL APPLICATION OF SKILLS

This study has also brought to light the difference between what the respondents perceive themselves to have skills in the creative, management and technical domains and the level of applications (higher level) of those skills in their area of working.

It has demonstrated the difference existing between the skills acquired and the skills utilised in the field of work by the respondents. In the case of female respondents, this difference between the perceived and the actual use of the skill is very low in the technical skills, while in the case of the male respondents, this situation is found in the management skills. In all other areas of skills, the gap between these two phenomena is high for the male and female respondents.

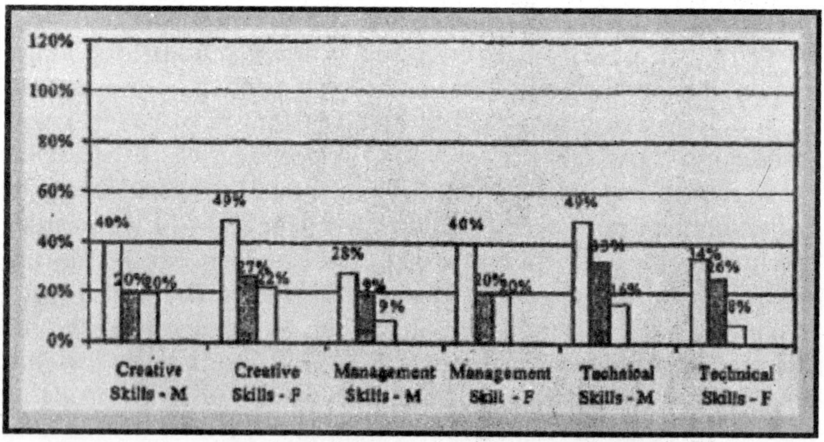

Fig. 5.1: Difference between the perceived and the actual applications of skills

The gap in the utilisation of the skills acquired by the respondents may be due to the lack of opportunity in the work area or due to want of time as most of the participants in the web areas of work are doing it as their additional responsibility. It is presumed that as the web development project of the university is getting advanced/matured, the need for development and management of sites would become more complex, which require full time professionals with specialisation in each branch of the web technology. In that context, the gap between the skill acquired and skill utilised would be narrow.

ACQUAINTANCE OF THE WEB DESIGNERS WITH THE IT INFRASTRUCTURE

The mastery in handling the technology and the familiarity with the hardware and software are considered as the essential parameter for the computing professionals. Tinkering with technology is one of the prime factors that determine the suitability of a person in the profession. This study has examined the level of acquaintance of the male and the female respondents in handling the multimedia hardware and the software associated with the web designing work. In the case of acquaintance with various workstations, a higher percentage of both male and female respondents have proficiency in handling windows 95 and windows NT. Gender difference is noticed only in the case of handling unit[7] in which case, the male respondents have higher proficiency than the female respondents. The same tendency is

Table 5.5. Gender Difference in Acquaintance with various Multimedia Infrastructures

Infrastructure	*Male*		*Female*	
Workstation	"Windows 9~	(91%)	Windows 95	(85%)
	Unix	(80%)	Windows NT	(69%)
	Windows NT	(73%)		
Hardware	"Flatbed Scanner	(83%)	Flatbed Scanner	(85%)
	Digital Video Cameras	(71%)	Digital Video Cameras	(61%)
	Slide Scanner	(60%)		
Software	"HTML Authoring	(93%)	HTML Authoring	(85%)
	Graphic Design	(82%)	Graphic Design	(78%)
	Desktop Publishing	(78%)	Desktop Publishing	(85%)
	Animation	(64%)	Presentation	(69%)

noticed in the case of handling the multimedia hardware where both the gender groups acknowledged a higher proficiency in handling flatbed scanner and the digital video cameras while the male members seemed to have gained high level expertise in handling the slide scanners. As far as the gender situation in the acquaintance with multimedia software is concerned, both the gender groups expressed a high level of acquaintance.

The above results make one to assume that female members of this study are no longer technophobes and they have already acquired confidence in handling the technology with ease.

CONCLUSION

Our study shows that like in any other IT profession in Germany, women are under-represented in web designing also. This lower participation of women might be due to the fact that the voluntary, unpaid and time consuming nature of the web designing job might be conflicting with the family and child care responsibility of women in the university. As this job requires constant learning and training, most of the women might find it hard to patch up with their already demanding commitments in their work and home. The findings of our study reveals that it is not the gender but the subject background of the individuals influences their participation in the web team of various organisational units in the university. Women's absence in the web team of the computer centre and their lower representation in the web team of the administration and the library coincide with the lack of women professionals with computing background. Among the 50 percent of web professionals with the computing background in our sample, only 5 percent are women. Since majority of the women have the subject background in science, their participation is visible in the web team of the biological sciences. It is seen from our study that the web development work requires both tech and non-tech professionals which encourages women with non-tech background also to get into this sphere of work. However, as the web matures, it would require professionals with more of technological background which could imply that the demand for non -technical professional is short-lived. A similar situation existed in the software industry during the 80s, when it was at the stage of infancy. As it advanced, it focused more on engineering and technological professionals rather than on non-engineering professionals[13]. It implies that the technological orientation is required for women at a larger level to cope with the fast changing web media environment. Our study reveals the participation of women both in the creation of web pages and in the implementation of the technologies signifying the equal opportunities prevailing in this work. Unlike the software industry where there is concentration of women only in the bottom line of the occupational hierarchy, in web profession, the presence of women is seen in all job categories. Our study points out the gender difference in the skill development pattern of the male and female members. Men seemed to be proactive in developing skills in the technical areas while women on the creative and management areas. The most required skill demands for the web based occupations regardless of the industry segment are a combination of creative, management and technical talents for the next three to five years. In that context, women's opportunities seemed to be brighter in this occupation. The larger acquaintance of women with various computing platforms, multimedia, hardware and software gives the impression that they are no longer technophobes and prepare themselves to take the technological route with confidence.

REFERENCES

1. December, John and Ginsburg, Mark (2G0O). "Introduction to Web Systems and Application". http://docs.rinet.ru:8083/CG13.2/ch7.htm
2. Information Technology Association of Canada (2000). "Women and Information Technology(WlNlT): Learn About IT Trends". http://www.witttnn.com/english/witit/learnabout/trends.html
3. WITT National Network (2000). "Profiles of women in IT:Multimedia/web". Canada.
4. Gantz, John(1996). "Web site design: Is it Art or Science?" *Computer World*. October 07. 1997.pp.l-2.
5. Employment Development Department, California (1996). "Labour Market Information: Web page Designers/Masters/Mistresses". *California Occupational Guide*. Number 559. Interest Area 5-A.
6. Melyrnuka, Kathleen (2000). "Bridging a gap for women in IT". *Computer World*, July 17. pp. 1-4
7. Spender, Dale (2000). The Digital Life Style for Women. The CPSR Newsletter, Vol. 18, Number 1. pp. 1 -6

8. Shortt, Denise, (200i). "Women crossing borders", http://www.globetechnology.com/wornan/pp.l-3
9. Wajcman, Judy (1998). The ferninisation of work: The case of management. *Current Research in Industrial Relations,* Vol.1. pp. 215-23.
10. Gill, Rosalind and Dodd Diane, (1999). "New Media: Working Practices in the Electronic Arts". Paper presented in the conference held at LSE, London, November 12th -14th, 1999.
11. Swanson, Gillan & Wise Patricia (1997). "Digital Futures: Women's Employment in the Multimedia Industries".
12. "Women's Research and Employment Initiatives Programme (WRE1P)", *Commonwealth of Australia,* p.219.
13. Spender Dale (2000). *The CSPR Newsletter*. Vo.18s. No.l. Winter 2000. pp. 1-6.
14. Strober, Myra H and Arnold, Carolyn L (1985). "Integrated Circuits/Segregated Labour: Women in Computer-Related Occupations and High-Tech Industries". In: Hartann, Heidi I., Ed. *Computer Chips and Paper Chips: Technology and Women's Employment*. Washington, D.C. National Academy Press. 1987. pp.136-182.

6

Women and Computing in Some European Countries

ABSTRACT

Computer Science is a relatively new discipline compared to well established disciplines like law or medicine. The computer industry has experienced a rapid and expansive growth in the last few years that educational institutions in some western societies cannot respond to their workforce needs. Women play in this situation a crucial role, since they represent a human resource potential in the IT labour market. Governments and the professional organisations in many countries and international institutions aim to encourage especially women labour enter IT professions to resolve the problem of shortage of workforce in the IT sector. Nevertheless, the enrolment of women in IT at educational institution level as well as professional level is not yet equal to that of men.

Our aim in this short paper is to show an approximate picture of women's participation in computing education and occupation in some European member states from a cross national perspective. The geographical focus of our study is the European Union.

***Keywords:** Computer Education, Computer Occupations, Gender and Computing.*

INTRODUCTION

The IT sector represents one of the fast expanding branches of the information economy and actually the most dynamic in the international labour market. During the second half of the nineties, this sector has experienced a huge demand for skilled IT labour force, while majority of the European member states did not have adequate supply to meet that situation. This unbalanced development between demand and supply of IT labour force has led the public and private sectors in many countries to initiate programmes which encourage young people to study computer science at the tertiary level (e.g. the state initiatives being, Frauen ans netz, werde-Informatikerin, etc. in Germany). Additional courses in private and public institutions also offer an opportunity for persons from other academic fields to join the IT-workforce (for example, initiatives from multinational companies like Cisco, Oracle or IBM in several countries and the E-Learning models of these companies attract people to IT-Trainings, OECD (2002)). These initiatives not only address the urgent working-force shortage, but also open up chances for women to gain access into the IT field and balance the gender inequalities prevalent in this industry. In this paper we will show participation of women in computer science at the educational institution level and in some areas of the IT sector in some EU Member States and initiatives that are being taken in the European area.

WOMEN'S PARTICIPATION IN COMPUTER SCIENCE EDUCATION AND IT RELATED PROFESSIONS IN THE EUROPEAN UNION

Participation of women in Computer Science education at the tertiary level differs among the European member states. A parallel situation can be observed in women's participation in IT related professions. In both the fields women's participation remains unequal to that of men in the countries, considered especially in the Netherlands and Belgium (Eurostat 2000).

Participation of female students in Mathematics and Computer Science Education at the Tertiary Level (University) in member states of the European

The proportion of female students in mathematics and computer science in the EU Member States is presented below (vide Table 1).

In Table 1 we can observe that the proportion of women studying mathematics and computer science strongly differs among the EU member states. While the Netherlands, Belgium and Finland account for less than 20% of female students in these academic disciplines, more than 30% of the students in Mathematics and Computer Science in Portugal, Italy and Sweden are women. Nevertheless this picture cannot give a clear idea of the enrolment of women in Computer Science, since in some

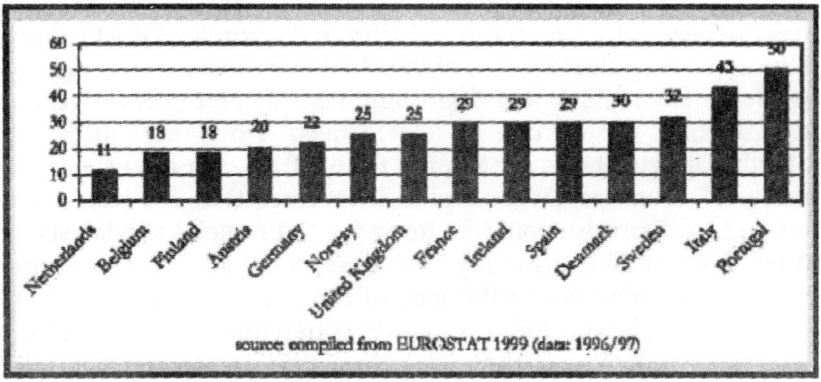

Fig. 1. Proportion of female students in Mathematics and Computer Science

countries (like Germany, s. Statistisches Bundesamt - Hochschulstatistik (2001)) the proportion of women studying Mathematics is much larger than those studying Computer Science. According to a recent study in Sweden (Swedish Ministry of Industry, Employment and Communications, 2000) 28% of the graduates from higher education IT Programs were women. The Norwegian University of Science and Technology introduced in 1997 a special quota system for women in computer science studies. The results of this project have been very positive: in the first two years, the percentage of female students increased to more than 30% (OECD 2002). In Germany, several initiatives from the state, but also from private companies (like IBM) encourage girls to study computer science (media girls, werde-informatikerin, Frauen ans Netz, D21, etc.) and retain them during their study years in this jet predominant masculine field (like "informatica feminale"). The enrolment of women in computer science studies has increased in the last years and actually 15% of the computer science students in German universities are women. In polytechnics this percentage is lower (13%) (Statistisches Bundesamt 2001).

Participation of women in IT related professions in Europe

The software industry is a key sector and it is the fastest growing sector in Europe (Panteli, 97), neveretheless women remain starkly under represented in all sectors of the computing industry. Though there has been an increase in the number of women entering IT occupations since the seventies, gender equity has not been achieved in this industry in the whole of the European Union. To gain a broad idea of the IT labour force in its complexity, we have to consider two important aspects. Not every worker in this sector is performing IT related tasks, since marketing, sales or other service tasks are related to this field. On the other hand, many IT workers are occupied in sectors that are not strictly related to IT production, like business or financial service sectors (OECD 2002). This difficulty to cope with the IT sector as a whole is an added obstruct to the lack of data about women available joining the IT labour force. An analysis of national statistics (IDPM Report, 1996) reveals that the proportion of women has fallen since the 1980s from 25 per cent to 19 per cent in 1993 and in 1996 it is between 21 to 22 per cent. Table 2 illustrates the status of women in the various IT related occupations in the UK during 1995 (Panteli, 97). The proportion of women is higher in consumer services (27%), followed by programming (22%) and system analysts (21%) whereas they represent a very low proportion in the management positions of the IT labour force (10% or less). Regarding the changing trends from 1994 to 1995 we can observe (vide table 2) that the proportion of women employed as IT operators shows a steeply decreasing trend. Programming and consumer services are sectors where the proportion of women decreased during this period of time. Nevertheless, women enrolment in some management positions, system analysis and technical support showed an increase.

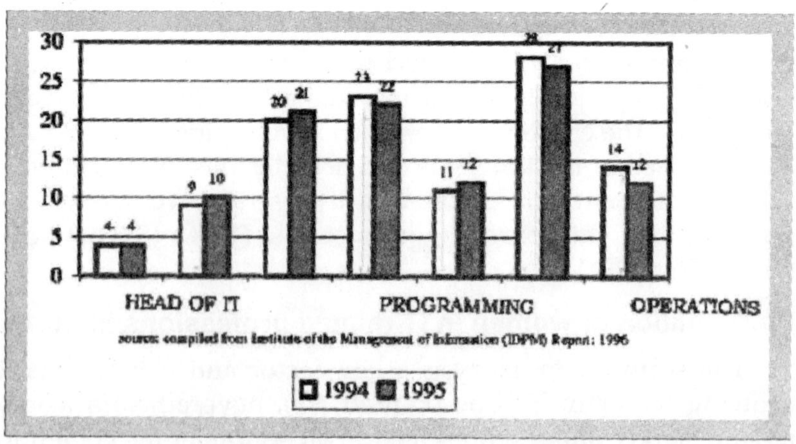

Fig. 2. Proportion of Women in the IT workforce in the UK (%)

Regarding Internet Networking, the last IDC study (2001) shows that only 5,6% of these engaged in networking are women in the twelve considered countries[1]. Nevertheless, according to this study, there are many differences between the countries. France is the country, in which women are best represented in

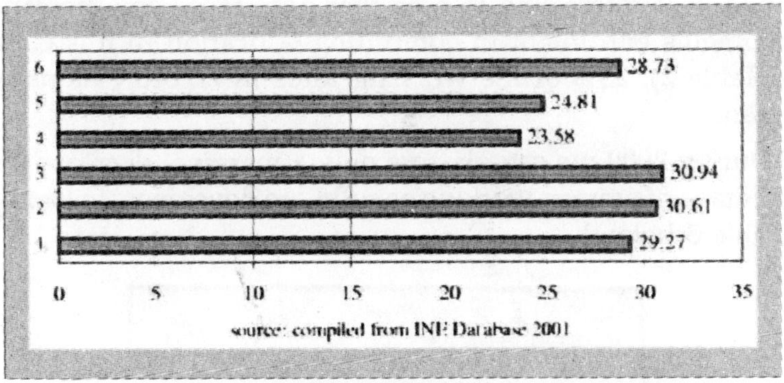

Fig. 3 : Proportion (%) of Women in IT professions in Spain (1 = 1995 – 6 = 2000)

this sector, followed by Spain and Finland. In France there have been several initiatives to support the enrolment of women in the IT sector (IDC 2001). In Spain women constitute 28.73% of the employees in the IT professions during 2000 according to data provided by the INE (Instituto Nacional de Estadistica) (see Table 3 below). The increasing trend in the participation of women in informatics related occupations in the last three years, after a decreasing tendency in 1998, is evident from the data of the INE (Instituto Nacional de Estadistica).

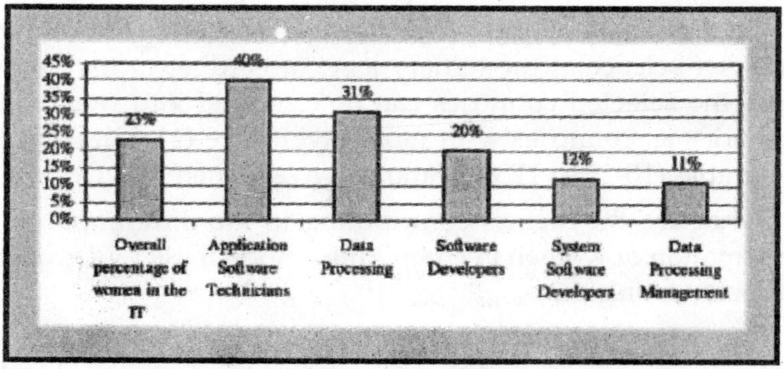

Fig. 4 : Proportion of Women in IT related professions in Germany (1993)

The proportion of women in the IT labour market in Germany was 23 per cent according to 1996 data (see Table 4 below). Application Software (40%) and Data Processing (31%) are the two fields where women are best represented. Nevertheless, in Data Processing Management there is an average of only 11% of women. It is interesting to note that despite the low percentage of women's enrolment in computing education in this country (see Table 2), 23% of the working force in IT professions were women.

During 2000 we can observe only a marginal decrease of the percentage of women working as software developers in Germany (s. Table 3 below).

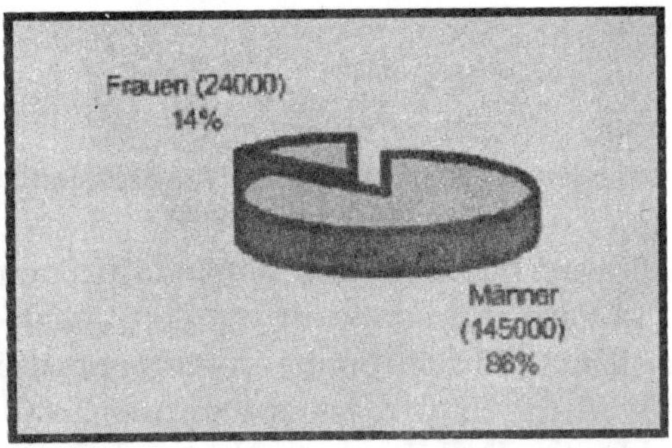

Source: Bundesanstalt fur Arbeit 2000.

Fig. 5 : Software Developers-Proportion of Women and Men

FACTORS INFLUENCING WOMEN'S PARTICIPATION IN COMPUTING (A CROSS NATIONAL PERSPECTIVE)

On the basis of the proportion of women graduating in computer science at the tertiary level (according to the Eurostat data), the selected countries can be classified into two distinct categories as countries with more favourable (21-40%) and less favourable (10-20%) IT educational environment for women.

What are the factors contributing to the differences in the participation of women in computing among these two groups of european countries?

Regarding the first category of countries, Spain shows a relatively favorable situation with respect to women's education in computing. This trend, to a great extent, is attributed to the feminisation of tertiary education that started in the seventies, especially in the beginning of the democratic system. Besides, competitive procedures in the entrance examination at the university admission play a favourable role in women's enrolment, since women tend to show better academic performance in pre-universitary admision tests than men (Garcia de Cortazar & Garcia de Leon, 1996)[2]. The relatively favourable situation of women's participation in computing in the UK, Ireland and Finland can be linked to the positive and salient situation of ICT sector in these countries. According to the OECD report "Measuring the ICT Sector" (2000) these countries are categorised under the high ICT intensity group, that indicates the relative importance of this sector to the total business sector regarding employment, value added, R & D and trade.

The second category countries viz. The Netherlands and Germany show less than 20% of women among graduates in computing (see Table 1). The lack of participation of women in computer science education in Germany and the Netherlands has been attributed in the literature to the influence of gender in the socialisation patterns (Famulla et al. 1993,). Gender roles in the family, in schools and in interaction with peers intervene influencing the attitudes of boys and girls in their career options. Moreover, coeducational practices in school have been identified as an additional factor influencing adversely women's participation in IT education (Kreienbaum & Metz-Gockel, 1992). Girls tend to take distance from those subjects near to engineering, that are regurded as masculine disciplines. This trend is already observed in the secondary educational level and it influences the future trajectories of women and their career orientation.But according to existing studies, family socialisation patterns seem to show a common trend among all the countries taken for analysis. Nevertheless structural factors inherent in each of these societies may contribute to gender based inequalities in the socialisation process in each country influencing contextually the study and vocational choices of men and women.

In the educational systems in these countries, mathematics and technical subjects are considered differently in the curricula. In Spain, for instance, the Ministry of Education have been supporting ICT projects in the primary, lower and upper secondary educational level since 1985, while the UK, Germany and Ireland began to improve these kinds of projects in 1998 and the Netherlands in 1997. There is no research that analyses the impact of these projects on the vocational trajectories of women and men, nevertheless, it would be plausible to argue that those women who are earlier introduced into the ICT field would tend to choose this discipline as a study option in the tertiary level.

Another important factor that could be related to the motivation to opt for this discipline is the situation in the labour market in each of these countries and the differences in the transition processes from education into working life. In Spain the unemployment rate among women was 23,2% during 1999, while the rest of the considered countries showed in the same year a lower rate than the overall average in the EU (10,9%)[3]. The motivation to choose computing as a vocational trajectory, maybe in all the countries, tends some extent to be influenced by work considerations. In contexts where unemployment rates are high it would have a stronger influence in women's vocational decisions. To the extent that computing as a study option represents a good chance to get a job in future compared to other options, women would tend to choose it in the tertiary level.

In short, from the above discussion we can observe a similar trend existing between the enrolment of women in computing education and their participation in IT occupations. In Germany enrolment of women in computer science education at the tertiary level has experienced a strong decrease since the beginning of the eighties, when women represented almost 25% of the student beginners (Bundesanstalt fur Arbeit 2001). Nevertheless, structurally persisting barriers for the enrolment of women in the IT sector have been identified in several studies (Henninger, 2001, Huber et al. 2001, Ruiz Ben, 2002). A more profound analysis of the current situation is nevertheless needed in order to facilitate implement action of the best practices that can be learned from other countries regarding positive enrolment and employment of women in this field. Therefore, the compilation of comparable data is an urgent demand to analyse the situation of women in the most innovative industrial sector now-a-days and furthermore to be able to ameliorate the unequal participation in computing between women and men.

REFERENCES

1. Bundesanstalt far Arbeit (2001). *Frauen und IT*. "Zukiinftsorientierte Arbeitsmarktpolitik". Eurostat (2000). Bildung in Europa. Luxemburg.
2. Famulla, G. E. et al. (1992) *Personlichkeit und Computer*, Opladen, Westdeutscher Verlag.
3. Kreinenbaum, M.A. & Metz-Gockel, S. (1992) "Koedukation und Technikkompetenz von Mddchen". Weinheim. Juventa.
4. Garcia de Cortazar, M. & Garcia de Leon, M.A. (1996). "Las Mujeres".
5. Ingenieras en Espaiia "in: M. Garcia de Cortazar & M.A. Garcia de Leon "Sociologia de las Mujeres espanolas." Editorial Complutense, Madrid, pp. 243-65.
6. IDC (2001) *Der Networking Fachkraftemangel*. "Wie Frauen helfen konnen die Liicke zu schliessen. Im Auftrag von Cisco Systems".
7. OECD (2000). *"From Initial Education to Work"* Paris.
8. OECD (2002). *ICTs and the Information Economy*, Paris, OECD Publication.

7

The Globalization of Gender in IT: A Challenge for the 21st Century

ABSTRACT

In the context of the current state of women in Information Technology (IT), this paper seeks to extend our understanding of the impact of occupational culture on gender relations in selected countries namely USA, UK and The Netherlands. The perspective adopted is one which takes account of the gender dimension of national cultures, notably masculinity and femininity. The evidence shows that gender segregation and under-representation seem to exist in both feminine and masculine national cultures suggesting that at least some elements of computing occupational culture transcend national boundaries.

INTRODUCTION

The low representation of women, in the field of computing, has received increasing attention during the past few years. Studies on this topic have been carried out in various countries and geographical regions in an attempt to highlight the trends in women's participation in this industry. In general, there is a consensus in the literature that the occupational culture of the computing environment has been a constraint for women's recruitment, retention and promotion in computing work. In this paper, we carry out a cross-national study on this issue. We believe that this study is important in helping us understand whether gender segregation needs to be dealt with at the national or global level. In particular, the paper examines and compares the level of gender representation and segregation in computing work across various countries by detailing the most recent statistics in this area. The paper then develops a discussion on the potential influence of the national culture and the occupational culture on gender representation and segregation in computing work.

THE OCCUPATIONAL CULTURE OF COMPUTING

Trice[1], (1993) who studied occupational cultures across various workplaces, defined 'occupational cultures' as collectives which consist of ideologies (emotionally charged and taken for granted beliefs) and cultural forms (mechanisms such as stories, rituals and myths which affirm and express these beliefs). Occupational cultures structure social relations, encourage ethnocentrism and could be dysfunctional as well as functional (Wright[2], 1996:82). As Wright puts it: "'...viewing computer work through the lenses of occupational culture suggests a way to unify seemingly disparate factors [on women's absence from this occupation] into a cohesive whole" (1996, p.81). In her study, Wright (1°96) provides an interesting account of the computing occupational culture by reviewing trie cultural history of computing, its masculine nature and its engineering basis. Her main arguments are presented and complemented by the work of other researchers in this section.

In many occupations, the pattern of gender segregation has been established through an historical sedimentation of role allocation, such as, for example, the clerical (female-dominated) sector and the engineering (male dominated) sector. Computing, which has only come into existence during World War II, might be seen as potentially less bound by traditions e.g. as men's or women's work, and, therefore, as a gender-neutral occupation offering opportunities to both men and women to enter and progress.

Contrary to this general assumption, however, the values and norms of engineering have been found to be especially prominent in computing and, therefore despite its newness, there has been evidence of gender segregation and ghettoization in this sector as much as in other longer-established technically-oriented and male-dominated professions. Indeed, the first computers were physically constructed by electrical engineers and, therefore, computing from its early years became a subordinate to electrical engineering. According to Trice (1993), because subordinate occupational cultures take on the ideologies and cultural forms of their dominant culture, the computing culture took on the occupational culture of electrical engineering. The latter comprises a style of calculation and a pattern of working that is predominantly mathematical and structured in nature. Turkle[3], (1984) argues that men are more likely to be comfortable with a 'hard' computing style that emphasises mathematical calculation, while women are more comfortable with the culture of simulation, working through interfaces that permit a 'soft', flexible style, allowing experimentation, a non-sequential and a non-hierarchical approach. The culture of calculation corresponds to the hard programming style which emphasizes a mathematical-driven structure with rigorous guidelines and procedures. By contrast, the culture of simulation adopts the soft programmmg style which allows for interaction, flexibility, trial and error and experimentation Wright[4], (1997a) finds that in computing workplaces both of these cultures could be evident although the culture of simulation is more evident among users who are, not-surprisingly, female dominated. Groups of computer professionals, on the other, are characterised by the culture of calculation and are male-dominated.

Other accounts develop an image of masculinity in computing and its effect on women (Grundy[5], 1996, Henwood[6], 1993; Wright, 1996). Hemenway[7], (1995) describes four 'forces' which make for discrimination and pressure for women in industries like computing. First, women with traditional feminine work styles, seeking consensus and team effort, are seen as less confident and capable than men; while those women, who emulate masculine behaviour, are seen as aggressive and are rejected by men for not conforming to feminine stereotypes. A second force is the tendency for employees to cluster with others like themselves. Tierney[8], (1995), in particular, reports networking advantages for 'the lads' specifically in the computing sector. Hemenway's third force is the reproduction of 'mental roles' of success in the image of senior males. This may lead to the potential of female candidates to be devalued through such comparison. Fourth, male behaviours (such as 'harmless' joking, laddis in conversation, discussion of male interests, and in extreme form harassment) are proved stressful and over time can erode women's self-confidence and ability to present themselves successfully.

In the same vein, Henwood (1993) argues that the reasons for women's exclusion from the IT industry is primarily due to the masculine culture of technology and the pattern of sex-segregation practices in this sector. Even today, women still perceive computing as a field for men. An interesting explanation of this trend has been advanced by Mclllwee and Robinson[9], (1992). They feel that the 'masculine culture' of the profession discourages women from entering it because it requires aggressive displays of technical self-confidence and hands-on ability for success. Women in this culture are particularly affected by the obsession with technology and hands-on activities, because the gender socialisation experienced by most women yields a distinct lack of experience in 'tinkering with electronics. Even when they acquire the necessary skills, women do not seem to become as comfortable or as obsessed as their male counterparts. The display required is that of masculinity, playing a role with which women are uncomfortable, even when they are capable of its performance. The work by Turlde (1984) and Wright (1996) also reiterates the fact that the exclusion of women from the IT industry is due to the alienation of women to this kind of technical culture.

What emerges from this literature is that computing carries 'progenetic' engineering and masculine characteristics. Even though other computing styles have been identified (e.g. the soft style of simulation), the engineering - masculine computing culture seems to be particularly predominant in organisations where computing work is the primary activity, such as software organisations (Wright, 1996).

THE POTENTIAL INFLUENCE OF NATIONAL CULTURE ON GENDER ISSUES IN COMPUTING WORK

The relevant literature has paid little attention to the potential influence of national culture and practices on gender integration or segregation in labour force. As we have shown in the previous section, computing is not a gender neutral occupation. In this section, we examine the potential influence of national culture on gendered patterns in computing work. This perspective embodies the idea that national culture as a social aggregate may develop sets of common assumptions and values about work and organisational patterns which are shared by its members. An important implication following from this view is that national culture and not only the occupational culture may exert influence on the values, styles and career orientation of computing staff in different countries.

National cultures comprise of beliefs and values which normally unconsciously govern people's perceptions and behaviour. Individuals with different national backgrounds have beliefs and underpinning values which hold different assumptions and expectations about relationships among people. Hofstede[10], (1980) who studied organisational cultures and individual behaviour in 53 countries, found that some societies are characterised by masculine features and others by feminine features. According to Hofstede[11], (1990:82):

> "Masculinity pertains to societies in which social gender roles are clearly distinct (i.e. men are supposed to be assertive, tough, and focused on material success whereas women are supposed to be more modest, tender and concerned with the quality of life): femininity pertains to societies in which social gender roles overlap (i.e. both men and women are .supposed to be modest, tender, and concerned with the quality of life)."

In this paper we aim to examine any national differences in gender-patterns of computing work. In particular, the first objective of the study is to explore any similarities and differences regarding the representation of women in computing science education across masculine and feminine countries. The second objective is to examine whether a) gender representation in IT and b) gender segregation differ between different countries.

RESEARCH APPROACH

For the purpose of our research, we selected three countries to participate in this international comparative study. These are: UK, US, and the Netherlands and they were chosen due to their masculine and feminine cultural characteristics. In terms of national cultures, the Netherlands ranked low (with 14) on Hofstede's masculinity index, while UK and the US scored higher (66 and 62 respectively). Therefore, the two latter countries, UK and US have clearly been identified as masculine and the Netherlands has been identified as feminine. Nation-wide statistics and other studies carried out in these different countries are presented and compared.

WOMEN IN COMPUTING EDUCATION

For the purpose of this study we compiled Table 1 which provides the representation of women in maths and computer science degrees at different periods of time. The Unesco statistics adopted by Wright[12], (1997b) were used to compile this information for US and the Netherlands. Since the Unesco report did not compile statistics about the UK, the Social Europe Supplement 3/93, which reports on the share of women among students on university computing science courses, was used to complement the table. Even though the Unesco and the Social Europe Supplement statistics do not correspond to the same periods of time, they do provide an indication of the trends in these countries.

Table 7.1: Cross National Comparison of Women's Representation of Graduates in Mathematics and Computer Science, 1975, 1985, 1990

Country	1975 % Women	1985 %Women	1990 % Women
US	32.3	39.4	36.-}
UK	25 (1970/	23 T1980)	13 11989)
Netherlands	9.9	14 0	12.9

In the US there has been an increasing share of women in computing science education from 32.3 % in 1975 to 39.4% in 1985. This, however, dropped to 36.4 % in 1990. The Netherlands experienced similar rising and then declining trends although the share of female students remains low overall. In contrast to these trends, the UK presents a gradual fall since the seventies. UK has experienced the steepest and long lasting decline of women taking computer science qualifications; this is evident in table 1. More recent statistics report that in 1995, women's participation in undergraduate courses with computer science as a major dropped to 11.9% (Siann[13], 1997) reinforces these declining trends.

The above statistics do not show the degree of collaboration and competition between boys and girls at school which are characteristics found respectively in feminine and masculine societies. They do suggest, however, that boys and girls in masculine as well as feminine countries do not study the same subjects. Instead, the representation of female students in computing science courses is lower in all countries with the US having the highest proportion, the Netherlands the lowest, and the UK the longest-lasting decline.

WOMEN'S REPRESENTATION IN COMPUTING WORK

There has been an increase in the number of women entering IT occupations since the seventies. However, women are underrepresented in this industry in all member states of the European Union and other countries. For instance, statistics available report that in the early 1990s no member state of the European Union had a percentage above 30% and in most cases it was nearer 20% (Social Europe[14], S3/93). International comparisons reveal a widespread tendency for the proportion of the female IT workforce to rise until the mid 1980s and then fall (Wright 1997a). Table 2 presents the representation of women in the selected countries over three decades: 1970s, 1980s and 1990s.

Table 7.2 : Trends in female shares of IT occupations

	1970S	1980S	1990S
United States (1) System Analysts	15% (1970)	23% (1980)	32%(1990)
Programmers	23% (1970)	31% (1980)	41% (1990)
United Kingdom (2) Analysts/Programmers		21H (1984)	16.45% (1994)
The Netherlands (3) System Analysts	5% (1979)	10% (1989)	8.9% (1993)
Programmers	8% (1979)	15% (1989)	13% (1993)

Sources : (l) Frenkel[15], 1990, Social Europe S3/93, Labour Force Statistics 1994[16] Social Europe S3/93; Tijdens[17], 1994)

This chronological analysis of gender has revealed that there has been little progress in the degree of representation of women in IT in the last three decades. Women have remained overall under-represented in this sector. The Netherlands has retained the lowest representation of women in IT since the 1970s. Even though the statistics available in the late 1980s were promising, forecasting an increasing trend, these have decreased again in the latest available figures of 1993. In 1993 in particular, the percentage of females had grown to 8.9% among systems analysts and to 13.5% among programmers (Tijdens, 1994). In brief, the Netherlands show trends that are increasing in the 80s and then decreasing again in the 90s.

The most detailed statistics on women in IT present the US situation. This is not surprising since the majority of the literature on this topic is based in the US. It is only in the last few years that researchers have begun examining gender issues in computing in other countries. US reports indicate increasing trends throughout the last three decades. The share of female systems analysts rose from 15% in 1970 to 32% in 1990 whilst the share of female programmers rose from 23% in 1970 to 41% in 1990. More recent statistics (Computerworld, 1995) report that in the US, women account for 37% of the IT professionals which although higher than the representation of women in any European country, it is 7% below the national average of women in the total workforce of the country.

In contrast, the UK presents a very gloomy picture with the shares of women declining not only in specific specialities, such as the one of analysts/programmers (table 2), but also overall. At present, the UK experiences a declining trend in the representation of women in computing work, for example, from a high of 25% women in the IT workforce in the UK in the 1980s, the proportion has fallen to a low of 19% in 1996. In 1984, the female share of IT professional occupations was 21% but this dropped to 19.5 % by 1989 (Social Europe S3/93). In 1991, there were reports that identified an even lower representation of women at 18% (LFS[18], 1992). Whilst this implied that fewer than two in ten professional jobs in computing (i.e. systems and data processing managers, analysts, programmers) were held by women, seven out of ten lower status computing jobs (e.g. data entry clerks, help-desk etc) were held by women (Grundy, 1996); Lander and Adams[19], (1997). Compared, therefore, to the Dutch experience, the UK reports a higher representation of women but also the most long lasting decline, evident in the 80s and throughout the 90s.

ANALYSIS

We begin this section by correlating the proportion of women receiving degrees in computing-related disciplines and the proportion of women actually employed in IT occupations. It is observed that for the UK and the Netherlands these two factors show a parallel trend. For instance, since the 80s in the UK there seems to be a downward trend in both the proportion of women awarded with computing qualifications and the proportion of women entering IT occupation. Furthermore, the increasing and then declining trend in the participation of women in computing education is replicated in the IT labour force. Following from these parallel trends, a possible explanation for the low representation of women in IT occupations is the decreasing number of female students who graduate with a computer science degree. According to researchers in this field, it is the image of computing as technical and male-dominated, the perception that computing work is a field for antisocial individuals, and the socialisation and identification of women themselves away from maths and science and thus not suited for such work which prevent the majority of females from pursuing computing as a career (Grundy, 1996; Siann , 1997).

However, although the declining number of female students who graduate with computing science degrees should be given serious attention, this should not be seen as the sole reason for the degree of female representation in IT occupations. This is reinforced by comparing the trends above for the US. For this country, the trend of female participation in computing education is not parallel to the female participation in the IT workforce of the country. Although the statistics available present an increasing representation of women in the IT workforce throughout three decades under consideration, the educational statistics show a declining representation as we move from the 80s to the 90s. Panteli et al[20], (1999b) have argued that due to diverse nature of IT occupations, there are in fact increasing opportunities for women to enter the industry from a wide range of backgrounds. During the late 40s and 50s programming was the major type of computing work, but in the 90s, IT also includes jobs in the areas of systems management, communications and networks, systems development, technical support, operations, user support and help-desk operations (NCC[21], 1992, 1997). The diversification of specialties and skills in this industry offers prospects not only for computing qualifications but also for those with business-like qualifications (Tijdens[22], 1991) or post-graduate IT degrees to enter IT occupations. Furthermore, a study by Carey[23], (1991/2) shows that 47% of all new entrants to computing work in the US were from other occupations within their employing organisations. Participation in computing education is a key factor which affects women's representation in the IT workforce. It is, however, believed that in addition to educational reasons, other factors have exerted an influence on the representation of women and their significance should not be neglected. For example, several researchers reported that gender segregation is very much predominant in this industry and it has absorbed the patriarchal power structure of the traditional engineering industries. The increasing trends in the representation of women in IT such as in the US case has not prevented gender hierarchy and inequality. The 1974 Computerworld[24], survey has reported that 99% of the women held the position of key punchers while 15% to 20% of them worked as business system analysts and programmers. Strober and Arnold[25], (1985) carried out an exhaustive research relating to women in the high-tech occupations in the US in the 70s and 80s. Their research has reiterated the fact that women remain far away from the most vulnerable and crucial occupations in the sector. They argued that various other environmental factors such as the emergence of the women's movement, the growing technical education, the initiatives from the government and computing organizations, and above all the implementation of equal opportunities in employment have not brought out a change in the occupational status of women in high-tech industries, such as IT.

A study by Kraft and Dubnoff[26], (1983) has also probed the extent of gender segregation in computing. According to this study, women have been better represented in software jobs compared to hardware jobs. However, even within software work-places, they have not assumed significant role and status. Most of them have been concentrated in the lower status jobs such as business programming, documentation and maintenance. Women in the upper level managerial and supervisory levels are in a minority. The study has identified that while 22% of women in the sample are managers of some kind, men are three times more likely to be in upper level managerial posts than women. This study has also brought to light the secondary status attached to women in IT management: women are often seen to supervise more women than men. Other studies (Donato[27], 1990, Frenkel, 1990) confirm that women are over-represented in some types of lower-level jobs (e.g. programmers and operators) and under-represented in higher level positions (e.g. project leaders and managers).

Studies on gender-based patterns of employment and work experience in IT have presented similar outcomes in the UK and the Netherlands. For example, in the UK, it was found (IDPM IT report 1996 in Panteli, et al, 1999b) that the presence of women declines on moving up the hierarchy. For instance, although in 1996 women constitute 11.7 % of management in all areas, only 7.3 % of heads of IT departments are women. Women are not only under-represented at the supervisory and managerial level but also in the higher ranks of the technical track. For example, although they constitute 26.9% of the total number of trainee programmers, only 8.3% of principal programmers are females. Similarly, although there are 25.5% female assistant technical analysts, only 6.2% of the senior technical consultants are female. The proportion of women reaches 40% and above only for those specialties that are related to administrative and support functions: e.g. help desk assistant 62.4%, help desk analyst 47.3%, help desk supervisor 47.1%, assistant user support analyst 44.2% etc. The proportion of women in the programming and the more technical-related occupations, reaches 25% or more in mainly junior positions (e.g. junior analyst programmer 26.2%), traineeships (e.g. trainee analyst programmer, or assistantship posts (assistant technical analyst 25%).

A Dutch study (Hoek and Riestra.[28]. 1989) shows similar findings: further to their quantitative under-representation, women occupy predominantly the lower segmentation of the job categories. In the majority of the organisations that participated in the study, the managerial, technical and designing jobs are occupied by men, while the processing and administrative jobs are occupied by women. Moreover, women end up in the so-called 'dead-end' functions and men in what it is called the "growth" functions. Grundy (1996) in the UK gave similar descriptions of such job segregation: 'messy' jobs for the women and 'pure' jobs for the men.

Overall, women are found to be under-represented and disadvantaged at the high-status and prestigious IT jobs in all selected countries. The implications of this are discussed below.

DISCUSSION AND CONCLUSION

The chronological and geographical analysis presented above, of the gender dimension during the last three decades in the four selected countries, has marked the predominance of male culture in computing and across its different occupational specialties. A closer look, at the status of women in different occupational specialties, shows that, despite their increased representation, women do not have equal access to the different levels of occupational hierarchies. They are over-represented in some types of lower-level jobs (e.g. programmers and operators) and under-represented in higher level jobs (i.e. project leaders and IS managers). Computing, therefore, has remained a gender segregated, male-dominated occupation.

Following from this finding, it can be said that the high-tech industries which are looked upon as the "great equalisers" do not give adequate berth for women's occupational development nor do they necessarily produce an integrated work force and equality of opportunities for men and women (Strober & Arnold , 1987). As was discussed in section 1 of this paper, the occupational culture of computing has been particularly vulnerable to influences from various sources and factors. Its links to traditional masculine environments, such as electrical engineering, the competitive and fast changing nature of work which exist and pervade across various countries and continents, all contribute to building and sustaining a masculine, male-dominated work environment. What we are finding in this comparative study is that the image of computing can override national values. In both feminine and masculine societies, women are not only under-represented but also experience similar barriers to their retention and career development in the field. The increasing number of structured tools and methodologies in software development, the competitive nature of work, the frequent tight deadlines and the project-based nature of workall contribute to a tremendous amount of pressure on requiring developers to work longer and unsociable hours. And it is often those who are able to cope with these demands and succeed that are promoted into the managerial positions (Knights and Murray[29], 1994). Moreover, the speed of technological change makes it difficult to catch up with technological advancements for those who take a career break, notably women who take maternity leave, and for those who can only work on a part-time basis, again mainly women with family responsibilities.

The above characteristics have been identified in various countries leading to the realisation that since similar patterns of under-representation and segregation are occurring in a number of countries, at least some elements of the computing occupational culture transcend national boundaries. Our findings support the findings of Gerpott, Dornsch and Kettler[30], (1988). They stated that in high-tech companies the sense of technological excellence overrides other considerations and engineers across national boundaries are more likely to share the culture of other engineers than their fellow countrymen, "...because scientific methods and standards are generally valid independently of country boundaries" (p. 456).

In the case of IT, offshore programming and globalisation contribute to the spread of the occupational methods and standards across the globe. From various reports, we understand that multinational IT organisations have transferred their North American culture to other parts of the world. To quote a Finnish researcher, (Vehvilainen[31], 1997:438): " ...there was a belief that the US training and testing could be applied in Finland as easily as the computer machines, IBM is known as an especially male-dominated company, the organisational of which ... has remained very male also in Finland" even when women have gaining increasing access in the labour force of the country. Similar accounts have been provided by researchers in other countries (e.g. Rafferty[32], 1997, Tiemey, 1995). Some suggestions, such as the increased availability of special training and career development programmes have been made in Panteli et al (1999a), but these and others require action.

We, therefore, think that multinational IT organisations have a responsibility and are in a better position to innovate in the way they do business and exert an influence with regard to the gender-patterns of work in various countries. This realisation should be the beginning rather than the end of the efforts made to building the IT skills for the 21st century. It should lead to more innovative ways of reorganising IS workplaces, developing career orientation programs and consequently to retaining and promoting those groups of people who might have felt neglected. Furthermore, IT organisations should formulate strategy that is comprehensive enough to incorporate considerations of a diverse workforce. This should be in the agenda of future research. This masculine-engineering driven occupational culture of computing is reinforced by the way work is done by it is also distributed across national boundaries contributing to a global phenomenon, that of a gendered IT profession.

REFERENCES

1. Trice H. (1993) "Occupational Subcultures in the Workplace". Ithaca. NY: ILR Press.
2. Wright, R (1996). "The Occupational Masculinin. of Computing". In Cheng, C. (Ed.*Masculinities in Organisations*, London: Sagè
3. Turkic, S. (1984). *The Second Self: Computers and the Human Spirit*, NY. Simon &Schuster.
4. Wright, R (1997a). *Women Computer Professionals: Progress and Resistance*, Lewiston. Edwin Mellen Press.
5. Grundy. F. (1996). *Women and Computers*. Exeter Intellect Books.
6. Henwood. F. (1993). "Establishing gender perspectives on information technology: problems. issues and opportunities. In Gendered By design: *Information Technology and Office Systems* (E Green et. al. eds). London: Taylor & Francis.
7. Hemenwav. K. (1995). "Human nature and the glass ceiling in industry". In Communications of the ACM 38. 1. 55-62.
8. Tierney. M. (1995). "Negotiating a Software Careen Informal Work Practices and 'The Lads' in a Software Installation". In Grint. K and Gill. R (Eds.) *The Gender-Technology Relation: Contemporary Theory and Research*. London: Taylor & Francis.
9. Mclhvee. J. S. & Robinson. J. G. (1992). "Women In Engineering: Gender. Power & Workplace Culture". SUNY: Albany Sational Computing Centre. *Salaries and Staff Issues in Computing 1992. 1997.*
10. Hofstede G. (1980). *Culture's Consequences: International Differences in Work-Related I Values*. Beverly Hills. Ca. Sage Publications.
11. Hofstede. G. (1990). *Cultures and Organizations: Intercultural Cooperation and its Importance for Survival*. London. Harper Collins Publishers.
12. Wright. R (1997b). "Women in Computing: A Cross National Analysis". Lander R and Adams. A (eds). *Intellect*. Exeter.
13. Siann. G. (1997). "We can. we don't want to: factors influencing women's participation in computing". Lander, R and Adams, A. (eds.) *op. cit.*
14. *Social Europe - Occupational Segregation of Women and Men in European Community - Suppliment 3/93. 70-76.*

15. Frenkel. K.A. (1990). *Women and Computing*. Communications of the ACM. 33. 11. 34-36.
16. *Labour Force Statistics*. UK. (1994).
17. Tijdens. K. (1994). "Behind the Screens: The Foreseen and Unforeseen Impact of Computerisation on Female Office Worker's Job". In Eberhart. T. And Wachter. C. (eds) Proceedings of the 2nd European Feminist Research Conference. Austria.
18. *Labour Force Statistics*. UK. (1992).
19. Lander. R and Adam. Alison. (1997). *Women in computing*. Intell Books.
20. Panteli.A. Stack. J.. Atkinson. M. and Ramsay. J (1999b). "Women in the UK IT Industry : An Empirical Study". *European Journal of Information Systems*, Forthcoming.
21. National Computing Centre. "Salaries and staff Issues in Computing" 1992, 1997.
22. Tijdens K (1991). *Women in EDP Departments*, la Eriksson. I.V. Kitchenham. B. A. and Tijdens. KG. (Eds) "Women, Work and Computerisation. Amsterdam. Elsevier Science Publishers B.V. (North-Holland).
23. Carey M L (1991/92). "Occupational Advancement from Within". *Occupational Outlook*. Quarterly. Winter. pp. 9-13.
24. *Computeworld's 9th Annual Salary & Survey*. "Unequal Opportunities". September 4.1. pp.70-72.74.78.
25. Strober. M II and Arnold. C. L. (1987). "Integrated Circuits/ Segregated Labour: Women in Computer Related Occupations and High-Tech Industries". In National Research Council (Ed) Computer Chips and Paper-Clips: *Technology and Women*'s Employment. Washington DC: National Academy Press.
26. Kraft, P. and Dubnoff. S. (1983). "Software Workers Survey". *Computernorld*. November. pp. 14.1-13
27. Donato, KM. (1990). *Programming for Change? The Growing Demand for Women Systems Analysts*. In Reskin B.F. and Roos, P.A. (Eds). Job Queues, Gender Queues: Explaining Women's Inroads into Male Occupations". Philadelphia: Temple University Press.
28. Hock, & and Riestra E. (1989). *Strategies and Education*. In Tijdens K, Jennings, M., Wagner, L and Weggelaar, M (eds), "Women, Work and Computerisation: Forming New Alliances." Elsevier. Amsterdam.
29. Knights, D. and Murray, F. (1994). Managers Dhided - *Organisational Policies and Information Technology Management*, Wiley Series in Information Systems. London. Wiley.

30. Gcrpott, T.J., Domsch, ML and Keller, RT. (1988) "Career Orientations in Different Countries and Companies: An Empirical investigation of West German." British and US Industrial R&D Professionals." *Journal of Management Studies*, 25:5, September. 439-462 Cornputernvrld's 9th Annual Salary & Survey." Unequal Opportunities". September 4. 1/70-72,74,78.

31. Vehvilainen, M. (1997). "*Gender and Expertise in Retrospect*: Pioneers of Computing in Finland". In Lander, R. and Adam, A. (eds). *op cit.*

32. Rafferty T (1997) "Factors that Attract Women to Careers in Information Technology - A Case Study in Ireland". In Grundy, A.F. Kohler, D., Occhtering, V. and Petersen, U. (Eds) *Women, Work and Computerization - Spinning a Web from Past to Future*. Berlin. Springer.

SECTION II

8

Women in the IT Profession in India—The Millennium Scenario

This article presents women's status in the IT sector in India from two approaches: Gender in IT (GIT) and Gender and IT (GAIT) (MacKenzie and Wajcman[1] 1993, Cockburn[2] and Ormond 1993). The former approach highlights the absorptive capacity of IT, and the latter approach looks into the gender segregation and gender sensitivity of the IT organisations. These two approaches generated such parameters as (i) proportion of women in the entire IT sector; (ii) women's status in the core and peripheral regions of the IT organisations; (iii) women's representation in the organisational hierarchy; (iv) working conditions; (v) training facilities; and (vi) levels of career path. Against this backdrop this article portrays the gender situation of the IT sector in India.

In India, IT is viewed as an important segment for the economic growth, giving rise to millions of new jobs and opening a gateway for women and men with right skills and aptitude to make inroads into this industry (Manu[3] 2000). It may be interesting to note that India has been sought as a port for software production and software marketing in the last five years by the global IT companies. Most of the top 10 software companies—including Wipro, Satyam and Infosys— get 70% or more of their revenue from the North American Market. This trend has generated an acute demand for Indian IT professionals (Kripalani[4] 2001). This IT revolution has also changed the gender calculus in India, one of the world's most traditional societies. In Indian society, the majority of women in the rural economies are still in the midst of poverty, illiteracy and lack bargaining power. However, the invasion of IT is offering new liberties to a small but influential group of women. These women are commanding unusual respect from family members, who grant them "male" privileges such as exemption from housework and a say in household finances (Yee, 2000). Women in India make up 31% of the official workforce and according to December 2000 estimates by HinduBusinessLine.com, women comprised 19% of the information technology work force in India, primarily within the software industry (AED[6] 2000). It is estimated that the prospects of employment in the software sector amounts to 2 million jobs in software production and another 2.2 million jobs in the IT enabled services by the year 2008 (NASSCOM[7] 2000). It is predicted that the male-female ratio in information technology jobs will be 65 men to 35 women in the years to come.

The Indian software industry is broadly grouped into three different categories depending on their areas of work: (i) industries in product development; (ii) offshore services; and (iii) onsite maintenance and implementation services. It is to be noted that both on-site and offshore development are specifically dependent on customer needs and generate new jobs in the service sector. The software product is the most vibrant of the three areas and involves a substantial amount of R&D as well as marketing (Heeks[8] 1998). Survey reports have shown that women are employed in larger proportion in the second and third categories of work. A high concentration of men (39.6%) as against women (21.6%) are placed in the high-end firms that involve software production, while a higher proportion of women are found in the low-end and IT enabled services that consist more of 'body shopping' and 'offshore software development'.

An analysis of the software professionals on the basis of their job positions have shown that fewer women are in higher-level positions such as project managers (5.56%), consultants (25%), and programmers/software engineers (45.31%) and there is a disproportionate representation of women in the IT-enabled services like the call services (60%) (Rothboeck[9] 2001). Similar such findings are seen in other studies also (Arun[10] & Arun 2002, Kelkar[11] 2001). There is a definite preference for men in senior management positions in IT. Women themselves opt for other parallel career tracks in the IT areas, such as, quality control, training, marketing and so on. In IT industry where workaholism is more the norm than the exception, women have had to work harder at achieving a good work-life balance which restricts women's choices in terms of better job opportunities.

There are tremendous opportunities abroad for the Indian software professionals causing greater mobility. The estimated migration rate in the Indian software industry is 38% and the mobility is towards the industrialised nations. The mobility rate of women IT professionals has also increased in the last five years. A survey report reveals that economic needs, social and cultural issues are pushing Indian women into taking jobs abroad. It is observed that two out of five applications that the US-based IT recruiters received are from Indian women.

Studies show that the professions of Indian women in technology is still low compared to a lot of other professions. In India, of IBM's 170,000 plus technical workers, about 20% are women. Women account for 11% of the engineers at IBM, six IBM Fellows, 20 distinguished engineers and 35 members of the IBM Academy of Technology. On the international level, eight IBM women are members of the Women in Technology International (WTO) Hall of Fame and there is no Indian women representation in this forum (Newindpress[12] 2003). Though the IT field has offered new opportunities, the beneficiaries are the urban youth. Many rural women communities areas have yet to reap the benefits of this technology in India. Though potential benefits for women from the IT industry are substantial, they are determined by intersections of class, caste, age, ethnicity, and race interests among the women themselves. However, there is a positive trend in IT education over the recent years. Until the last decade, the percentage of women engineers was very low. Currently the numbers have overwhelmingly increased from 1% in 1975 to 10% in 1990 (IIT[13] 2000). There is a spurt in the number of women entering the primary and the tertiary level of IT education in India. The proliferation of IT institutions, and the growing IT labour demand attribute to women's advancement in IT (Suriya[14] 2002). Government initiatives and financial support from banks and other funding agencies encouraged young males and females to gain access to computing technology, which serves to bridge the gap between the gender groups in IT education and IT employment. Since the demand for technical professionals continues to be strong in the IT industry, women are not seen as competitors to men. Skills and experiences have come to matter more than anything else in the software sector.

A gendered perspective of the IT sector in India shows that it creates opportunities for women though it also has reproduced gender inequalities seen in the broader fabric of society. Although women are equally qualified and equally capable, they do not appear to compete on equal terms even in a modern 'high-tech' sector. Such a situation warrants a reform in the gender policy framework. Where IT based policies are planned and implemented, a gendered perspective is required. Only then, it is likely that IT policy will help tackle and transform the asymmetry in social and economic power relations, enhance the quality of women's lives both in household and the labour market, and create a true process of development.

REFERENCES

1. Mackenzie D. & Wajcman, J. (1993). *The Social Shaping of Technology*. Milton Keynes. Philadelphia. Open University Press.
2. Cockburn C. & Ormond, S. (1993). *Gender and Technology in the Making*, London: Sage.
3. Manu, J. (2000). "Software Wars: China Vs India". NewsWeek, Oct. http://www.silicontaiga.org/home.asp?artld=385
4. Kripalani, M. (2001). "A Power Play India Can't Afford to Lose". *Business Week Online*, http://www.businessweek. com/bwdaily/dnflash/jan2001/nf20010131_804.htm
5. Yee, CM. (2000). "India's Other Tech Revolution: Women Find New Independence". *Technology Journal of Asia*, October 30.
6. Academy for Educational Development (2000), "Women and Information Technology in India: A Case Study,"
7. NASSCOM (2000). *Indian IT Enabled Service Providers Directory 2000*. New Delhi. India. NASSCOM
8. Heeks R (1998), "The Uneven Profile of Indian Software Exports" *Development Informatics Working Paper Series No.3*, IDPM, University of Manchester.
9. Rotheoeck S. (2001). "Labour in the New Economy: The Case of the Indian Software Labour Market". New Delhi: ILO.
10. Arun, S. & Arun, T. (2002). "ICTs, Gender and Development: Women in Software Production in Kerala". *Journal of International Development*. Vol. 14. pp. 39-50.
11. Kelkar, G. (2001) "Information Technology and Gender Relations in India". Bangkok: Asian Institute of Technology, *Gender and Development Studies*.

12. Newindpress.com (2003). "Women in IT: Neither seen, nor heard". *Newindpress.com*. May 19.
13. Indian Institute of Technology (2000). "Women in the Engineering profession in India-The Millennium Scenario".
14. Suriya M. (2002), "Impact of Technology on Women's Life in the Developing World: Fact or Fiction". In Women in Computing Around the World: The ACM-W Ambassador Program, Grace Hopper Celebration of Women in Computing Panel.

9

Measuring Gender Equality in the Information Society: A Case Study from India

INTRODUCTION

Information society has been in the global agenda for about two decades. International conferences, workshops, projects and programmes are centering around this phenomena invariably in all the countries of the world. The common concern is (i) how to make this 'information society' a place for all; (ii) how to balance the 'information haves' and 'information have-nots'; (iii) how to close the digital divide caused by the technological revolution? As rightly stated by the UN's Administrative Committee, we are profoundly concerned at the deepening maldistribution of access to resources, and opportunities in the information society. This widening inequalities leads to a new type of poverty called information poverty that leads to a new form of electronic feudalism. The question before us is: (i) what should we do to realise the desirable scenario? (ii) how can we help the millions of the deprived in the country? (iii) how can we use digital technologies to improve their livelihood? At the same time, we must be conscious that the new technologies are going to stay; no one can wipe them away from it. We must also realise that, it would be impossible to provide the same level of access to ICT tools for all the people. The slogans like 'information for all', 'IT for all' will remain only a slogan as long as the other socio-economic variables remains the same. How are we going to deal with this skeptical situation? There is also a growing concern that women are at the bottom of the digital divide and the question is how to leverage them and to make them be equal partners in this knowledge based information society.

PROBLEM STATEMENT

India has emerged as a superpower in the ICT Sector and

also in building an information society for all. Integration and application of ICT in various sectors have gained momentum in this country in the last two decades which is visible from both production (for instance, in the development of its software industry) as well as the consumption pattern (with significant investments in e-government applications, and attempts to push ICTs out into rural areas) (Heeks, 1996; Bhatnagar and Schware, 2000)[1]. This situation has facilitated unprecedented job opportunities not only in the corporate IT and ITES sectors but also in the government departments, and in the community information centres. In recent decades, India has witnessed a shift from depending upon the so-called male-centric formal employment to women-centric informal employment. For instance women-owned businesses have grown at a faster rate in the private sector (USAID)[2]. Though the general ICT situation seems to be very much promising in the Indian sub-continent, a close analysis is required to find the suitability of women to participate in the information society. Without explicit gender analysis and incorporation of the results into policies, programmes and projects, it is unlikely that the results will have positive impact on women (Marcelle, 2000)[3]. Without direct intervention, gender equality will not occur. This study is an attempt to examine whether the ICT policies and ICT capacity building programmes initiated by India are gender sensitive and whether they facilitate women to derive the maximum benefits out of the information society.

RESEARCH QUESTIONS

The present study has the following research agenda. It attempts to find answers to some of the key questions : (i) does the patriarchy and the power relations in the agrarian and industrial societies are carried over in the information society? (ii) How do socio-cultural customs, infrastructural and access barriers restrict women from accessing and using ICTs? (iii) Do women have the e-readinesss (education, training and skills) required to function in the Information Society? (iv) What is the proportion of women in the knowledge and content creation industries? How severe are gender disparities in ICT employment? (v) Why do they occur? (vi) are there gender differences in access to and control over financial resources which affect participation in the information society?

E-READINESS OF WOMEN TO PARTICIPATE IN THE INFORMATION SOCIETY

It is widely felt that the development of an information society begins with having a literate society and a information conscious society. While literacy refers to "the minimum capacity both to understand the moral implications of and to act upon the demands of competence of what a particular society defines as responsible participation of a person [in a] society"; information literacy refers to the ability to access, evaluate, and use information from a variety of sources". Information conscious society, on the other hand, is a society in which people realise the importance of the need to access information. More so, towards an information society, the society must be information literate. In fact Garfield (1993:231)[4] imagines the information society to be "when all people in all parts of a society have rapid access to information they need". Moore (2000: xii) believes that it is only when all members of the society are able to build continuously on a foundation of basic knowledge and can be able to develop and renew skills that a society needs. Based on the above discussion, it is noted that participation in the information society will be remote in the absence of information literate population.

As far as the Indian situation is concerned, women's participation in this new society is hampered by many factors, including time-constraints, low-literacy levels, low-awarness and social norms (Agarwal , 1994). According to 2001 census, female literacy is 54.16% as against male literacy of 75.85% in India. The enrollment of girls in educational institutions decreases as educational level goes higher. In particular, the percentage of girls enrolled to total enrollment is 43.6% in primary, 40.1% in middle, 37.1% in secondary level and 34.8% in higher education according to the statistics of 1997. The enrollment of girls in Engineering/ Technology/Architecture at Graduation level (in 1998) is 0.58 million as against 2.85 million boys. The low enrollment of women in the science and technology impedes their participation in the new society. In addition, a series of social and cultural norms constrain women's access to ICT, especially in common use facilities, such as cyber-cafes, tele-centres and phone shops. In many culturally conservative societies, women are often not allowed to go out without supervision to public venues where men are present or seek help from male users or staff. This situation calls for the intervention of the various government and non-government agencies to devise capacity building programmes to achieve : (i) technology fluency; (ii) mastery of analytical skills; (iii) ability to use technology innovatively; and (iv) ability to develop, find and use information and knowledge to improve one's life and expand one's choices among the masses especially among the women community.

The relevance of women's participation in the information society is also emphasized by the Geneva Declaration of Principles (GDP) which states that: "We affirm that development of ICTs provides enormous opportunities for women, who should be an integral part of, and key actors, in the Information Society. We are committed to ensuring that the Information Society enables women's empowerment and their full participation on the basis on [sic.] equality in all spheres of society and in all decision-making processes. To this end, we should mainstream a gender equality perspective and use ICTs as a tool to that end."The following sections illustrate the efforts taken by the government of India to realise the objectives of the Geneva Declaration Principles (GDP).

PROMOTING IT LITERACY AT THE GRASSROOT LEVEL: INITIATIVES OF GOVERNMENT, CIVIL SOCIETIES AND CORPORATES

Most of the countries in the world are rapidly moving into the information society with varying degrees of e--readiness. India has initiated some catalytic, pro-active and enabling steps to spread computer literacy by undertaking such programmes as (i) enabling literacy and education for the masses; (ii) fulfilling local information needs of the people (iii) educating citizens about their duties; and (iv) enabling women in technology. The first programme aims at spreading computer literacy to the school teachers and students besides equipping the schools with computer labs. The second programme aims at establishing networking and knowledge sharing centers such as 'citizen service points', cyber cafes and information kiosks in order to establish the linkages between the government and the citizens using the internet facility. The third one aims at educating the citizens on various welfare programmes. In addition to these generic programmes, the Indian government also has come out with a large programme for promoting women's literacy. For instance, an IT literacy programme specially directed towards spreading literacy among women was launched by the year 2001. Government also has encouraged the NGOs to set up B2C (business to consumer) and B2B [business to business] websites to promote interest of women doing business in the state.

The role of NGOs in proliferating the computer literacy among the rural women is noteworthy. Specific mention may be made about the initiatives taken by Datamation, MSSRF and SEWA. Datamation establishes that education and awareness through information is an indispensable input in the process of empowerment to facilitate women's decision- making capacities and capabilities to participate in governance. SEWA Bank in India uses the development communication wing of Indian Space Research Organisation (lSRO) to remote villages. Discussions on topics like women in development, nursery raising and forestry management, savings and credit are beamed to different villages through the use of satellite cable. The viewers can phone their enquiries which are answered promptly by a panel of experts. The M.S. Swaminathan Foundation (MSSRF) has established a high tech village information center in the state of Pondicherry in India. Villagers congregate around the center to get connected with the local news. Women get information about the markets and health from this center. Distance education is yet another significant areas where women stand to gain tremendously. Internet and television broadcasts opens up avenues for women to continue with their education at their own pace and from the confines of their homes. The project 'Putting ICTs in the Hands of Poor Women' was initiated by Datamation [NGO] in 2002. It is one of the initiatives, which has been recognized as the 'Most Promising Social Entrepreneurs 2002' by Digital Partners. The Seelampur project entails 'Putting ICTs in the hands of the Muslim women' in a slum area in Delhi has directly linked the use of ICTs to the alleviation of their poverty. This project seeks to modernise the vocational skills of Muslim women in the area in bead-making, dress-making, carpentry, and embroidery and lend marketing support to help them enhance their incomes. Datamation is in the process of developing 50 multimedia CDs focusing on skills enhancement, women's empowerment, and life skills. The CDs will be shown via the existing cable network. The project entitled IT Enabled Education for Rural Women (Tel-Nek) was initiated by an International NGO in 2001 The content of the course includes, Windows basics, MS -Office, Pagemaker, Graphic Designing etc. Local language softwares like Nudi, Baraha, i-Leap along with hardware basics, e-mail, Internet were also included. The course also focuses on IT security, computers and society. The training course is done in Kannada, the local language, and teaching manuals are also in the same language. Tel-Nek is keen on providing its current trainees, especially women, with teleworking opportunities. Future plans include, setting up of a Tele-centre, to provide facilities in training, data entry, and also double up as an Internet cafe. The project entitled 'Sumangali Seva Ashram IT Education Program for Women and Children' was initiated by Sumangali Sewa Ashram (SSA) in 2002. It is implementing an IT Education program for children and women.

BUILDING KNOWLEDGE WORKERS OF THE RURAL WOMEN: INITIATIVES OF THE GOVERNMENT, AND THE CORPORATES

The UN World Conference on Women, Beijing and Beijing +5, Gender Caucus of WSIS 2003 and many other national and international forums have reaffirmed the need to focus on gender equality issues through ICT use, since lack of access to ICT is considered as one of the major impediments towards achieving an information society. It is also recommended that 'government and other stakeholders should provide the necessary conditions to ensure women's equal access to information and knowledge as well as ensuring their equal role as producers and decision-makers, in all aspects related to the shaping of ICT policies and frameworks'. Government of India has taken conscious efforts to build the technical manpower through such initiatives as: (i) upgrading Industrial Training Institutes for providing training of skills for data entry, marketing, transcription, call centres, content creation and data processing; (ii) expanding Training Centre for Unemployed Educated Youths; (iii) establishing IT Open University; (iv) setting up premier Indian Institute of Information Technology to impart high quality IT education and training to the people and (v) setting up Digital Media Library that would be a central storehouse of digitalised data containing government records, industry information and information on education, tourism and archaeology. In the year 2001, nearly 7929 colleges for general education and 2223 engineering and professional colleges were enrolling 36.9% of women in higher education. ICT organisations across the world are moving beyond their traditional roles of delighting the customer and meeting bottom lines. Indian IT companies too are moving in the same direction and giving precedence to their social commitments or what is called corporate social responsibility (CSR). A look at the scene in India reveals innumerable examples of corporate paying close attention to social issues and venturing into philanthropic endeavors. While a majority of the companies concentrate on the children of the disadvantaged communities, only a very few concentrates on the girl-specific ICT training programmes. For instance, Moksha is inspiring the industry with Project Prerna, under which it is educating young girls of "Navajeevana", with computers by providing the necessary hardware and training faculty. The girls are being made aware of the importance and relevance of computer education in their future career aspirations. The NIIT is aiming to change the life of India's citizens through computer education. It has initiated projects such as Hole-in-the-Wall experiment, a brainchild of NLLTian and R&D chief Dr. Sugata Mitra, where slum children have successfully learnt to navigate the 'Net and "Web-enable" themselves. NIIT has also developed special I-write and I-learn packages for the physically challenged, under a programme called Computer Assisted Teaching and Rehabilitation [CATERED). Another programme initiated by the company is NIIT BOOT IT, a television-based distance learning project, to bring computer education free to the homes of millions of Indians. In an attempt to bridge the digital and gender divide, NIIT has also launched initiatives such as World Computer Literacy Day and International Women's Month. NIIT has also got underway an AIDS prevention and control program—a joint effort between NIS, USAID and the Government of Tamil Nadu. A unique project with the National Association of the Blind [NAB], Bangalore, has been initiated, where NIIT made available its SWIFT India courseware for conversion into Braille and provided its faculty for training. The Cognisant Technology works closely with academia in providing advanced developmental programmes for faculty and defines curricula and syllabi. The company also helps colleges and universities to set up solution labs and knowledge centers. TCS has developed computerised programmes to address the adult literacy problem in India. The company has undertaken special adult education projects in the states such as Andhra Pradesh and Tamil Nadu. With a strong belief, that India's educational system need to be strengthened, Polaris has set up "Ullas" trust which gives monetary aid to students who cannot afford education on their own. Partly funded by employees of the company, Ullas has sponsored more than 2000 students scattered across 132 schools in Chennai City. It is also providing them free computer training at its office premises.

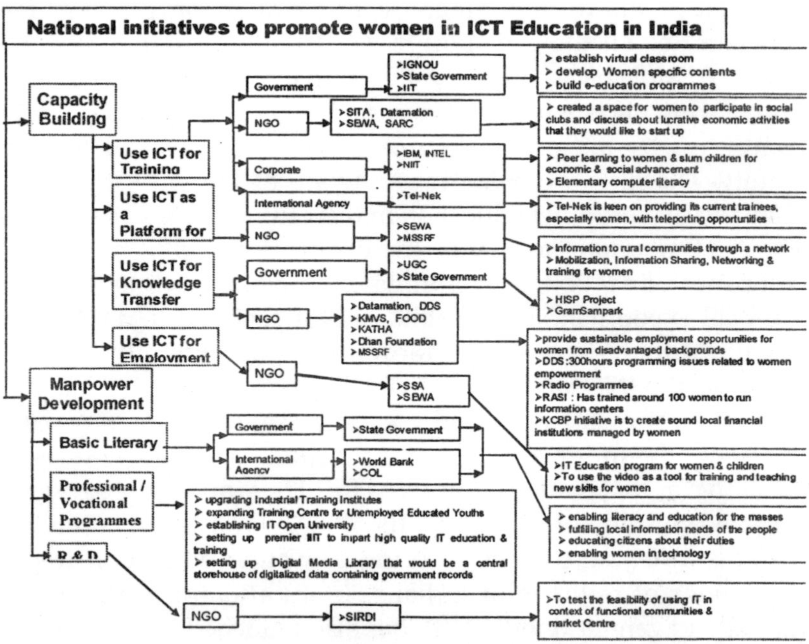

LEVERAGING WOMEN IN KNOWLEDGE BASED HIGH-TECH INDUSTRIES

The technology revolution is changing the gender calculus in India, one of the world's most traditional societies (Chen, May Yee, 2000). Women find new independence. Women play a larger part in the expansion of software market in India and they constitute 45% of the high tech work force. Women account for

50% in the engineering colleges as well as in the software training sectors. In the organisational hierarchy, more women have occupied the responsible and high-profile positions but a few have climbed all the way up. The number of women executives has multiplied in the last few years (Kishori Gopal Krishnan, 2000).

The Indian software industry is growing in three different directions viz: (i) industries involved in product development; (ii) offshore software services ; and (iii) on-site maintenance and implementation services. Based on the size of the employees, the IT companies are classified as high, middle, low-end companies.

The software sector in India has created a tremendous amount of new forms of work of different qualities. It is estimated that the future prospects of employment in the software sector amounts to 2 million jobs in software production and another 2.2 million jobs in IT-enabled services by the year 2008 (NASSCOM, 2000).

Though IT sector has offered equal employment opportunities to the gender groups, differences are noticed in the types of activity that men and women software professionals specialise in (table 4). Surveys among the software professionals showed that a high concentration of men exists in export software firms, while women are present in higher proportion in domestic low-end and IT-enabled services. This implies that at the entry level itself, there is a marked gender differential in access to employment in this sector.

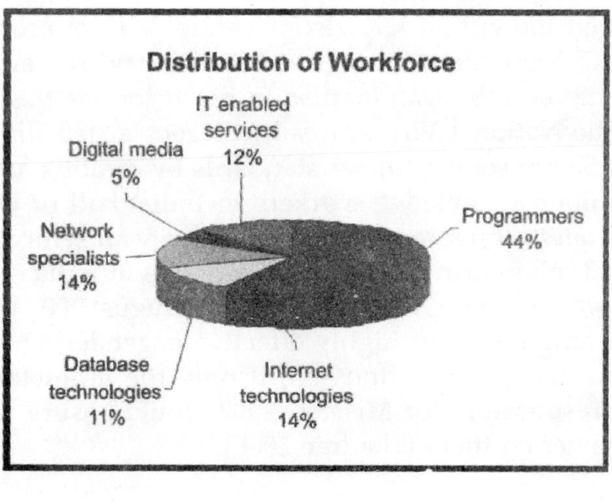

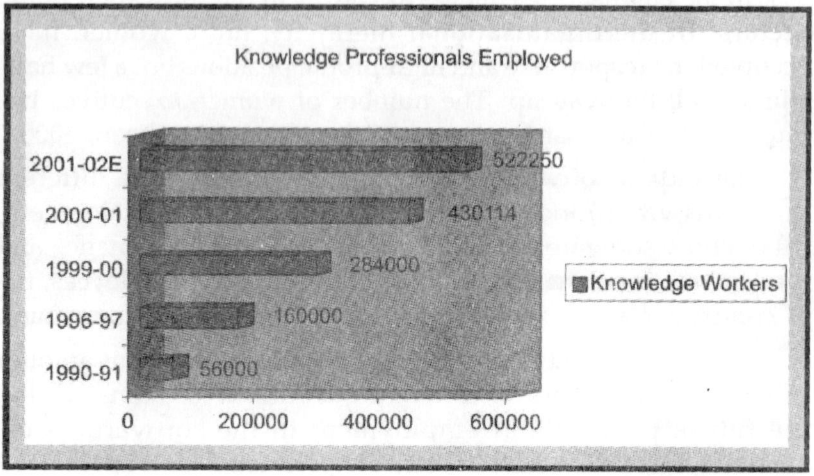

GENERATING EMPLOYMENT OPPORTUNITIES FOR GRASSROOT WOMEN IN IT-BASED SERVICE INDUSTRY

According to Amartya Sen the Nobel Laurate in Economics, gender equality could be achieved only if the human capabilities and enhancing opportunities are increased for both men and women alike. He emphasized that without equality in capabilities and opportunities, women cannot be on the same level playing field with men in the knowledge society. In keeping with the suggestions of this great economist, several economic empowerment initiatives have been undertaken in various regions of India to benefit women community. Special mention could be made about the virtual knowledge centre projects promoted by the MSSRF foundation located at Pondicherry. The architect of this foundation MS Swaminathan in his vision for Mission 2007 and for the National Virtual Academy, goes a step further than Amartya Sen in setting higher standards by creating an army of over 1 million knowledge workers in India, half of which are women from the grassroots. Building capacity and empowerment of over 1.2 million rural knowledge workers in India – one man and one woman in each village – by 15th August 2007 is perhaps the most ambitious but highly effective engendering effect the world will have ever witnessed, if only the multistakeholder partners responsible for Mission 2007 would ensure recruiting and empowering them (Shadrac 2006).

In Andhra Pradesh (South India), e-Seva project was initiated during 2002 in order to generate IT-based employment opportunities for the rural women. This project, which is run by the West-Godavari District Administration in Andhra Pradesh State, India has established Web-enabled rural 'e-Seva Centres run by self-help groups of women from the poorest segments of society. Under this project web enabled rural kiosks—e-Seva centres—have been set up and are managed by women. The project enabled these groups to become "information leaders" and act as change agents. The e-Seva Centres run on a district portal that allows access to various citizen services ranging from issuing various certificates to disseminating information about governmental programmes. http://www.westgodavari.org. MACTCS (Mutually Aided Co-operative Thrift and Credit Societies) is one of the most successful initiatives in Andhra Pradesh that works towards economic empowerment of women. Over 5.4 million women have organised themselves in 380 thousand groups and they have accumulated savings of the order of USD* 900. They have also got loans and grants from the State Government and National Bank for Agricultural Rural Development Bank (NABARD) to the tune of USD 62 million, thus making their bank finances at USD 172 millions.

Basic data regarding village information kiosks

Number of mandals covered	10
Number of grams Panchayats benefited	300
Benefited Population (approximately)	45000
Trained MACTCS members	150
Village Information Kiosks	11

(These Kiosks are at : Medchal, Keesara, Maheshwaran, Ibrahimpartnam, Godumakunta, Parvatapur, Ghatkesar, Hayatnagar, Shamirpet, Chevella and Manchal.)

MANAGE (National Institute of Agricultural Extension Management) has set up a village information kiosks project to provide information technology for farmers and farm families at their door step. Each village information-kiosk provides services to about 25-30 villages, i.e. around 20,000 to 30,000 population. The village information-kiosks are located on the roadside and are at central villages where people normally travel.

Agriwatch.com has given free access, to their website to all the 11 villages. Besides normal websites, the rural community in these villages is using multimedia CD learning packages for making pickles, learning about maternity and child health, importance of child education, issues regarding child labour, nutritional aspects and also expert comments on crops. The CD on pickle preparation (which is in local language) is a big hit in all the 11 villages.

In Kerala (South India) a six-month training course in desktop publishing and hardware assembling is organised by the district government (Kasargod, India) for the below-poverty-line families especially women as a part of its computer literacy and self-employment training programme. Nearly 200 such enterprises have been established by employing 4,000 previously-unemployed women from below-poverty-line families. The Government of Kerala also has launched "Delivering IT @ School: Divine Computers of Vadakara", India, to deliver computer education to school students at subsidised rates. "TechnoWorld Computer Centre" is yet another initiative of the Government of Kerala (Mallappuram, India) is offering training in Data entry and DTP for the self-help group of women in order to outsource jobs from the government departments. These initiative enterprises show how ICTs can directly deliver fundamental development benefits – jobs, incomes, skills and empowerment – including delivering such benefits direct to poor communities.

Akshaya Project (Kerala, India) embarked on 2002 is an yet another project endeavor to 'bridge the Digital Divide' and to propel Kerala as India's foremost knowledge society, This initiative started in the district Mallapuram with a vision to ensure that every family (urban and rural) in the district should have at least one member who is computer literate. With this purpose, the Government set up a number of computer training centers amounting to 560 in number with capital funding. As of April 2004, Malappuram was declared as the first computer-literate district of the country with 0.65 million families linked with 615 Akshaya e-centres and high speed broad band internet connection. The scheme has covered 0.55 million people out of which 60 percent are women. Within a span of three years, the project proposed to set up 6000 information centres, generate 50,000 employment opportunities and increase investment opportunities to upto Rs. 500 crores in the state.

In Tamilnadu (South India) the 'Inter-city Marketing Network of Women Entrepreneurs' project has set up a communication network among the women's community-based organisations (CBOs) to market their produce. The CBOs are provided with cellular phones, and women have been trained to maximise the use of telephones for selling not only in their immediate neighbourhoods but also reaching new markets within the city. The impact is that poor women from CBOs constrained by pressures of time and mobility are able to assess and aggregate market demand by trading through their peer CBOs, and evolve cost-effective mechanisms to increase business turnover by making the most of business networking (Gurumurthy 2004). Village Knowledge Centres (VKC) have been established across the state of Tamil Nadu in order to support the online transaction of the rural women. Rural women are thus encouraged to visit the centre to access information, especially on the issues relating to reproductive and child health, and for income generating activities. A website called Oddanchatrammarket. com was launched in the Biovillage Centre at Kannivadi, Tamil Nadu. Oddanchatram is a small town, located in a region that produces large quantities of vegetables, fruits and flowers. The knowledge centre here focuses on rural vegetable producers, and this website uploads market price on real time basis so that the reach and bargain of the local producers will become larger.

The civil society initiatives implemented in the southern states of India have opened new vistas of opportunities for rural women in the areas of (i) ICT-enabled marketing, (ii) knowledge empowerment and (iii) production capabilities. As we continue our journey in gender mainstreaming, the work towards achieving the Millennium Development Goals, the learning points from Beijing+10 Plan of Action review, and the regional efforts in South India are welcome steps. The best example is the Indian Finance Minister's P. Chidambaram's reference to gender in his budget speech on 28 February 2005: "Last July I promised to consider gender budgeting. Honourable members will be happy to note that I have included in the budget documents a separate statement highlighting the gender sensitivities of the budgetary allocations under 10 demands for grants. The total amount in Budget Estimate 2005-06, according to the statement is Rs. 14,379 crore. Although this is another first in budget making in India, it is only a beginning and in course of time, all departments will be required to present gender budgets as well as make benefit-incidence analyses."

WOMEN WEAVING THE INTERNET WORLD IN INDIA

Both Indian men and women value the Internet for its efficiency and its strength as a gateway to inexhaustible reserve of information and experiences, and thus have their own interests and reasons to use the World Wide Web. It is also interesting to note the shifting use pattern of internet use among the gender groups. Since 2004-05, the percentage of online users has increased by 54% to 38.5 million users - male online users increased in absolute numbers but dipped from 72% (2004-05) to 68% (2005-06) and women numbers increased from 28% in 2004-05 to 32% in 2005-06 [12.32 million]. The estimate for the male female ratio in the next 2 years is that it will be closer to 60:40 ratio but will still

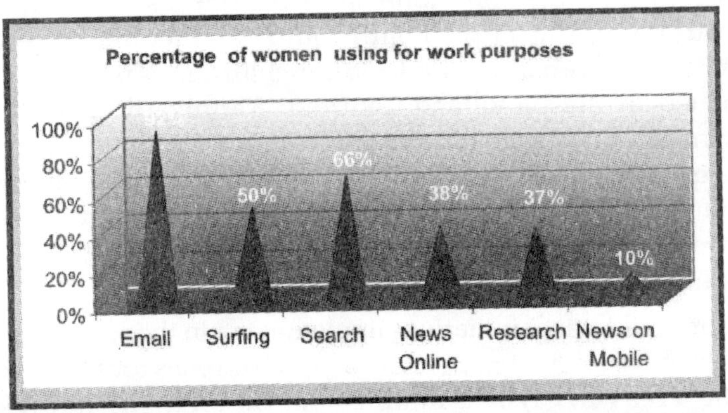

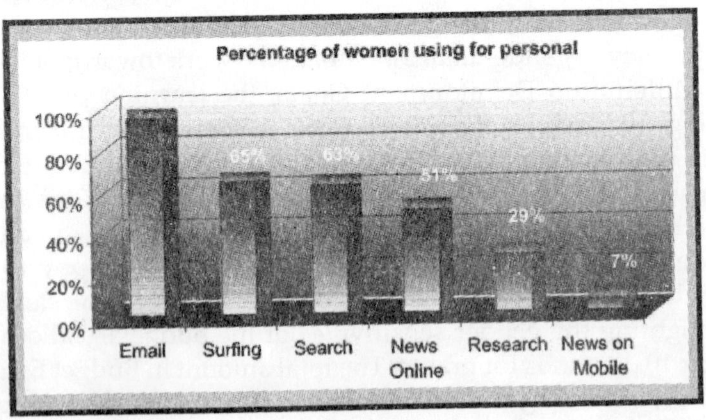

Source: IAMAI

result in the absolute numbers of men being higher than women. However, there seems to be marked difference among the gender groups in their purpose of using online. According to IAMAI survey report on women's online use gender divide among the users seems to be narrowing.

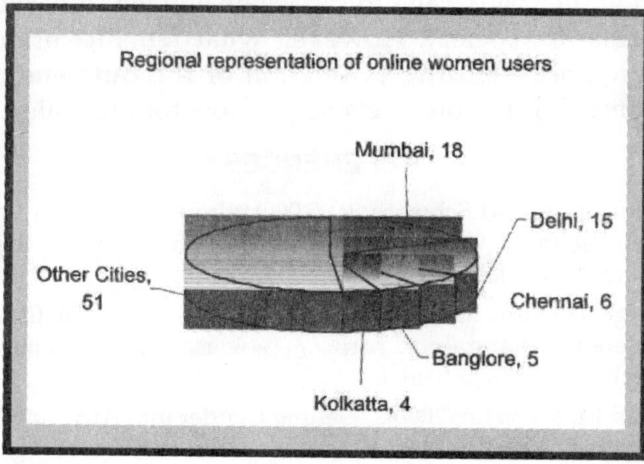

The above Graph explains that a large majority of the women use internet services for emailing (Perosnal: 96%; Work: 92%); searching (personal research: 65%; work: 66%); surfing (personal: 63%; work: 50%); online news (personal: 51%; work: 38%); research (personal: 29%; work: 37%); chatting (personal: 44%; work: 26%); matrimonial (15%); and religious and spiritual information (17%). It is observed that there is a correlation between the e-readiness of the region and the prevalence of gender equality. For instance, in regions where the ICT factors (viz. ICT infrastructure, IT manpower and the software and hardware) are strong, the digital gender gap seems to be small. A gender analysis of the internet and cyber case uses are among the metropolitan population in India.

CONCLUSIONS

This study brings to limelight the gender concern of the Indian government and other stakeholders in providing the necessary conditions to ensure women's equal access to information and knowledge as well as ensuring their equal role as producers and decision-makers in all aspects related to the shaping of IT policies and frameworks. It also dispels the myth that the information society is the birth-right of the urban and elite segment of the population. A national mission has been set up to work towards the fulfillment of the vision of the Geneva Declaration Principles (GDP) viz: to transform women as "key actors in the information society". A plethora of national and regional initiatives have been taken up in the last decade to capacitate women to participate in the information society. However, what remains undone is a systematic and scientific evaluation of the outcome of these programmes which would be a helpful tool for the policy-makers.

REFERENCES

1. Bhatnagar, S. and Schware, R. (2000). "Information and Communication Technology in Development Cases from India". Sage Publications. New Delhi.
2. George Deikun, Mission Director, USAID India, at Bizwomen's Conference, Bangalore. http://www.usaid.gov/in/newsroom/speeches/aug06_5.htm
3. Gillian M. Marcelle (2000). "Getting Gender into African ICT Policy: A Strategic View".

10

Demand and Increasing Opportunities for Women in Indian IT Sector—A Gender Approach

ABSTRACT

Information technology offers many new opportunities that offer women in developing countries a lifeline for economic, social, and political empowerment. Information technology can be an important tool in meeting women's basic needs and can provide the access to resources, and thereby assist women in their current economic activities including farming, trade and entrepreneurship and thus lead women out of poverty. However, in the most development strategies, inclusive of the different policies for the women empowerment, the emphasis is still on planning and appraisal but not on implementation, on investment but not on operations. Hence, the success of the development policies requires the awareness and the involvement of women which could be created by the appropriate institutions at the grass root level. Since IT sector provides multiple benefits like dissemination of knowledge, information, employment, etc.—unlike the other projects dealing with any one objective—and thereby reverses the causes of poverty and removes the obstacles of development, appropriate institutional setup is very much important to the empowerment of women. Appropriate institutional arrangements benefit from the inflow of physical capital tend to acquire and reach the rural women. Appropriate institutions, in addition, help to distribute the benefits equitably and more important, they will contribute to the sustainability of the programs.

Hence, this paper aims to present a picture of effective institutional framework and to point out the general components of institutional developments that reach women and reverse the obstacles of their development. A detailed description of the two components - first, concerned with broad institutional arrangements and second, describing the specific institutional characteristics—are discussed in this paper.

INTRODUCTION

The central question of this study concerns the opportunities and challenges to women's use of information and communication technologies (ICTs). This includes issues of access, the benefits and the role they can and do play in the production and dissemination of information. Recent developments in the fields of information and communication technologies (ICTs) are indeed revolutionary in nature. Information and Communication Technologies (ICTs) are for everyone and women have to be an equal beneficiary to the advantages offered by the technology, and the products and processes, which emerge from their use.

Women representing 50 percent of the world adult population and one third of the official labour force perform nearly two-thirds of all the working hours and receive only one-tenth of the world income and own less than one percent of world property (WCUNDW, 1980a: para 14). Now development practitioners and international organisations alike are beginning to realise that women possess a wealth of untapped indigenous knowledge and human capacity that is essential for sustainable development. It is generally believed that IT is one of the best equal opportunity areas that provide wider opportunities for women to enter and succeed in this industry, and therefore, they are consistently identifying innovative ways that ICTs can be used to empower this marginalised segment of the global community.

However, the validity of these claims requires certain pre-requisites regarding a transition in attitudes towards the gender approach. Firstly, there should be an adequate proportion of technically trained female labour force and secondly, the permeation of an alternate gender culture, that needs as a process of de-learning and re-learning from the new work environment for both men and women. To illustrate the gender situation in IT, one has to view 'the women in technology approach' and 'the women and technology approach'. The former approach tries to involve more women via equal access to education and employment; while the latter has a broader focus on the nature of technological work.

The women in technology approach advocates a weariness of the 'add women and stir' approach which insists on imparting skill to women to survive in the world of new technology. This approach considers only the problems of women in their socialisation, aspirations and their values; but not on the broader questions of whether and how science and its institutions could be reshaped to accommodate women. The women and technology approach, whereas, looks into the gender segregation of skills and jobs, and the gender sensitivity of the organisation in particular. According to this approach, women have to enter into such work with loss of identity or integrity by altering the masculine practices of the occupations.

Issues

Based on the above arguments this paper aims to access the status of women in Indian IT sector. The analysis highlights the growth of Indian software industry and the growing demand for the IT professionals in the near future. New opportunities for women employment are also identified by viewing the distribution of employment in IT sector and also the distribution of women in various service sectors. Moreover, by adopting certain common indicators like proportion of women in various types of IT industry, segregation of women in different levels of employment in IT sector, the gender situation is also measured.

GLOBAL VIEW OF IT SECTOR

The number of people with access to the Internet in the world grew exponentially from fewer than 20 million in 1995 to more than 400 million in 2000. This number is expected to reach one billion by 2005. The number of web sites also grew rapidly from fewer than 200 in mid 1993 to about 20 million in late 2000. Since the early 1990s, the web has been the mainstream environment for creating and disseminating digital information. Today, ICT is the fastest-growing industry in the world and it is poised to become the largest in the world. Global spending on ICT is projected to grow from US$2.2 trillion in 1999 to US$ 3 trillion by 2003, providing many niche opportunities for service providers in developing countries. Establishment of a national ICT infrastructure and policy framework is a prerequisite for developing countries to participate in the emerging global ICT business (UNDP, 2001a).

STATUS OF INDIAN IT SECTOR

India is one of the top 10 countries in the world in the production and supply of high skilled IT manpower. Of the microsoft employees 34%, whereas 17% of Intel scientists in the USA are Indians. Moreover, the co-founder of the Sun Microsystems, the founder and creator of Hotmail, the GM of HP, the president of AT&T are also Indians.

The IT sector in India has created employment opportunities in wide varieties of areas like telecommunications, banking, shopping, education, health, business, etc. the computer occupations are also expanding at the faster rate both within and in a wide range of industries. In addition, the Internet also generated new jobs in areas like the design, maintenance, and management of sites on the World Wide Web. Therefore, real employment opportunities are there that women may be able to access opportunities that they never had earlier.

In India, according to the NASSCOM annual industry survey, the IT Software and Services Industry is projected to employ 650,000 IT professionals by March 2003. This reflects a growth of 24.4% from the last years employment of 522,250. Of the total, almost 205,000 are working in the IT software exports industry; 160,000 are employed in IT enabled Services; 25,000 in the domestic software market and over 260,000 in user organisations.

It could also be reported that the success of IT sector mainly falls in the fields of Software production and exports. The status of Indian Software Industry during the recent period is given in table 1.

Table 1: Production and Export of Indian Software Industry (in million US $)

Year	*Total Production*	*Domestic Consumption*	*Export*
1989-90	197	97 (49.24)	100 (50.76)
1994-95	835	350 (41.92)	485 (58.08)
1995-96	1224	490 (40.03)	734 (59.97)
1996-97	1755	670 (38.18)	1085 (61.82)
1997-98	2700	950 (35.19)	1750 (64.81)
1998-99	3900	1250 (32.05)	2650 (67.95)
1999-2000	5700	1700 (29.82)	4000 (70.18)
2000-01	8750	2450 (28.00)	6300 (72.00)

* values in the parenthesis are the % to the total.

Source: Kumar 2000, p.5

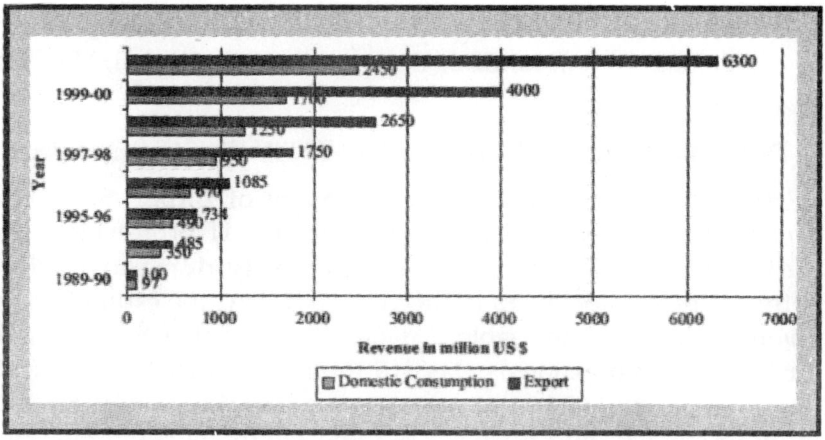

Fig. 1. Consumption and Export Revenue of Indian Software Industry

Reasons for India's Supremacy in Software Export

The mystery behind India's success in providing efficient software and the hyper growth of Indian Software exports are as follows:

- Indian software companies have the unique distinction in efficient software solutions with cost and quality advantage, using state-of-the art technologies, having the capacity to handle large projects and, above all, the ability to execute timely deliver.
- Corporate giants in U.S., Europe and Japan are increasingly looking towards India's cost-effective, high quality software solutions.
- A World Bank funded study in the U.S. confirmed the vendors rated India as their number one choice for outsourcing. For example, Citibank in U.S., Barclays Bank in the U.K. Or Hong Kong and Shanghai Bank in far East depend on software engineers in the silicon valley of India for their efficiency in operating the ATM Machines.
- Even British Airways, Singapore Airlines, American Airlines, Swiss Air etc. outsource their work to a group of software engineers in India for running their airlines on schedule.
- The list of software multinationals operating from India reads like a who's who of global software giants -IBM,

Microsoft, Novell, computer Associates, Oracle, AT&T, Fujitsu, Motorola, EDS, Computer vision, Digital, Hewlett Packard.

DEMAND FOR SKILLED MANPOWER IN THE IT SECTOR

In view of the increasing supremacy of Indian Software exports, there occurs a rising demand for the IT professionals in India. NASSCOM has estimated the likely demand for the Software professionals up to the year 2008, and the estimates are given in the following table. It was estimated that the demand for Software professionals was 115 thousand in 2003 and it will likely to be tripled in the next three years. i.e. it will be 300 thousand in 2006 and further it become 370 thousand in the year 2008.

Estimated Demand for Software Professionals during 2002-2008:

Year	*Estimated Demand*
2002	1,15,000
2003	1,50,000
2004	1,95,000
2005	2,50,000
2006	3,00,000
2007	3,40,000
2008	3,70,000

Source: NASSCOM - McKinsey 1999, report published in The Hindu, 6th February, 2001.

According to another survey of the NASSCOM, the demand for software professionals is expected to be approximately 1.1 million people and there will be one and a half million jobs in IT enabled services by 2008. However, the supply of software professionals, based on current trends, is projected to be 885,000 by 2008. And thus there will be a potential shortfall cf 235,000 people by 2008, if current trends of intake of technical talent into the IT workforce continue. In addition to the Software professionals, there will be a growing demand for professionals in the other IT related sectors. Hence, in order to meet the growing demand, the supply has to be increased. However the supply of ICT oriented professionals, trained from the approved educational institutions, are not sufficient to meet the rising demand.

Therefore, though India has a large talent pool, with 167,000 engineering students and 1.54 million graduates passing out of India's educational institutions annually, still some gaps will remain. Hence, it is also important that educational institutions in India should partner with private training institute to impart intensive training on specific skills required by the industry. This is particularly important in the ITES sector, since it is imperative for professionals in the sector to have the required linguistic skills and the appropriate domain/functional expertise. The IT industry on its part must provide appropriate training opportunities for these students through internships. (Mr. Kiran Karnik, President, NASSCOM)

STATUS OF WOMEN IN THE IT SECTOR IN INDIA

The newness and the expanding nature of computer industry in India has given an impression that it would be relatively immune to gender typed pattern of occupation and would

Gender-Wise Distribution (%) of IT Professionals in Different Firm Types

	High End	*Middle End*	*Export End*	*Domestic Low-end*	*IT Enabled*	*Total*
Male	39.6	9.4	35.4	8.3	7.3	100
Female	21.3	17	27.7	12.7	21.3	100

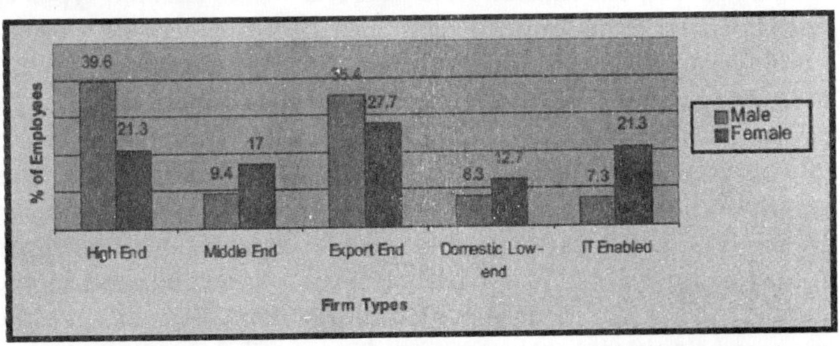

Fig. 2. Gender Distribution (%) of Professionals in Different Firms

maintain gender equity in its occupation. However, existing information reveals that, like in other sectors, gender segregation is very much predominant in the IT sector. An ILO survey confirmed the prevalence of gender inequality among the IT professionals in the Software industry in India by showing how women are relegated to the less prestigious and low paid jobs. Based on this study, the gender-wise distribution of IT professionals in different types of firms is given in the above-mentioned table.

The high-end firms undertake Software products and Development, R&D, turnkey solutions and strategic technical alliance by employing qualified engineering graduates, mostly Ph.Ds and post graduates with technical multi-skills. The Middle-End firms under take development of Software package, offshore services, and alliances for market access. This category of jobs employs engineering graduates who are geographically mobile and possess managerial multi-skilling. The Export End firms undertake onsite services, maintenance and implementation, alliance with labour contractors, etc. The Domestic End jobs require only certificate holders with pure technical, coding and maintenance skills. The IT Enabled and Domestic End firms undertake low skilled routined jobs, inclusive of data entry and continous partnership with the clients. The employees in this category of firms are considered as workers in the back office.

It is evident that the major portion of women employees are employed in the Domestic Low End and the IT enabled types of firms. These firms employ 12.7 and 21.3 per cent of women employees, whereas the male workers in these firms are only 8.3 and 7.3 per cent respectively. The proportion of women IT professionals in the High End and Export End firms are 21.3 and 27.7 as against 39.6 and 35.4 per cent male IT professionals. This clearly indicates that the largest segment of women are clustered in the Low End jobs while the smallest segment of women are found at the higher end which reflects a larger extend of the gender divide in the IT sector. And, therefore, women have not assumed significant role, status and responsibilities, though they are better represented in the IT sector.

WOMEN'S WORK STATUS IN THE INDIAN IT SECTOR

It is reported that the proportion of women, engaged into various IT based industries in India, is portrayed in the following table:

Proportion of Women in the IT based Sector in India

Sl.No.	*IT sector*	*M/F Ratio*	*Type of Work and Skill requirements*
1.	Software Industry	81:19	Software development and designing, customisation and adoption of Software.
2.	Telecom Industry	60:40	Technical and creative work-required highly qualified engineers.
3.	Airlines	20:80	Customer Services-Required communication, language and software skills.
4.	ITES (Medical Transcription)	55:45	Demands in linguistics and functional/domain skills.
5.	BPOs	51:49	Indian BPO is predominantly voice-based (out-bound calls).

Different estimates propounded that about 79 percent of software professionals in software companies were men, whereas 21 percent were women. However, the ration is likely to be 65:35 (male: female) by the year 2005. This ratio is reversed in the ITES sector where the ratio of males to females is 35:65. Also, in spite of only 12.5 per cent women employees in the total IT sector and more than 45 per cent women employment in the ITES sector is a welcome change, since it attracts more women to train in this field. According to a Dataquest-IDC survey in October 2002, NIIT employs the highest number of women by 29 per cent followed by the top Software companies like TCS employing 20 per cent; Wipro employing 19 per cent; Infosis employing 17 per cent of the women while Rolta India employing the lowest number of women at only 4 per cent.

WOMEN IN THE ORGANISATIONAL HIERARCHY OF IT SECTOR

In addition to the lower absorption of women in the higher side IT firms, there occurs the gender segregation also in the organisational hierarchy. The proportion of men and women in the different types of employment are as follows:

Gender Segregation in the Organisational Hierarchy

Position	*Male*	*Female*	*Total*
Call Services	40	60	100
Software Engineers	54.69	45.31	100
Consultants	75	25	100
Project Managers	94.44	5.56	100
Total	67.13	32.87	100

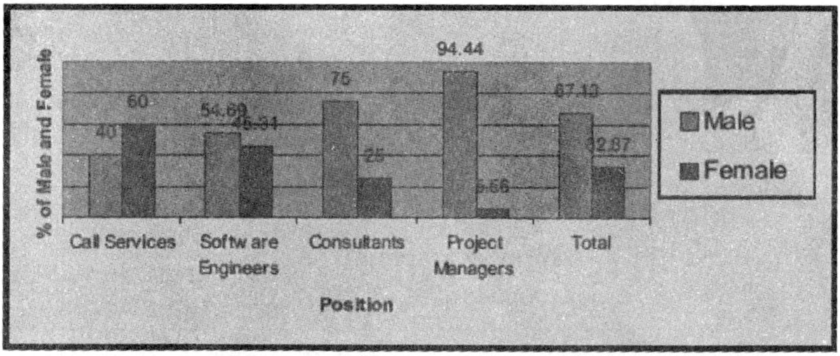

Fig. 3. Distribution of Men and Women in various Organisational Hierarchy

The above information reveals that women are over-represented in some types of lower level jobs like call services and programmers; and under represented in the higher levels jobs. The job ahead survey conducted by Dataquest confirmed this fact. This may be due to the fact that Indian women have lower access to resources such as education, information, mobility, health and leisure and rest as compared to men. Result of which is the Lack of developing their capabilities and, therefore, still remains lower than men in the job market. Also, due to the prevailing gender socialisation factors, women are mostly associated with the secondary markets.

OPPORTUNITIES FOR WOMEN IN IT SECTOR

Since the contribution of women in the IT sector is still marginal, no doubt, women had greater opportunity in the ICT industries to meet the growing demand for IT professionals. With the growth in the IT industry, there is a corresponding growth in the employment opportunities in the areas of systems management, communication and network, systems development, operations and users support etc. Viewing the diversification and content of jobs, it is expected that there is an expanding opportunities for women at different levels of hierarchies. However, the gender inequalities, concerning the low representation of women in the most rewarding areas have to be removed. Hence, what is required are education and proper training for the women. Since, the overall median age of the software professionals was only about 26.5 years, the younger professionals will have a bright chance to be absorbed and accommodated in the IT industries.

OBSTACLES FOR THE PARTICIPATION OF WOMEN IN IT SECTOR

Though women have greater opportunities for getting employment in the IT related industry, their involvement is far behind as compared with the men. The common obstacles and challenges of women's low participation in IT sector may be broadly grouped into three groups viz., Inadequate infrastructural facilities, Social and cultural factors and the Structural factors.

(i) Inadequate infrastructural facilities

First, the most important factor in improving the ability of women to enable the advantages of the opportunities offered by the IT sector is education; especially the engineering and technical education at the higher level. In India, the female literacy rate is only 54.16 per cent as against the male literacy of 75.85 per cent (Census 2001). Moreover, the enrolment of girl students at the higher level of education has declined. i.e. 43.6 per cent in primary, 40.1 per cent in middle, 37.1 per cent in secondary level and only 34.8 per cent in higher education. Also, there has been a wider gap in the male-female enrolment in engineering/technical graduation in India and thus the low enrolment of women in the science and technology which impedes their ability to occupy higher positions in the IT organisations.

Secondly, apart from the literacy, as English is the world- wide dominating language in the IT sector, language is another major obstacle to women in IT sector because majority of the women in the rural areas know and are familiar with their local language but not in English.

Thirdly, since increasing women's access to ICT involves increasing availability of communications in the areas in which they live, the slow growth in the extension of infrastructural facilities like satellite communication in the rural areas is also one of the major barriers of women's access to IT. Hence, emphasis is needed to be on common use facilities, such as, cyber-cafes, telecenters and phone shops and other forms of public access in places convenient and accessible to women.

Next, beyond the basic access to education and other infrastructural facilities, equipped skills are very much required for the women's role in IT as users, creators, designers and managers. Hence, apart from the formal education, the informal IT training is needed to equip with the IT skills for the full utilisation of IT opportunities.

(ii) Social and cultural factors

A series of social, economic and cultural norms and values constrain not only the women's access to engineering and technical education at the higher level, but also women's access to ICT, especially in the common use facilities. In many culturally conservative societies, women are often not allowed to go out without supervision to public venues where men are present or seek help from male users or staff. Also, there is not only restrictions at the entry point, but there are many barriers in the work place and lack of self confidence blocking women from moving up in the ladder of the organisational hierarchy.

Moreover, marriage is found out as a point at which the shrinkage of women from the career pipeline has started. It is because, childcares and housework remain women's responsibilities irrespective of their income, educational level or employment. This places a greater burden on women and restricts women's choice in terms of better opportunities.

In addition, insecurities like eve teasing, harassment, in public and working places lacks the mobility from their work place, is also one of the major obstacles for women's career advancement in the working condition.

(iii) Structural factors

Even though the Government has initiated various programs for the women's welfare, a concrete program for the access to ICT is yet to be implemented. Hence, in the women welfare programs, special considerations to expand the women's access to ICT are needed. This may be initiated through NGOs and various training programs to impart computer and communication knowledge to women for utilising and exploiting their opportunities in the IT sector.

CONCLUSION

Having realised the importance and opportunities of women's access to ICT, it is the appropriate time to ensure the inclusion of gender concerns in the national IT policy. In order to ensure women's ability to take advantages of opportunities presented by IT, gender and development policy-makers need to consider these issues. The gender and IT policy-makers join together to formulate appropriate IT programs that meet the needs of women and implement the women targeted programs to expand the IT training and awareness to women. A worthfull action and complimentary activities are urgently needed to utilise and exploit the opportunities for women in the IT sector for their economic, social and political empowerment, and to keep women in the mainstream, equally and more equitably.

11

Globalisation and ICT Employment Opportunities for Women in Business Process Outsourcing in India

ABSTRACT

The cross-border export of services or outsourcing has expanded dramatically in recent years, owing to advances in network technology, high-speed data networks and substantial increase in bandwidth capacity. The business process outsourcing (BPO), an offshoot of globalisation or internalisation of information-technology-enabled services (ITES) has generated new employment opportunities in a wide spectrum of activities including finance, banking, insurance, human resources, e-trading, healthcare, mortgage services, credit card services, asset management, customer care, real estate, sales and marketing web-enabled services. Out of the large number of BPO service providers from the developing countries, India has demonstrated its visibility because a large segment of its skilled workforce is English-speaking. This study is an attempt to identify the extent to which this new sector has benefited women in India and to measure the opportunities and challenges that women encounter in this new form of work. This study makes an evaluation of the extent to which the escalation of labour demand, the transformation of work culture and the diversification of the professional characteristics of the BPO sector have attracted women to enter into this new area of the ICT profession. It examines the gender roles in the various sub-sets of BPO sector and also the gender differences and similarities in the pattern of knowledge and skill acquisition in the BPO workers. Further, it is an attempt to review the BPO market through a gender perspective in order to suggest ways to improve the women's participation in this new sector. And to establish the impact of globalisation on women's employment opportunities in ICT-related sectors.

INTRODUCTION

Globalisation or internationalisation of business process is not a new phenomenon in the digital economy. One of the major outcomes of the rapid internationalisation of information-technology-enabled services (ITES) has been the practice of BPO, including remote management services that can be performed away from client's locations through ICT (UNCTAD 2003). Recently, an increasing number of enterprises in the developed world are opting for outsourcing in developing countries thereby providing these countries with an opportunity to exploit higher added value niches. As a consequence, some developing countries like India have emerged as major players in BPO, providing services such as software application and development, finance and account management services. Studies have reported that India has been successful in exporting software and services; most exports are to the USA (57%), followed by Europe (22%) and others (21%) (Mark Kobayashi 2004).

India's BPO outsourcing sector has grown by almost 60 percent since 2000 and is projected to be the fastest growing segment of the IT market in India over the next five years. It is reported that half of the world's largest 500 companies and government agencies contract out their business process services to India and the number of companies outsourcing more than 3 percent of their IT budget to India rose from 32 percent in 2000 to 62 percent in 2001 (Hillary 2004). As per available estimate, the outsourcing centres in India employ more than 170,000 workers and have the potential to generate direct employment for one million workers in the next five years (UNCTAD 2003). It is noted that outsourcing plays a big role in creating job opportunities and the Indian BPO sector. In this context it is felt essential to identify the extent to which this new sector has benefited women in India and to measure the opportunities and the challenges that women encounter in this new economy. Besides, an analysis of the BPO market through a gender perspective is required at this juncture in order to device strategies for involving more women in this new economy from different strata of the Indian community.

RESEARCH BACKGROUND

The status of women in the BPO based occupations has received greater attention in the recent years and the discussions are directed towards both the upsides and the downsides of women working in this new profession. The focus of most of the existing literature has been centred around the following thematic categories: (i) changing labour market conditions, (ii) women friendly organisational culture (iii) changing role of women in the field of technology and (iv) the closing of the gender-based digital divide in the BPO related occupations.

Regarding labour market conditions, it is observed that, unlike other IT branches of work, this new sector (BPO) is based on diverse skills and it generates a demand for employees having a solid foundation in communication, technical skills and customer relations (NASSCOM 2004), (Spender 2000), (Melymuka 2000). This professional demand is an added incentive for women to gain access into this profession. The International Labour Organisation (ILO) in its report on 'Gender Issues in the World of Work' also has reiterated the positive impact of technological change on women's employment (ILO 2000). Due to their innate sense for communication and customer service skills, women are making a difference in the BPO sector and, through their performance, women have placed themselves in vital positions in the labour market. The reason for this optimistic trend is that this new profession opens its gateway to a wide range of professionals with diverse skills, not just computer scientists. Women with fresh degrees in arts, science, mathematics, business administration and even medieval history can also enter and progress in this profession.

As far as the organisational factors are concerned, research has shown that workplace culture plays a substantial role in shaping women's involvement in the labour market. (Gill 2000). The individual autonomy, equal opportunities, 'comfortable, causal, friendly and professional atmosphere', 'family-like collaborative community characteristic of the workplace[1], the 'avenues for constant learning' and above all 'the fewer gender-related issues' are considered as the motivating factors for women to enter the BPO based profession in large numbers.

Regarding women's role in BPO, studies have pointed out that women's presence is noticed in the wide spectrum of BPO reiated activities. The survey reports also have confirmed that women have experienced 'an exhilarating sense of achievement, impact, satisfaction and opportunity for creative freedom[1] in the BPO based work. This is because in other branches of IT, the work is crafted around men whereas in this profession the work is crafted around both men and women. It is also deiieved that the nature of work in the BPO sector liberated women from the old stereotypes and gender-related obstacles in the work place and thereby unleashed great energy and talent into workplace (Napier 2000), (WOW 2001), (Cohen 2000).

Contrary to the above discussion, there are a few studies which focused on the downsides of women's position in the BPO related occupation (Taggart & O'Gara 2000). They highlight issues such as: (i) lower representation of women in critical areas of work; (ii) polarisation of gender roles in various segments of the BPO; (iii) women's lack of necessary skills in technology; (iv) and lack of opportunities for updating skills in their work. With regard to women's presence in different areas of work, it is stated that though women constitute a larger proportion of BPO based workers, the top slots always go to men. Women's lack of acquaintance with a wide range of skills and their inability to update their knowledge in state-of-the-art technologies are cited as the cause for their lower representation in vital areas of work.

The foregoing studies brought into focus two important aspects: one is about the existence of mixed career opportunities for women in new economy and the other one is about lack of studies on the status of women in BPO related activities.

GENDER TECHNOLOGY RELATIONS WITH RESPECT TO BPO INDUSTRY

Each period of technological change carries with it high expectations of societal and organisational restructuring that will favour the disadvantaged. This holds true for information and communication technologies in general and the business process outsourcing, in particular, as the latter is the offshoot of the former. It is presumed that IT and its related industries will create new windows of opportunity and accelerate social mobility for new entrants like women in an institutional framework that is not as yet shaped by traditional power relations. The fast expansion of the IT labour market, the need for diverse talents, the shift in the demand from technical to more general management and business skills and the government's and employer's initiatives to improve women's representation in the IT sector have created an image that IT is one of the best equal opportunity areas 'that provide wider opportunities for women to enter and succeed in this industry'. Nevertheless, the validity of these claims is yet to be established through empirical analysis. For such a gender transition to take place certain prerequisites have to be met. First, there should be an adequate proportion of technically trained female labour. Second, for the permeation of an alternate gender culture, there needs to be a process of de-learning and re-learning from the new work environment for both men and women (Haraway 1997), (Cockburn 1 993). This, in turn, has to facilitate changes in families that will support the demands of the job or, in the absence of which, there is a need for the industry to make alternate provisions to meet the family responsibilities of women.

Even as early as the 1980's, research that centred on the effect of new technologies on women's jobs spawned a whole body of literature which explored the relationship between women and technology. Of all the approaches, the following two are widely adopted.

- The women in technology approach focus on the 'exclusion of females from computer work, with change expected to come about via equal access to education and employment' (Gill and Grint, 1995), and (Webster, 1996) and
- The women in technology approach which explore 'the nature of technological work, its development over time and its articulation with changing gender relations' (Henwood 1993).

Women in technology approach simply try to involve more women, whereas, the second approach has a broader focus on the nature of technological work. These different approaches have also been identified in the literature on women and science (Fox-Keller 1986), (Wajcman 1993) and (Grundy 1994). The philosophy of the 'women in technology approach' is that, given the right encouragement and opportunities, the girls will gladly become scientists, computing professionals or engineers and engage in the present work practices of these fields. This approach locates the problem in women (their socialisation, their aspirations and values) and does not ask the broader questions of whether and in what way science and its institutions could be reshaped to accommodate women. The equal opportunity recommendations, moreover, ask women to exchange major aspects of their gender identity for a masculine version without prescribing a similar 'degender' process for men. (Wajcman 1993)

Henwood (1993) also advocates a wariness of the 'add women and stir' approach and argues for the frameworks which address the many ways in which technology and gender interact. Henwood suggests that access to skills is not enough to secure a permanent place for women in the technological workplace and that the source of the inequality needs to be addressed. (Battel 1994), on the other hand, does not deny the relevance of this argument but adopts a more pragmatic view point: The difficulties surrounding women and technology involve wider social questions than computer courses alone can hope to solve. Therefore, the means, the know-how to 'break through the barriers which make the computer as a machine meaningless' to women must be made available to them. (Grundy 1994) acknowledges that in spite of the superficiality of the add-more-women approach, it must nevertheless be implemented as it is a precondition to the 'emasculation' of computing.

Women and technology looks into the gender segregation of skills and jobs and the gender sensitivity of the organisation in particular. It aims to alter the masculine practices of these occupations so that women could enter into such work without any loss of identity or integrity (Grundy 1994). Women should not be required to 'play the game' or accept working conditions such as ten hour days, frequent weekend work or travel, in order to fit into the computer culture (Dain 1991). (Wajcman 1990) advocates that what is needed is a transformation in the nature of paid and unpaid work as well as looking at the impact women can have on technology and technology on women. Drawing from this approach, the following parameters have been used to analyse the gender regime in the IT sector of the sample nation's proportion of women across various IT occupations/sectors, working conditions, practical gender needs of women, learning and career paths. Based on the above theoretical background, the gender situation in the area of Business Process Outsourcing is analysed and presented in the following sections of this paper.

STATEMENT OF THE PROBLEM

India commands a competitive edge in the BPO sector due to the favourable supply of qualified people with relatively low wage rates. It is not only emerging as a major service hub for the global market but also has the strength to retain its status on vital factors such as: (i) possessing a high quality scientific and technological workforce; (ii) maintaining a superior quality in IT/ITES export services; (iii) building the largest telecom network; (iv) establishing a number of export processing zones; (v) improving the level of IT penetration in the Indian economy; and (vi) creating IT clusters in the major urban centres in the country (NASSCOM 2000), (NASSCOM 2003). All these factors have encouraged multinationals like IBM to locate their operations in India for providing services to their overseas clients. But the question is to determine how far the escalation of demand for BPO workers acted favourably for the wide-spread participation of women in this new sector.

OBJECTIVES OF THE STUDY

Based on secondary sources, this study seeks to examine the situation of women working in the BPO sector in India. The focus of the study is (i) to identify the organisational and demographic profile of the employees in the BPO sector in India; (ii) to assess the gender profile as well as the occupational profile of the workers in the various segments of the BPO operations; (iii) to present a quantitative and the qualitative analysis of employment potential generated by BPO, particularly for women; (iv) to develop a comprehensive understanding of the various aspects of gender disparities in this new economy and (v) to identify policy implications for equal opportunities. In short, this study is an attempt to develop a holistic perception of the structures, policies and practices of the BPO sector from the viewpoint of women's opportunities in this sector.

TRENDS IN THE PARTICIPATION OF WOMEN IN THE BPO SECTOR

Women's position in the BPO sector has seen both positive and negative trends in the last decade in the Indian sub-continent.

Studies have presented BPO industry as a key player in the creation of jobs for women in various categories. It was expected that the global expansion of software and IT-enabled services would broaden the job prospects for women and also would facilitate their working from anywhere and at anytime, capitalising on network technology. The proportion of men and women being employed in the leading firms that handle BPO activities in India is presented in Table 1.

Table 1: Proportion of women in the Indian BPO sector workforce

Sl.No.	*Indian BPO*	*Women %*	*Men %*
1.	TracMail India	35	65
2.	Infowavz International	40	60
3.	Wipro-Spectramind Services	49	51
4.	ICICI	60	40
5.	Daksh E-services	60	40
6.	GE	60	40

Source : Dataquest, April 2002

It is interesting to note that out of its total workforce of 5000 employees, Wipro-Spectramind Services has women to men ratio of 49% to 51%; Infowavz International has a total of 1000 employees, of whom 380 are women, which is approximately 40% of the workforce. TracMail India with an employee base of over 1800 agents has 35% women, while ICICI One Source with a base of over 2400 employees has 60% women in its workforce. Daksh E Services also claims that 60% of its employees are women (Aggarwal 2003). According to the Deputy Director of the Confederation of Indian Industries (Cll), a minimum of 40 percent of the newly created jobs by the EPO sector are taken by women in India (Mitter, 2001).

COMPARISON OF EMPLOYMENT PROSPECTS FOR WOMEN IN IT AND BPO SECTORS

Recent research and projections have indicated that the employment potential for women in this emerging sector is more promising than in the traditional manufacturing sectors (Mitter, 2004). A comparison of labour market potential offered by the traditional IT sector and the new BPO sector shows that the latter is more women friendly than the former. This can be better illustrated by viewing the labour market situation in both the sectors. The gender situation in the tradition IT sector is presented in Table 2.

Table 2: An Overview of Gender Participation in the IT Sector

Sl.No.	*IT Sector*	*Women %*	*Men %*
1.	NUT	29	71
2.	Rolta India	4	96
3.	Infosys	17	83
4.	TCS	20	80
5.	Wipro	19	81

Source : Dataquest, April 2002.

A close examination of the employment pattern in the IT sector reveals the widening of gender gaps in this area of work. It is evidenced that barring a few firms like the NUT, they have employed women in the range of 17-20 percent in their companies. For instance, top software companies like Infosys, employ 17 percent women, TCS employs 20 percent, and Wipro employs 19 percent women. Rolta India employs the lowest number of women at 4 percent. The national average of women being observed in the IT sector is less than 20 percent (Mohit 2004). On the contrary, the BPO sector employs over 60 percent of women in their workforce which is a welcome change from the point of view of women's employment in the IT industry.

COMPARISON OF THE EDUCATIONAL ATTAINMENT NEEDS OF THE IT AND BPO SECTORS

Evelyn Fox-Keller (2002) observed that the outsourcing of IT-Enabled Services has been immensely beneficial to both women and men, especially those who have limited skills or lack of resources to invest in higher education. One of the factors that have motivated a larger section of middle class women with an urban background to join the labour force in the BPO sector may be its decreased emphasis on technical qualifications. A comparison of the educational background of the employees in the IT and BPO sectors is presented in Table 3.

Table 3: Educational Attainment within the IT and BPO sectors

Sl.No.	*Educational Background*	*BPO INDUSTRY %*	*IT INDUSTRY %*
	Technical		
1.	Engineering	6	57
2.	M-Tech	3	10
3.	MBA	8	5
4.	MCA	6	12
	Non Technical		
5.	Diploma/Certificate	14	5
6.	Graduate	51	4
7.	Post Graduate	10	5
8.	Others	2	2

Source: NASSCOM INDIA, 2002.

The above data shows a sharp contrast in the educational attainment of the employees in the sectors. For instance, the proportion of employees with technical qualifications is higher in IT industries than in the BPO, because one needs to be an engineer or a technocrat to get employment in the IT industry. On the contrary, the entry requirements for the BPO sector is much more flexible which is found to be convenient for women. Any degree with communication and soft skills are the prerequisites to enter the BPO sector. The enforcement on the technical and hard science is one of the factors that deter women from entering into the labour market in the traditional IT sector while the reverse is true in the case of BPO sector. The other motivating factors, for women to join the BPO sector in greater numbers, may include easy access and greater flexibility in work organisation; perceived scope to combine family with career, and apparent advantages in terms of equality and empowerment. Further, the nature of work is considered conducive for women's engagement as it does not involve any physical exertion. Notwithstanding these advantages, the feminising profile, the stress free environment as well as the women suited nature of work have been subjected lately to growing criticism.

THE GENDER SITUATION IN THE VARIOUS SEGMENTS OF BPO

BPO services span finance, banking, insurance, human resources, e-training, health care, mortgage services, credit card services, asset management, customer care, logistics and distribution, real estate, sale and marketing, and web related services. Table 4 illustrates the spectrum of BPO service activities in India and the employment requirements in each segment of the BPO operations.

BPO is emerging as a booming sector in India, with a wide spectrum of services and a range of clients which generates direct and indirect employment opportunities. For instance, the service offered by BPO ranges from back office operations to content development. The clients range from airline companies like Delta and British Airways for reservation and frequent flyer services, to financial companies like Citigroup for credit card payment and collection services, to retail stores, like JC Penny and Lowe, for on-line shopping services, to cheque printers like Deluxe for data processing services. An attempt has been made here to examine the organisational profile of men and women working in the various segments of BPO sector.

Table 4: BPO services in India (in million USD)

Services/ Segments	*1998-1999*		*2001*	
	Employed	*Amount*	*Employed*	*Amount*
A. IT Enabled Services				
(i) Back office operations/ RevenueAccounting/ Data entry/Data Conversion	9700	97	260000	4370
(ii) Remote maintenance and Support	1600	15	180000	3105
B. Medical Transcription/ Insurance				
(i) Claim Processing	3800	32	160000	2530
(ii) Call centres	1400	9	100000	1380
(iii) Database services	1000	10	100000	1495
(iv) Content Development	5500	62	300000	5750
Total	23000	225	1100000	18630

Source: NASSCOM, India (1999).

CAREER PROSPECTS FOR THE GENDER GROUPS IN MEDICAL TRANSCRIPTION SERVICE

An analysis of the gender situation in the BPO sector shows that medical and legal transcription is one of the areas where women tend to make a significant contribution. At present, there are about 200 medical transcription firms in India employing some 10,000 transcribers, many of them women (Economist 2001). For instance, a case study of women's status in a medical transcription unit called SEMA in Kolkata shows that women receive a very large share of remote processing jobs especially in the transcription work.

CAREER PROSPECTS FOR THE GENDER GROUPS IN SOFTWARE-EXPORT SERVICE

Software export is another area where women are employed in the managerial and technical grades of BPO based companies. In the technical and managerial categories, the proportion of women varies from company to company and it is usual to find women occupying at least 20 to 25 percent of the technical and managerial jobs. There is no evidence of discrimination either at the point of recruitment or in career progression. Women with engineering degrees or with Masters Degrees in Charted Accountancy experience equal opportunities in export-oriented units such as CAD world, HCL, and Cognizant. However, the positive aspect of the export-oriented software sector towards women employees has not been accepted unequivocally by the women leaders in the Trade Union. According to them, only a few urban based upper and upper-middle class women have been favoured by this sector and not others.

CAREER PROSPECTS FOR THE GENDER GROUPS IN BACK-OFFICE FUNCTIONS

As the recent volatility in the US economy has affected the volume of e-business in software, most of the IT companies, like Infosys, have shifted their market to the back office functions which involve basic and advance level activities. BPO vendors, who offer data and accounting services, require people with typing and clerical skills. The next level of back office functions involve rule-based and decision making processes which require a certain level of discipline and focus. According to Miner (2000), the routine and discretionary works are taken up by women and the advanced level of operations are handled by men.

CAREER PROSPECTS OF GENDER GROUPS IN WEB DESIGN AND CALL CENTRES

Yet another area where women workers in India have found a market niche, both nationally and internationally, is in web site design. The growing incorporation of the Internet into business operations has led to this new window of opportunity, in which the stereotyped image of femininity can provide women with comparative advantage. Women are considered to be better creators and designers, familiar with layouts and colour matching, and are considered to be more suitable for this profession. Call centres are another important segment of the BPO sector which attracts a larger proportion of women into its workforce. Last year alone more than 100 call centres were established and it is interesting to note that multinationals such as British Airways or American Express have operated their services through call centres in India. The emergence of e-governance has also prompted establishment of call centres that are geared to answering queries in relation to obtaining and processing of government forms. There seems to be a correlation between the skill requirements and the gender preference in the call centre business. When the call centre service provider is involved in direct contact with clients, as with telemarketing, e-publishing, and customer support, they prefer employees to have excellent communication skills, knowledge of the client's languages, their mindset and native industry. On the other hand, when the service provider offers consulting or advisory services, complex specialised business skills and relationship-building skills are required. As the skill and knowledge requirements increase, the cost of the employees providing the services also increases. It is evidenced from the survey reports (Data Quest, 2003) that women find employment in online customer relation support services while men are employed in the consultancy services.

The above section presents the preference of women and their employment opportunities in the various organisational structure of the BPO sector. Though the general employment situation seems to be favourable to women as it absorbs a larger section of the educated but unemployed youth, it is not free from the patriarchal power structure prevailing in the traditional industrial sector. The following section deals with the gender situation in the occupational hierarchy of BPO sector.

THE GENDER DIVISION OF LABOUR IN THE BPO SECTOR IN INDIA

While both men and women derive benefits from the participation in BPO sector, there is evidence that such benefits exist on a gender-based continuum. A study, on 'Housekeepers to the world' focused on labour market potentials in BPO sector in India, has pointed out the prevalence of gender division of labour in the call centres (Chengappa and Goyal 2002). The findings of this study reported that men were found as leaders of the industry and experts in terms of discussing the future growth and challenges in developing the industry. In contrast, the women interviewed were not in positions that were higher than that of an entry-level worker. The one exception to this was a female vice-president. However, she worked for a company that trains women on how to be effective customer service representatives. She was not in a direct position of power in terms of owning a call centre or serving as an agent for influencing policy surrounding the development of this industry. This article has brought to light the fact that women are to be seen, but not serve as active agents in the decision-making sphere in BPO sector. Another study by UNCTAD 2002 also confirmed this phenomenon. The findings of the empirical studies undertaken by Vijaya Bhaskar and (Ghosh 2001), showed that there are clear signs of labour market segmentation by gender in BPO sector, where women are engaged in low paid and less skilled occupations, thereby reinforcing or aggravating the existing gender inequalities in the labour market. It has been observed that while the proliferation of BPO draws more educated women into paid jobs and reduces the problem of educated unemployment to some extent; it has not brought any major transformation in aggregate employment patterns (Ghosh 2003). A study by (Mazumdar 2004) reviews the role and position of women workers in the call centres and the nature of career prospects open to women within the firm/ industry. The job requirement in this sunrise industry is that of 'computer telephonists', who are usually cailed 'agents' rather than telephone operators The findings revealed that the call centre agents who are mainly women having been involved in highly repetitive and 'dead-end' jobs, and they are have very low career prospects.

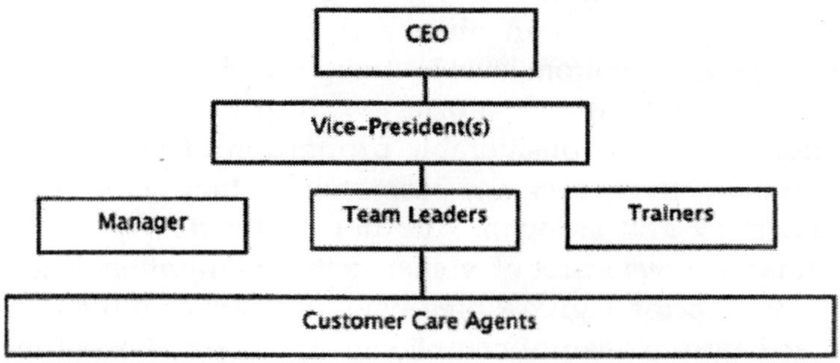

Fig. 1 : Organisational Structure of a Typical Call Centre

The study by (Ramesh 2004) among the call centre agents also demonstrated that vertical mobility on the job ladder becomes an issue to more than half the women agents in the call centres. It identified that a considerable proportion of women agents prefer to continue at the level of agents (bottom line work) and are not actively seeking any vertical mobility in the job ladder.

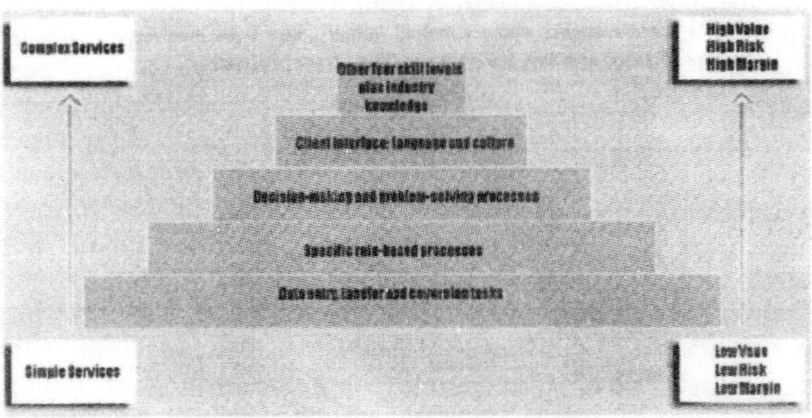

Fig. 2 : BPO hierarchy of Services

Source: E-Commerce and Development Report 2003 (UNCTAD 2003).

This voluntary acceptance of low-end career is mainly due to the caring commitments and household bindings of these women workers, where they find promotion as an undesirable preposition with added responsibilities and greater 'rigidities'. The managers consider this category of staff as the substratum of the organisation as they are happy to stay with the firm as agents. In this respect firms are found to be capitalising on gender divisions by actively recruiting women that they perceive will not be interested in promotion. It has been observed that this preference for continuing at the bottom level is stronger with those women who are in the upper age categories, with grown up children. In addition to this, a considerable proportion of younger agents also do not actively seek any promotion as they consider the job as transitory and stopgap. Another by (UNCTAD 2003) also confirms the lower status of women in the organisational hierarchy of the BPO sector. Figure 2 presents the pyramid of BPO services arranged by the levei of complexity. The proportion of women decreases as the complexity of the occupational level increases.

GENDER CONCERNS IN THE BPO INDUSTRY IN INDIA

The general image about the BPO sector is that it is 'stress free', and 'women-friendly' which needs to be justified from the case studies. A few surveys have listed the prevalence of career opportunities, the congenial work environment, the comparatively easy access to a job, the lack of insistence on experience or a series of academic degrees, perceptions of higher career prospect, flexible work hours etc as the positive factors for women's employment in the BPO sector. But it is not without its perils. In the firms studied (Ramesh 2004), the attrition of women workers is found to coincide with their engagement, marriage or pregnancy. The other obstacles that prevent women's progress in this sector include the lack of access to training; lack of clarity on the career growth path; grave working condition; night shifts; stress and strain of work; hassles due to typical timings of work; low wages and occupations in less visible areas of work. Women are viewed as 'organisational isolates', segregated from career structure of the broader organisation in which they work. In this regard, call centres share many similarities with other female-dominated occupations. It is also observed that BPO has favoured only young, educated, unmarried and urban based women. This kind of bias in recruitment is suggestive of a disquieting trend of an increasing polarisation within society and within the workforce where a considerable chunk of women's work in the new economy is accessed by the fairly well-off and educated sections of society.

The picture will become more gloomy when considering the overall Socio-culturai background in Indian context, which constrains an average women's access to information and new technology, via such sites as cyber cafes, tele-centres and even phone booths. This situation calls for monitoring of the gender differentials in the areas of recruitment, skill sets, training and mentoring. Policy-makers need to ensure that women receive the same opportunities and encouragement to acquire skills that could equip them for more complex and specialised job Training in the skills saleable in the international market is required for the benefit of women. The Outsourcing Institute in the US has observed that there is a changing pattern of areas being outsourced to Internet and intranet services owing to the increase in e-commerce activities. Thus if women are to increase their share in these services, they have to be increasingly exposed to and trained in Internet skills. Moreover, the BPO related firms are located in the urban centres and thereby the bulk of educated women in the population are denied the opportunity of taking part in this growing labour market. Table 4 illustrates the clustering of BPO companies in the first tier cities in India.

The above table illustrates the urban centric nature of BPO industry which is not reachable by rural women youth. Initiatives are in progress to set up internet kiosks as a step towards bridging the gender based digital divide in the country. These kiosks will be a media not only for providing multiple services like telephony, e-mail, voice mail etc, but also for imparting skills in data processing apart from supporting the e-governance initiatives at different levels.

Table 5: The Back Office Landscape in Indian Companies: Locations and Focus

City	*No. of Companies*	*No. of Employees*	*Focus Areas*	*Companies*
Bangalore	35	1,09,500	Chip design, software bio informatics, call centre, IT consulting, tax processing	Intel, IBM, SAP, SAS, Dell, CISCO, Tl, Motorola, HP, Oracle, Yahoo, AOL, E&Y, Accenture, Wipro, Infosys, Msource, Thomson Financial

Delhi	53	73,000	Call centres, transaction processing, chip design, software, knowledge services	GE, American Express, ST Microelectronics, WIPRO Spectramind, Daksh, Convergeys, McKinsey, Smart Analyst, Evalue Serve
Mumbai	45	62,050	Financial research, back office software	Morgan Stanley, Chigroup, TCS, Mphasis, I-Flex Solutions
Chennai	35	51,000	Software: transaction processing animation knowledge services	World Bank, Ford, Standard Chart and, ABNAmro, Cognizant, Polaris, EDS, Pentamedia, Graphics, SmartAnalyst, Office Tiger, Mckinsey, Scope e-Knowledge Centre, Datamatics, Lason, Vision Healthsource
Hyderabad	24	36,500	Software, backup office, product design	HSBC, Microsoft Satyam, GE
Kolkata	29	7,300	Consulting, Software	PWC, IBM, ITC, Infotech, TCS
Pune	6	7,300	Call centres, chip design, embedded software	Msource, Cdac, Persistent systems, Zensar

Source: Ravi Kumar, Sunday Express, February 8, 2004.

CONCLUSION

It is observed that there is a proliferation of trade literature on BPOs that have projected the employment potential of this sunrise sector and also the changing work environment. But the number of studies that provide an in-depth analysis of the labour market implications for women's advancement in this new economy is limited. Initiatives are needed to promote research in the areas of gender dimensions in this new economy. An investigation of the gender situation in the various segments of the BPO industries indicates that women's share in the back-office operations, medical transcriptions, software-export service, web service and call centres is on the increase although it is restricted to the urban based upper and upper-middle class women. Despite the fact that this sector absorbs a larger section of the unemployed women youth, it is not free from the patriarchal power structure prevailing in the traditional industrial sector. Studies have reported that women's invasion of the BPO sector has not improved their power relations in this new sector. There are clear signs of gender divisions of labour and women are relegated to low status and low paid jobs. Although the BPO sector has opened the opportunity for unemployed educated women, it has not brought any transformation in the employment patterns. The vertical mobility of the women on the job ladder becomes an issue in this sector and women are getting stagnated in highly repetitive and 'dead-end' jobs. Besides, there remain several blocks (access to education, infrastructure and finance) in the way of women wishing to participate fully in the BPO industry. Efforts should be taken to (i) encourage the participation of women at ail levels of BPO services; (ii) enhance women's awareness of BPO opportunities, and (iii) improve their technical and managerial skills (through training) and their self-confidence (by involving them in decision-making levels) to enable them to generate sufficient income and to significantly improve their quality of life.

REFERENCES

- Aggarwal, B. 2003. "Women Power Coming of Age". Cyber India Online Limited, New Delhi.
- Battel, Roisin 1994. "Women and technology: A place for hard-ware". Adams, A., Emms, J., Green, E., OwenJ (eds), Proceedings of the 5th IFIP International Conference on Women, Work and Com-puterization, 2-5 July 1 994, *Breaking Old Boundaries: Building New Forms*. Manchester. pp. 397-404.
- Chengappa, R & Goyal, M. 2002. "Housekeepers to the world". *India Today*. Vol. 27. pp. 36-49.
- Cockburn, Cynthia & Ormrod, Susan 1993, *Gender and Technology in the Making*. Sage Publications. London.
- Cohen, May 1997. "Cracking the glass ceiling". *Canadian Medical Association Journal*. Vol. 157. pp. 1713-1714.

- Dain, Julia. 1991, "Women and computing: some responses to falling numbers in higher education". *Women's Studies International Forum,* Vol. 14. No. 3. pp. 217-225.
- Economist 2001. "Back office to the world". 3 May 2001. The Economist. London.
- Fox-Keller, Evelyn. 1986. How gender matters: Or, why it's so hard for us to count past two. In: Hardin, J (ed), *Perspectives on Gender and Science.* Falmer Press. London.
- Ghosh, Jayati 2003. "Globalisation, Export-Oriented Employment for women and Social Policy: Case Study of India". Mimeo. Jawaharlal Nehru University. New Delhi.
- Gill, Rosalind & Grint, Keith. 1995. *The Gender Technology Relation: Contemporary Theory and Research.* In Keith, Grint & Rosalind, Gill (eds). The Gender-Technology Relation: Contemporary Theory and Research. Taylor & Francis". London.
- Gill, Rosalind and Dodd, D. 2000. "New Media: Working *Practices in the Electronic Arts."* Final Report Submitted to Director General V. European Commission. Brussels.
- Grundy, Frances. 1994, 'What is to be done? A feminist critique of science', *Technology and Computing.* Vol. 1, No. 1, pp. 21-32.
- Haraway, Donna. 1997. *Feminism and Technoscience.* Routledge. New York & London.
- Henwood, Flis. 1993. "Establishing gender perspectives on information technology: Problems, issues and opportunities". In Eileen Green, Jenny Owen. & Den Pain, (eds). *Gendered Design? Information Technology and Office Systems.* Taylor & Francis. London.
- *International Labour Organization 1998.* "South-East Asia and the Pacific Muitidisciplinary Advisory Team SEAPAT.". 1998 'ILO/ SEAPAT's OnLine Gender Learning & information Module', in: ILO, Gender issues In the world of work - Emerging gender issues in the Asia Pacific region", http: / /www.ilo.org ' pu bl ic / enq1ish / region/as ro/mdtmamia/train ing %I'unit2; as ialfp.htm
- Kelkar, G. & Nathan, D. 2002, "Gender relation and technological change in Asia', Current Sociology. Vol. 50. No. 3. pp. 427-447.
- Mazumdar, Indrani. 2004. "Neither Mental Nor Manual Labour: Service Factories of the New Economy". Mimeo. Centre for Women Development Studies. New Delhi.
- Melymuka, Kathleen. 2000. "Bridging a gap for women in IT. *Computer World.* July. pp. 1-4
- Mitter, S and Sen A.2000. "Can Calcutta become another Bangalore?." *Economic and Political Weekly.* Vol.35. No.26, pp. 2263-68,

http://www.woridbank.orqqender/diqitaidivide /'offshore.htm [15 July 2004]

- Mohit. Chhabra. 2004. "The DQ-IDC India Salary Survey '04'". Dataquest. http://www.dqindia.com/content,top_stories/2004/104100601.asp [15 July 2004]
- Napier, JoAnn. 2000. Technology With Curves: *Women Reshaping the Digital Landscape*, Harper Collins. Toronto.
- NASSCOM 1999. *The Information Technology Workforce*. National Association of Software and Service Companies. New Delhi.
- NASSCOM 2000. "Nasscom for immediate Action to Increase Supply of Knowledge Workers, 2000: Press Release". National Association of Software and Services Companies, New Delhi.
- NASSCOM 2003. "Knowledge Professional". National Association of Software and Services Companies. New Delhi.
- NASSCOM 2004. "Indian ITES-BPO Industries". National Association of Software and Service Companies. New Delhi.
- Ramesh, Babu. P. 2004. "Cyber coolies in BPO: Insecurities and vulnerabilities of non-standard work". Economic and Political Weekly. Vol. 39. No. 5, January. pp. 492-97. Ramesh, Babu P. 2004. "Labour in Business Process Outsourcing: A Case Study of Call Centre Agents". NLI Research Studies Series, No: 051 /2004, V.V. Ciri National Labour Institute, Noida.
- Spender, Dale. 2000. "The digital life style for women". *The CPSR Newsletter*. Vol. 18. No.1. pp. 1-6, Available: http://www.cpsr.org/publications/newsletter/issues/2000/Winter2000/spender.html
- Taggart, Nancy and O'Cara, Chloe. 2000. "Training women for leadership and success in IT". Academy for Educational Development, http://www.Proiects:aed.org/techeauity/techknowfinal.pdf [1 5 July 2004]
- UNCTAD. 2003. Business Process Outsourcing Services for Economic Deveiopment, in: UNCTAD, *E-Commerce and Development Report 2003*. United Nations Publication, NewYork and Geneva, http:. /www.unctad.org.'commerce
- UNCTAD 2003. op. cit.
- UNCTAD 2003. op. cit. p. 140.
- Vijaybaskar et al. 2001. "Labour in the New Economy: Case of the Indian Software Industry". *The Indian Journal of Labour Economics*. Vol. 44. No. l.
- Wajcman. July 1990. "Women, Technology and Work". *Refractory Ciri*, Vol. 35. pp. 7-10.

- Webster, J. 1996. *Shaping women's work: Cender, employment and information technology*. Longman. Great Britain.
- WOW 2001. "Women on the Web Conference held at Hamberg". Germany, March 8-10. 2001.

12

Gender Democracy in Digital Economy: An Indian Experience

INTRODUCTION

One of the parameters for participating in the e-society is the capability to build technical manpower. The spurt in the growth of knowledge economy or e- economy, in the last two decades, have enforced the developing nations including India to concentrate more on the human resource development. As these countries have skipped the agricultural and industrial revolution, they worked hard to catch up with the IT revolution by building their manpower and network infrastructure. India, a country freed from foreign yoke 55 years back, is emerging as one of the world class leaders in IT with 220,000 world class IT professionals rolling out annually. According to the NASSCOM annual survey, the IT industry has employed 650,000 IT professionals in 2003 representing an increase of 24.4% over the previous year. The demand for the skilled manpower in the IT sector is projected to be 235,000 by 2008. Though India has a large talent pool with 167,000 engineering and 1.54 millions of non-engineering graduates passing out of India's educational institutions annually, there remains a shortage of skilled labour force. It is also estimated that the demand for IT trained manpower in India will grow up to 370,000 in the year 2008 (The Asia week May 18, 2001). The question here is, how these skill shortages are to be managed and what is the share of women in the manpower development process in the Indian sub-continent. This implies that in order to achieve gender-democracy in the e-society, equitable participation of the gender groups in IT education and IT employment is considered as an essential input factor.

STATEMENT OF THE PROBLEM

It is generally believed that IT is one of the best equal opportunity areas 'that provide wider opportunities for women to enter and succeed in the computer industry'. Nevertheless, the validity of these claims is yet to be established through empirical analysis. For such a transition in attitudes toward gender to take place, certain prerequisites have to be met. First, there should be an adequate proportion of technically trained female labour force. Second, for the permeation of an alternate gender culture, there needs to be a process of de-learning and re-learning from the new work environment for both men and women. In essence, the family life of a woman and her professional commitments adapt to one another. To illustrate the gender situation in IT, one has to view 'the women in technology approach' and 'the women and technology approach'. The former approach tries to involve more women via equal access to education and employment; while the latter has a broader focus on the nature of technological work.

OBJECTIVES OF THE STUDY

This study attempts to find answers to such questions as: (i) Where are women in the IT industry? How do they benefit?; (ii) How has the IT industry changed women's position? Is there any change in the gender division of labour as a result of women's employment in the IT industry? And is there any change in women's mobility due to IT industry? (Mobility is a measure of gender relations). The findings of this study would throw light on the distribution of women's work in the IT sector and illustrate the (i) position of women in various service sectors; (ii) opportunities for women in the new economy; (iii) and the impact of changing organisational structures on women's work. The gender situation is measured by adopting various common indicators like (i) the proportion of women in the various subsets of the IT industry; (ii) segregation of women across the high-medium and low-end jobs; (iii) types of jobs undertaken; (iv) working condition of the organisation; and the (v) facilities to learning and career progression.

TRENDS IN THE PARTICIPATION OF WOMEN IN IT INDUSTRIES

Women's position in the IT sector has seen both the positive and negative trends in the last decade in the Indian sub-continent. There are studies that have highlighted the fast track that women have made in the IT related industries. Women's composition in the IT workforce has risen from 10% in 1993 to 18% in 1998 which is much higher than the national average of 12 percent (NASSCOM 1999). To a great surprise, the entry of women has shot upto 21 percent in 2002 (NASSCOM, 2002) and it is expected to go up to 35 percent by 2005. The following table illustrates the wide-spread participation of women in the various segments of IT industries.

Table 1: Distribution of women among the subsets of IT

Sl.No.	*IT Sector*	*F/M Ratio*	*Type of Work and skill requirements*
1.	Software industry	19:18	Software development not just design, customisation and adaptation of software.
2.	Telecom Industry*	40:60	Technical and creative work. Required highly qualified engineers.
3.	Airlines	80:20	Customer service. Required Communication, language and software skills.
4.	IT-Enabled service Sector	45:55	Demands linguistics and domain skill.
5.	BPO**	49:51	Indian BPO is predominantly voicebased (outbound calls).

Source: DATAQUEST, April 22, 2003.

The high rate of women employees in the ITES and BPO sector is a welcome change from the low 12.5 percent women being employed in the IT industry. According to a Dataquest-IDC survey in October 2002, the highest number of women was employed by NIIT at 29 percent while Rolta India employed the lowest number of women at four percent. Top software companies like Infosys employs 17 percent women, TCS employs 20 percent and Wipro employs 19 percent women. The massive incorporation of women into paid work and their positions of authority in the IT industry have improved their social status. Though the above statistics has shown a rosy picture of women in this sector, a further investigation is required to know the existing situation in the various regions of the IT related sector in the country.

GENDER COMPOSITION OF IT WORKFORCE IN FIRMS OF DIFFERENT SIZES

The composition of male and female IT workers, in firms of different sizes and activities, needs to be analysed in order to identify their level of participation. State-level survey reports indicated that the employment opportunities opened for women are relatively higher in the IT sector when compared to other industries. Out of 28,109 employees surveyed from 156 firms in Mumbai, it was noticed that the percentages of female workers were 32.1 percent in the IT firms and 12 percent in the other firms. Not only in terms of numbers but also in positions of power and authority women's status is higher in the IT related industries than in the non-IT sectors. It is evident that the IT industries have opened a gateway for women's entry as well as for their career progression compared to other non-IT sectors. Figure 1 is illustrative of the advantageous situations that women have experienced in the software sector than in other traditional banking and media sectors.

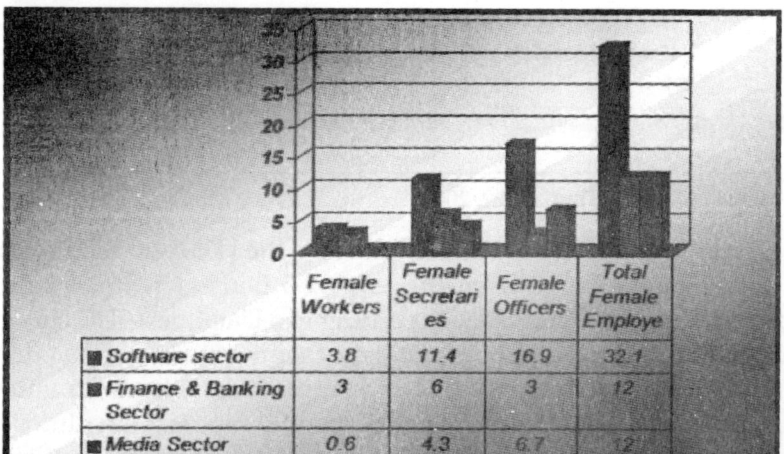

	Female Workers	Female Secretaries	Female Officers	Total Female Employe
Software sector	3.8	11.4	16.9	32.1
Finance & Banking Sector	3	6	3	12
Media Sector	0.6	4.3	6.7	12

Source: Teleworking, Economic and Political Weekly, 2002.

Fig. 1 : Distribution of Women Workers among IT and Non-IT Sectors

The next issue that needs to be addressed is whether the IT sector offers equality of opportunities for both men and women in their roles and responsibilities. Before investing the response of the industries to gender factor, it is necessary to find out the transformation that has taken place in the areas of gender technology relations, traditional gender roles in the society, attitudinal changes in the gender groups with respect to their professional choices, social, political and economic pressures on gender participation in the national economy etc. For centuries together women were allowed to play a secondary role both in the domestic and public spheres. But the sudden changes that have taken place in the areas of globalisation, media, knowledge management and the compulsion on the part of the individual nations to response to the changing situation directly and indirectly enforce them to develop their human capital irrespective of the gender, caste or creed. Now the question before us is, does this changing global situation have brought any positive change on women's situation in this new economy. Since the key pillars of this new economy (knowledge based industries) is based on expertise in infostructure, corporate intelligence, high-tech infrastructure etc, it is interesting to find out where do women figure into this competitive industry? Have they been able to participate on equal plane with their male counter- parts in all spheres of IT based industries? What were the factors both contributing and deterring their progress in this sunrise industry?

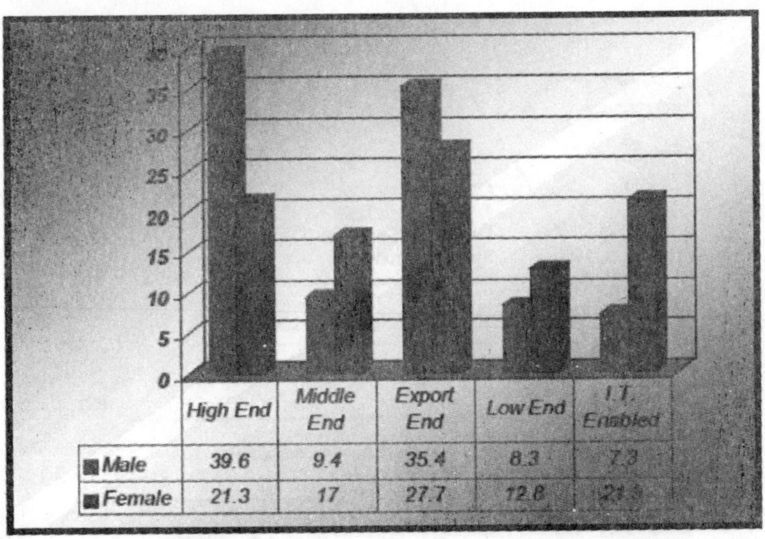

Source: International Labour organisation, New Delhi, 2001.

Fig. 2 : Distribution of Women in IT Firms of various Types and Sizes

ILO has recently undertaken a survey to identify where are women in this most competitive industry. It has analysed the gender structure in more than 100 IT firms located at the major metros in the country. The main purpose of this survey was to find out the type of firms where women are mostly accommodated and the kind of activities that women are involved in the software development. Figure-2 explains the areas where women have dominated in the IT sector.

It is noted that a major segment of women are clustered in the low-end jobs; while a minor segment of women are found at the high-end jobs reflecting the gender divide in the IT industry. Though women are better represented in IT sector, they have not assumed significant roles and status. Most of them have been concentrated lower strata of job categories, such as, coding and programming; and only a minor percentage is presented in the development part of IT. ILO report clearly indicated that the high-end firms that undertake software products, R&D, turnkey solutions and strategic technical alliances prefer to employ men to women. The professional demands in this area of work are mostly engineering graduates, PhDs and post-graduates with technical multi-skilling. The proportion of women with such

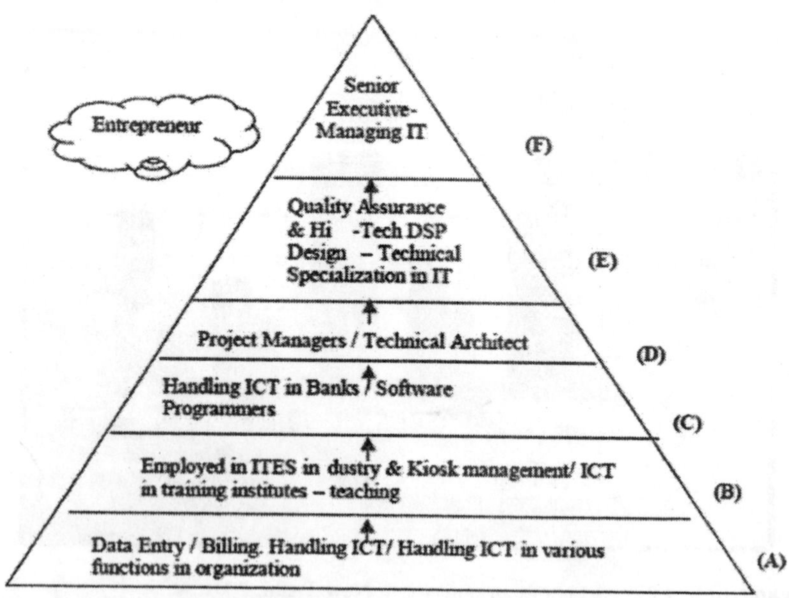

Source: WICT in India and china.htm.

professional background is less and, therefore, they are relegated to less prestigious and low-paid jobs. For instance, the IT-enabled and domestic, end firms, that perform low skilled, routinised and back office jobs-employed more women, since they require only certificate holders with pure technical, coding and maintenance skills. Women's representations outnumber their male counterparts in these low-skilled and low-paid jobs. The male and female ratio of the IT workers in the organisational hierarchy is diagrammatically shown below:

The above situation supports the hypothesis that IT industry is not in any way different from the other industries and women have not enjoyed any special status or privilege in this industry. It is noted from the above diagram that higher the hierarchy, the lower will be the number of women and vice-versa. The reasons for this under representation may be owing to various educational, social, political, cultural and individual factors and, therefore, efforts should be made to analyse the gender technology variables such as the status of (i) gender socialisation, (ii) gender bias in access to ICT, (iii) gender preference to technical education, (iv) parental encouragement, (v) availability of role models, (vi) support from family and institutions and the (vii) cost of high-tech education etc. Among these various factors that deter women from occupying positions of authority and power, let us give priority to the educational factors at the first instance.

TRENDS IN THE PARTICIPATION OF WOMEN IN THE TECHNICAL EDUCATION

Literacy Level of Girls and Women in India

It is widely observed that lack of access to basic education and literacy for girls and women in India is the foremost obstacle to their access to IT job opportunities. Education and literacy are low for both men and women, with women's literacy rate at only 51.4%, compared to men's 74.5%. While enrollment rates have increased at the primary level for boys and girls, upper primary enrollment drops off, particularly for girls. Moreover, only 48% of girls stay in the system until the secondary level. These statistics also vary widely between specific states within the country, where particularly the Northern and Eastern states have the lowest health and education indicators. The following census substantiates this statement:

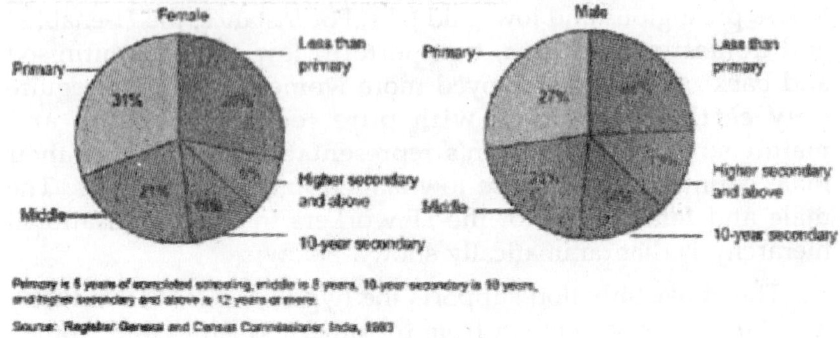

Fig. 1: Literacy level of Indian Women according to 1991 Census.

Computer and Media Literacy Levels of Women in India

As most Indian women lack literacy and basic education, more advanced or specialised IT education is out of the reach of poorer women and only realistic for those middle class women and elite who can afford it in some form. Currently IT education and

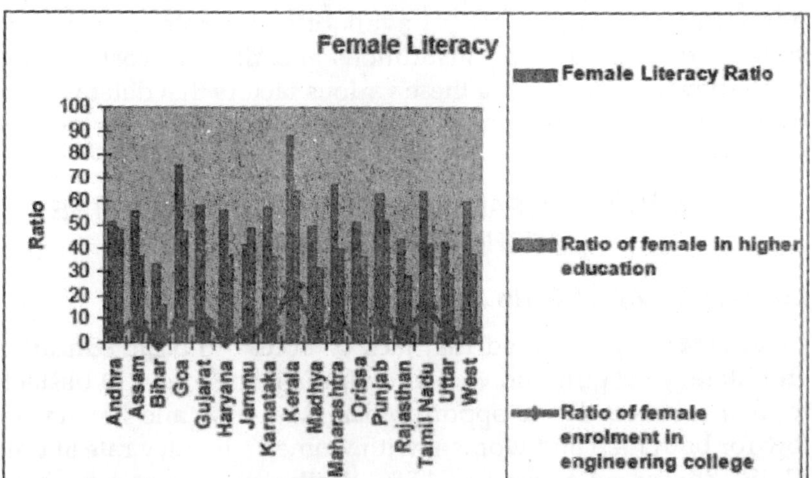

Source: i4donline Events.htm

Fig. 4 : Proportion of Women's Participation in IT Education.

training is available in degree programs in engineering colleges and universities and in diploma and certificate courses at polytechnics, and commercial and government training centers.

Due to cost and selectivity of admissions at the universities and engineering colleges, most Indian women are able to access IT training through training centers or women's polytechnics. However, not surprisingly, the quality of the training varies with each option. As the job market has become more competitive, certificates from training centers, or even diplomas in IT subjects from polytechnics, often do not equip job seekers with the competitive skills to guarantee a job, not to mention a well-paid job. Moreover, the majority of women pursue their studies in the humanities and business rather than IT-related fields. Women make up 88% of the students in the arts, science and commerce, while education and law account for 4% of women students, and engineering accounts only for 1%. Figure-4 illustrates the status of women's education in general and engineering education in particular.

A close examination of the graph clearly indicates that the states like Kerala (24.19%), Tamil Nadu (15.35%), Punjab (10.36%), Andhra Pradesh, and Maharashtra are marching ahead in the field of ICT while the state like Bihar, Uttar Pradesh, Orissa are lagging behind. Uttar Pradesh, with a low female literacy level, low female enrolment in higher education, and low female enrolment in technical colleges is still lacking behind in providing basic infrastructure to utilise full potentials of ICT. The lopsided gender ratio in the IT industry begins in academic institutes itself, as "there are far fewer women candidates as compared to men in engineering and management institutes". (Dataquest, 2002)

NATIONAL LEVEL INITIATIES TO INVOLVE MORE WOMEN IN IT SECTOR

The marginalisation of Women in IT Education and IT employment in India is a major concern among the Indian administrators. To stay in the global competition, human resource development becomes the area of top priority. State-level programmes have been launched to train and develop the IT skills among the women community based on the market demand. For instance, Government of India through its "National Programme for Education of Girls in Elementary Level (NPEGEL) with an outlay of US$ 230 Million and reach in 21 States has created enough synergy to improve rural female literacy and gender gap in the educationally backward blocks. Institutions like NIIT through its "SWIFT JYOTHI FOR WOMEN" program target one-million non-computer literate women in India and educate them on ICT. The efforts of CISCO, HP, IBM and Datamation can't be under-estimated in this regard. Internet-enabled "cyber incubators" are emerging to provide counseling and training support to larger numbers of small businesses over the long distances from multiple sources. The encouragement from the government sector; the financial support from the nationalised banks; and the scholarships programmes introduced by the leading IT industries serve as an impetus for both men and women to enter into this course in large numbers. For instance, in the year 2001, nearly 7929 colleges for general education and 2223 engineering and professional colleges were enrolling 36.9% of women in higher education (degree and above level).

Fig. 4 indicates the increase in the enrollment of girls for higher education.

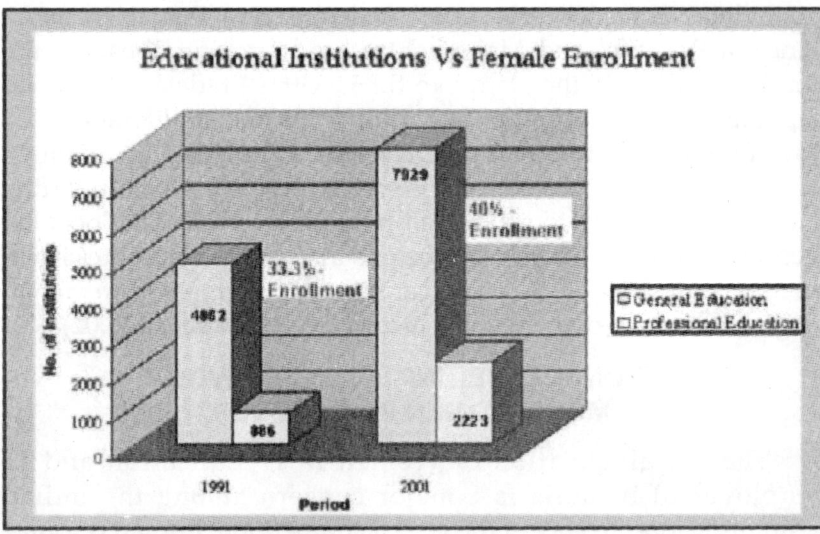

Source: census 1991 and 2001.

Fig. 4. Growth Pattern of Women In Higher Education

One of the major problems faced by women is the access to IT education. It is seen that access to IT is limited to a certain class of women only. Access to IT education and training is highly skewed towards urban centered, English speaking masses with a high socio-economic status. The central government plans to upgrade the higher education institutions providing IT education and training will establish more IITs throughout the country and improve the regional engineering colleges. These efforts should strengthen the caliber of IT training available to Indian elites, but will have little impact on the majority of women. The major criticism is that while women form the majority among the deprived community, the government has not taken concrete efforts to uplift their status in technology. The way things are moving would only widen the gender-based digital divide and it is a serious concern, which calls for the attention of the policy-makers. As rightly observed by Kofi Annan, the Secretary-General of the UN, at the first world submit on information society that the so called digital divide is actually several divides: a technological divide in infrastructure, a language divide with much of the content in English, a gender divide for women in many nations, a commercial divide where e-commerce reaches only some. Indeed, the digital divide is the biggest non-tariff barrier to world trade today. It is difficult to captivate the digital divide precisely. From a policy angle, a specific absolute cut-off line may be drawn to denote the minimum level of IT knowledge required for any individual, especially the women, the most suppressed and deprived community. Any shortfall denotes the distance to be covered by the individual suggesting that the state should initiate suitable steps to rectify the situation. This perhaps opens up a new area of further research (Elango, 2003).

Status of National and State-Level IT Policies on Gender Issues:

Policies formulated in this direction are also silent on gender issues. For instance, in 2000, the Indian government created a 'Working Group on Information Technology for Masses'. However, the working group's report with recommendations for how to broaden access to "the common man" does not specifically mention women. The recommendations call for activities related to access, education, and awareness raising of the importance and benefits of IT opportunities that if implemented, which will also benefit women. However, targeted strategies for ensuring female access and training are not discussed. To close the gender divide, gender responsive e-governance should be implemented. Funds should be raised to support women's initiatives in ICT base entrepreneurship and other economic activities. Digital marginalisation has to be addressed squarely at the policy level. This necessitates more and more of social inclusion process by way of conscious state policies adopted in favour of promoting women's education and participation in IT sector. Digital divide distribution and IT deprivation index is to be developed to see the level of access that women gained in the digital economy. The following explains how the strength of women gets decreased in the IT field over the years due to want of support system.

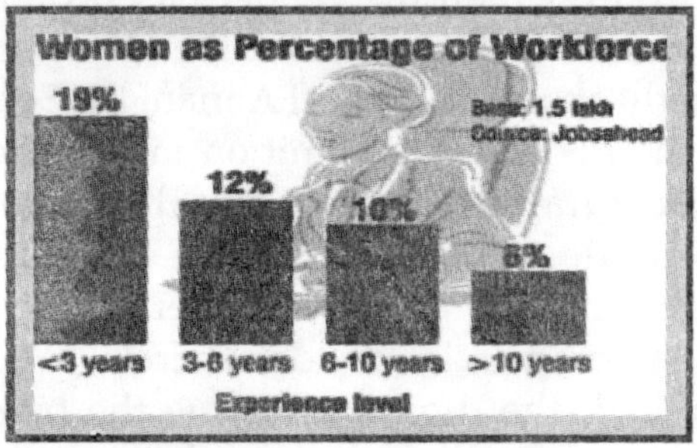

However, it needs to be realised that training in ICT by itself cannot be an answer and elixir to all problems facing women development but it does bring new information resources and can open new communication channels for the marginalised communities.

IMPACT OF SOCIAL AND CULTURAL FACTORS

Vittal (2003) observed that in order to empower women in the IT sector in the real sense, it is necessary to investigate the social impact of IT sector on the women's community. Empowering women in the real sense implies that their position should be strengthened in the family and in the society; adequate support system is to be built up both at the private and in the public spheres. This requires a lot of cultural and attitudinal change in the mind-set of the people to accept women's progression. In this context, Mr. Vittal has indicated the emergence of 'metro-sexual men', men who are sharing the responsibility of the family which might help women to be an active agent in the IT workforce. The drop out level after getting employed and not able to sustain employment has been a matter of concern. This drop out effect is because of the cultural and social barrier faced by even educated women today. It is a fact that women deliver 100% both at work

& home. Entering a marriage phase or encountering a child birth forces many women to drop out of IT. "Marriage-Baby" phase for women is the most crucial part of their work life which forced them to drop from their jobs. Graph-5 explains how the drop out rates of women gets increased with their marriage and childbirth. It is because childcare and housework remain women's responsibilities, irrespective of her income, educational level or employment. This places a great burden on women and restricts women's choices in terms of better job opportunities. Though women employed in the IT industry are relatively free from domestic drudgery, this is a class-specific phenomenon restricted to a few in high level jobs whose domestic responsibilities have been transferred to women of a lower economic class. The opportunities offered by IT have only benefited a privileged few. The above table shows that only a few women rule in the workplace well into marriage. Married women outnumber men in low-experience categories, but in 10+ years'—the stage at which serious seniority should come in—a large number of women either opt out of their careers, or accept less demanding roles. The Jobs ahead survey also substantiates the fact that the drop-out rate of

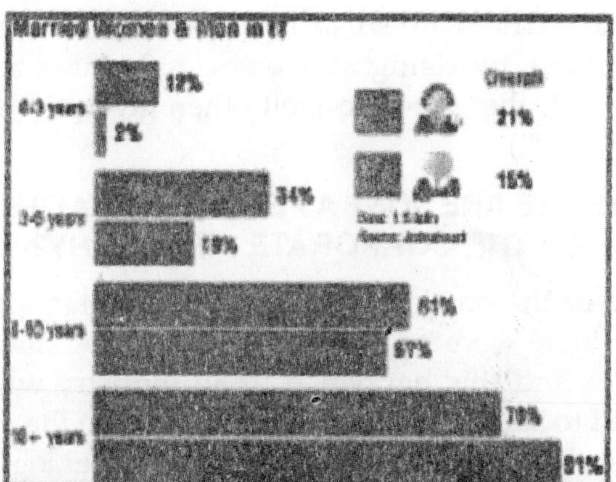

MARRIAGE AND FAMILY COMMITMENTS PINCH: Few women rule in the workplace well into marriage. Married women outnumber men in low-experience categories, but in 10+ years'—the stage at which serious seniority should come in—a large number of women either opt out of their careers, or accept less demanding roles.

***Source*:** DATAQUEST JOBS AHEAD SURVEY.

women increases with their advancement in experience. There seems to be a negative correlation existing between the women's presence in the IT workforce and their years of experience. Lesser the year of experience, larger will be the proportion of women and vice-versa. Women were not able to continue their job with sustained interest due to various interruptions happen in their life which force them to drop out from their aspiration of building a better career in IT.

To overcome this, the society at large should bring about proper understanding in the family life and support work going women in shouldering some of her burdens. In nuclear families, husband has to support this cause. Organisations have to bring about more pronounced flexi timing at work, even to the extent of supporting women to "work from Home", with investment in ICT infrastructure and flexible compensation packages. This trend is already noticed to tap the vast potential that experienced women would have which otherwise could go untapped, if they drop out due to cultural and social pressure. This emerging trend shall certainly bring about a substantial decline in Women being unemployed and getting back to household chores.

The social barriers are so strong and women who manage to enter workplaces by rising above societal biases are probably very strong and, therefore, do well when given the opportunity. (Data Quest, 2002)

WHY THERE ARE JUST A FEW WOMEN AT THE TOP OF THE CORPORATE HIERARCHY?

A study of the entries getting into the Dataquest magazine reveals that there were no women CEOs getting into the Top 10 IT companies and this happened in an industry where women are supposed to stand shoulder to shoulder with the men (Figure-6). What is it that keeps Indian women from making it to the top rung of authority in the country's IT sector? Or is it the IT sector that has not recognised and rewarded women well enough for their efforts? Or will maturity only come with age and experience, and it is because of the industry's nascent youth that women are yet to reach the top rung? Or is there a glass ceiling and despite whatever is said, is it not really a level playing field as far as women are concerned?

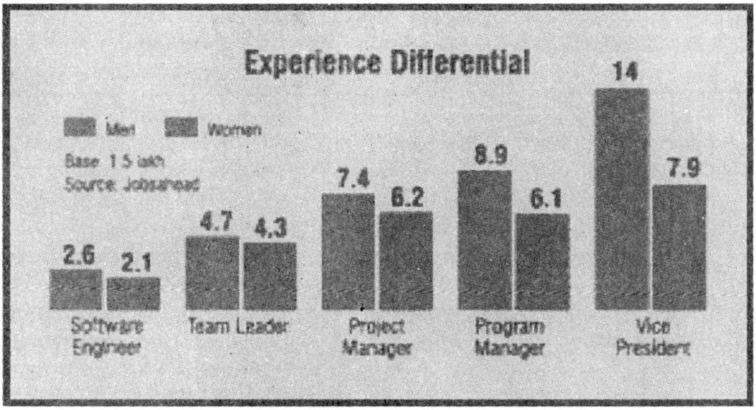

Fig. 6 : Status of Women in Organisational Hierarchy

The other perspective for the lower status of women at the top of the corporate hierarchy can be explained by the fact that the number of women entering the IT industry has been lower than men (Balu Doraisamy, president of HP India). It is argued that the lopsided gender ratio begins in the academic institutes itself (Mita Brahma, HR Head of Nucleus Software). It is further stated that more than impediments at the workplace, it is women's personal choices and abilities to cope up with family and social pressures that decide whether they rise above the ordinary or quit the workplace prematurely. Some of the HR managers of the opinion that only a very few women IT professionals are passionate about their jobs as compared to men (M L Taneja, V-P, HR of HCL Infosystems). Because men typically do not exit careers, so all of them are bound to stick on well over 10 years. "As against that, women exit the workforce, either by choice or because of their circumstances" (Mittal of Jobsahead).

Obstacles for carrier development in the IT sector

Several surverys have been undertaken to take stock of the common problems that women have encountered in their workplace in order to sort out the remedial measures. According to the 'prevalence survey' over 80% of the employers said that there is no discrimination and there is no gender preference. Another survey reported that out of the 500 employers interviewed, about 80 employers said that there was gender preference in terms of subcontracting or outsourcing, out of which

Table 10: Barriers For Women's Progression in IT Carrier

Sl. No.	*Barriers/ Issue*	*Survey report*	*Employers remarks*
1.	Gender preference Or gender bias	Prevalence Survey	Out of 500 employers, 80 confirmed gendered preference in outsourcing or sub-contracting. No =80%. Yes=20%
2.	Burnout Syndrome	Prevalence Survey	The routine nature of the job forced women to switch jobs (Airlines employees)
3.	Lack of confidence	IBM Survey	Women have the ability, education and experience to handle challenging jobs, but what they lack is confidence
4.	Differences in the way men and women approach technical subjects	IBM Survey	Women possess soft skills while men have technical skills
5.	Assignment of Priorities (family Vs Profession) Padmaja Krishnan, Xansa	Dataquest Survey	Proportion of women in the IT workforce is 19%, but at senior position 6%. There is a smooth going from the fresher to the team leader and project leader stage. Growth of women IT professionals stop at the team leader stage
6.	Glass ceiling (H.R. Rajasekar VP Mistral Software)	Dataquest Survey	No discrimination towards women IT professionals
7.	Social factors (Mita Brahma, HR Head of Nucleus Software)	Dataquest Survey	Since many women manage to enter the workplace by rising above the social biases, they are strong and do well when given the opportunity
8.	Performance Robert F Danbeck VP-HR at IBM India	Dataquest Survey	Indian women make better engineers; they have qualities like strong team playing abilities, the capacity to juggle a variety of issues, flexibility and creativity in abundance

Source: Results of the Prevalence/ IBM Survey

47 stated their gender preference. Out of 47, 7 preferred women and 40 preferred men. If there was no gender preference for

outsourcing, one would imagine there would be no gender preference for employment. Software is the only sector, barring one or two instances, which said that they prefer women. As regards gender bias, nearly 40 out of 500 (8%) affirmed gender bias against women.

Moreover, access to jobs is more or less restricted to the urban-based upper class youth. What are the advantages that women enjoy in the new forms of work? It reduces the hard choices that women have to make. The strategies to draw more women lies in improving the manner in which work is conducted without jeopardising the quality of workers' lives. The following table illustrates the barriers that women have encountered in their efforts to progress in their career in the IT sector.

DIGITAL REVOLUTION – A TOOL TO ELIMINATE THE GENDER BIAS

It is widely accepted that IT is one of the panacea for empowering women to take an active part in the digital society. Liberating access to IT is the key factor for economic, social and political empowerment of women. Women within developing countries like India are in the deepest part of the digital divide. The gender gap in the digital divide is perhaps the most neglected issue in recent times. If access to and use of information technology is directly linked to social and economic development, then it is imperative to ensure that women in India, understand the significance of IT and use them. If not, lack of access to information technology becomes a significant factor in the further marginalisation of women from the economic, social and political mainstream of our society. This necessitates the condition whereby women have to make use of information technology, not only for getting themselves empowered but also for avoiding further marginalisation. The following model has been suggested for empowering women to take an active part in ICT and be an integral part of it. Government of India has promoted several programmes to promote women's empowerment in ICT. A few of them inclues: 1. Establishing Technological Park for women; (2) National Assessment for on women friendly technology on drudgery reduction, tools and implements and income generation for women. (3) Exhibition on women in science (4) Women in Information Technology. In conclusion, these protective gender-sensitive legal measures should be extended to the ICT sectors and reflected in ICT policies from the national, regional to international levels.

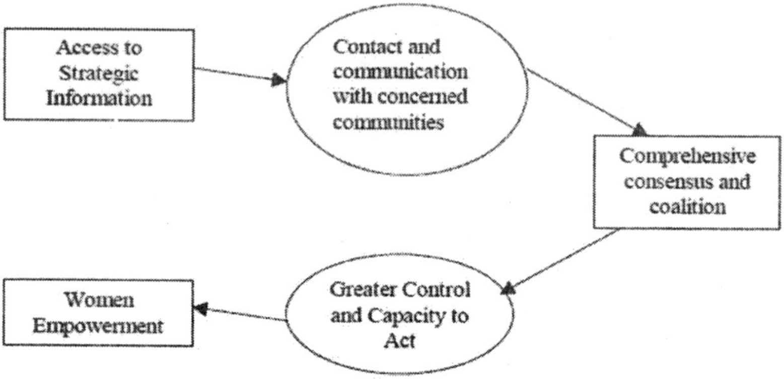

ICT – Women Empowerment Model

CONCLUSION

While technology has the potential for leveling the playing field on a global scale, it is also responsible for contributing to the digital divide. Despite modernisation and technological developments, the traditional gender roles remain firmly entrenched in all levels of the Indian society. The research question is what is the impact of the socially constructed traits on women's participation in information technology sector. As gender roles are firmly enriched into the society, how women in India moved into the IT labour force, and how do they navigate between these spheres? These are the serious issues which needs further investigations. The goal of empowerment of women, however, can be achieved only if the countries and states implement some adequate policies, which emphasize on the enhanced female participation in education sector to get benefited from ICT. It is saddened to note that " women constitute 50% of the population but do 60% of works, earn one-tenth of the income and own 1/100 of the assets" (http://www.uneca.org/aisi/aisi.htm#gender). The question before the entire nation is how to close the digital divide among the gender groups which caused due to various factors, including lack of resources, illiteracy and low levels of education (APC.ORG).

REFERENCES

- Balaka Baruah Aggarwal. "IT Women Come to the Fore". DATAQUEST. Tuesday. April 22. 2003.
- "Teleworking in India" *Economic and Political Weekly*, 2002.
- Rothboeck, S; Vijayabaskar, M; & Gayathri, V (2001). "Labour in the New Economy: The Case of the Indian Software Labour Market". International Labour Organisation. New Delhi, 2001. p. 34.
- Rajalakshmi,R (2003). "The Emerging Trends of Women in Information Technology". In: *Women, Information and Communication Technology in India and China*. The Hawke Research Institute, Adelaide, South Australia, November 5-7. 2003.
- "Gender and ICTs: What difference does it make?" Apc.org
- Artee Aggrawal. "State initiatives in Gender Empowerment through Information and Communication Technologies - With special reference to Uttarpradesh" Giri Institute of Development Studies. Lucknow, Uttar Pradesh. 1st Seminar. 14th October, 2003. Putra World Trade Centre. Kula Lumpur. Malaysia.
- Elango, R (2003). "Empowering women in Information Technology". In: The International Conference on women in the digital era: opportunities and challenges. December 10-12. Annamalai University. India.
- Vittal (2003), "Strategies to empower women in the IT sector" In: The International Conference on women in the digital era: opportunities and challenges. December 10-12. Annamalai University. India.
- Manjiri Kalghatgi and Rishiseth (2003). "Why just a few women on top?" *DATAQUEST*, Monday, June 30, 2003.

13

Gender-based Digital Divide in the IT Sector in India

INTRODUCTION

It is generally believed that IT is one of the best equal opportunity areas 'that provide wider opportunities for women to enter and succeed in this industry'. Nevertheless, the validity of these claims is yet to be established through empirical analysis. For such a transition in attitudes toward gender to take place, certain prerequisites have to be met. First, there should be an adequate proportion of technically trained female labour force. Second, for the permeation of an alternate gender culture, there needs to be a process of de-learning and re-learning from the new work environment for both men and women. In essence, the family life of a woman and her professional commitments adapt with one another. To illustrate the gender situation in IT, one has to view 'the women in technology approach' and 'the women and technology approach'. The former approach tries to involve more women via equal access to education and employment; while the latter has a broader focus on the nature of technological work.

The women in technology approach advocates a wariness of the 'add women and stir' approach which insists on imparting skill to women to survive in the world of new technology. This approach locates the problem in women (their socialisation, their aspirations and values), but does not ask the broader questions of whether and in what way science and its institutions could be reshaped to accommodate women. Whereas, the women and technology approach looks into the gender segregation of skills and jobs and the gender sensitivity of the organisation in particular. It aims to alter the masculine practices of these occupations so that women could enter into such work without any loss of identity or integrity. What is needed is a transformation in the nature of paid and unpaid work, as well as looking at the impact women can have on technology and technology on women. Drawing from this approach, the following parameters have been used to analyse the gender regime in the IT sector in India – the proportion of women across various IT occupations/sectors, working conditions, practical gender needs of women, learning and career path. The actual situation can be evaluated from the published literature available on this theme.

RESEARCH QUESTIONS

This study attempts to find answers to such questions as: (i) Where are women in the IT industry? How do they benefit? (ii) How has the IT industry changed women's position? Is there any change in the gender division of labour as a result of women's employment in the IT industry? Is there any change in women's mobility due to IT industry? (Mobility is a measure of gender relations). The findings of this study would throw light on the distribution of women's work in IT sector and illustrate the (i) position of women in various service sectors; (ii) opportunities for women in the new economy; (iii) and the impact of changing organisational structures on women's work. The gender situation is measured by adopting various common indicators like (i) the proportion of women in the various subsets of the IT industry; (ii) segregation of women across the high-medium-and low-end jobs; (iii) types of jobs undertaken; (iv) working condition of the organisation; and the (v) facilities to learning and career progression.

STATUS OF WOMEN IN THE IT SECTOR IN INDIA

It is reported that the proportion of women, in various IT based industries in India, is in the order of 19% in software industry; 40% in telecom industry; 80% in airlines; 45% in ITES; and 50% in BPOs. The high rate of women employees (45 percent on an average) in ITES sector is a welcome change from low 12.5 percent women being employed in IT industry. According to Dataquest-IDC survey in October 2002, the highest number of women was employed by NIIT at 29 percent while Rolta India employed the lowest number of women at four percent. Top software companies like Infosys employs 17 percent women, TCS employs 20 percent and Wipro employs 19 percent women. The massive incorporation of women into paid work has marginally increased their bargaining power and undermined the legitimacy of men's domination as providers of the family. While women in positions of authority in the IT industry have improved their social position. The issue to be addressed is which categories of women are benefited through this sector? To which class of women does this help? What also came out quite well in the case studies is that there were different kinds of women. There are women who are top software programmers who can go to silicon valley and there are women who have to rely on Internet kiosks to start self-employment.

JOB OPPORTUNITIES FOR INDIAN WOMEN IN THE IT SECTOR

The IT sector in India has created employment opportunities in areas such as telecommunications, banking, shopping, education, health and business. In addition, the internet has also generated new jobs in areas like design, maintenance and management of sites on the World Wide Web. There are real possibilities that women may be able to access opportunities they never had before. According to a prediction by the National Association of Software and Services Companies (NASSCOM), by 2008 there will be one-and-a-half million jobs in the IT Enabled services. If 50% to 70% of these jobs were to go to women, the impact will be tremendous. There is going to be such a shortage of skills that women will have to be included.

GENDER SEGREGATION IN THE IT SECTOR

When one examines the employment situation of women in industrial societies from a national and international viewpoint, one encounters forms of inequality between the genders, which have remained fixed despite wide-reaching changes. The phenomenon of gender segregation in the workplace remains valid regardless of profession or differing social and cultural factors on which the different systems of work are based. The computer occupations are expanding at a faster rate both within and in a wide range of other industries. The newness and the expanding nature of the computer industry has given an impression that it would be relatively immune to gender typed pattern of occupation and would maintain gender equity in its occupational distribution. However, an examination of the exisiting studies reveals that gender segregation is very much predominant in this industry, and it has absorbed the patriarchal power structure of the traditional industries. For instance, an ILO survey conducted among the IT professionals in the software industires in India has revealed the prevalence of gender inequality in its various forms. It has also show-cased how women are relegated to the less prestigious and low-paid jobs.

Table 1 : Gender-wise Distribution of Professionals in Different Firm Types (Percent)

	High End	*Middle End*	*Export End*	*Domestic low-end*	*IT Enabled*	*Total*
Male	39.6	9.4	35.4	8.3	7.3	100
Female	21.3	17.0	27.7	12.8	21.3	100

The high end firms undertake software products, R&D, turnkey solutions and strategic technical alliances. The professionals employed in this area are engineering graduates, mostly Ph.Ds and post-graduates with technical multi-skilling. The middle end firms undertake development of software packages, offshore services, and alliances for market access. This category of job demands engineering graduates who are geographically mobile and possess managerial multiskilling. The export-end firms undertake onsite services, maintenance and implementation, alliances with labour contractors etc. The domestic end jobs require only certificate holders with pure technical, coding and maintenance skills. The IT-enabled and domestic-end firms undertake low-skilled and routinised jobs. The employees in this category of firms have to work in backoffice. The nature of job includes data entry and continuous partnership with the clients. The above table illustrates that women's representation outnumbers their male counterparts in low-skilled and low-paid jobs.

DISTRIBUTION OF WOMEN'S WORK IN THE SUBSETS OF THE IT SECTOR IN INDIA

What is the position of women in different sectors? The women in Mahendra British Telecom were engaged in some very different and creative kinds of work. One woman had entirely done the Y2k for the company. For sometime, she even worked from home when there was a crisis at home. These were highly qualified women. There the ratio of women to men staff is about 40:60 while in the airlines sort of work it is about 80:20. This type of work has a much wider range of jobs that women do than those available in the electronics industry.

Table 2 : Segregation of women among various subsets of IT

S.No	*IT Sector*	*F/M Ratio*	*Type of Work and Skill requirements*
1.	Software Inudstry	19:81	Software development not just design, customisation and adaptation of software
2.	Telecom Industry*	40:60	Technical and creative work. Required highly qualified engineers
3.	Airlines	80:20	Customer service. Required Communication, language and software skills
4.	ITES (Medical Transcription)	45:55	Demands in linguistics and functional /domain skill
5.	BPO**	49:51	Indian BPO is predominantly voice-based (outbound calls)

Mahendra British Telecom

Wipro-Spectramind (TE: 5000; W/M ratio: 49:51%).

Infowavz International (TE: 1000; W/M ratio: 40:60).

TracMail India (T:1800; W/M ratio:35).

ICICI One Source (T:1800; W/M ratio:60:40).

Dash E-Services (W/M ratio: 60:40)

GE (W/M ratio: 60:40)

GENDER SEGREGATION ACROSS IT AND NON IT OCCUPATIONS

A comparative analysis of gender segregation in IT and non-IT industries in India (Mumbai based survery) has revealed that the IT industries are less segregated by gender than the other industries. Not only the proportion of women in the IT industries are higher, but their position in the organisational hierarchy are also better than the other non-IT sectors. To some extent, the IT industries are more accommodative to women's career development than the other non-IT sectors.

Table 3: Distribution of Women Employees by various Sectors (%)

Job Categories	*Software Sector*	*Finance and Banking Sector*	*Media Sector*
Female workers	3.8	3.0	0.6
Female secretaries	11.4	6.0	4.3
Female officers	16.9	3.0	6.7
Total female employees	32.1	12.0	12.0
No. of establishments	76	56	24
No. of employees	12278	8631	7200

N.B. Based on the survey conducted in Mumbai.

GENDER SEGREGATION IN THE ORGANISATIONAL HIERARCHY OF IT SECTOR

Table 4: Position of Men and Women in various Organisational Hierarchy

	Position	*Male*	*Female*	*Total*
(i)	Call Services	40.00	60.00	100
(ii)	Software Engineers	54.69	45.31	100
(iii	Consultants	75.00	25.00	100
(iv)	Project Managers	94.44	5.56	100
	Total	67.13	32.87	100

The above table have confirmed that women are overrepresented in some types of lower level jobs (call service and programmers) and underrepresented in higer level jobs (consultants and project managers). The continud underrepresentation of women is pointed out by Job-ahead survey conducted by Dataquest. This may be due to the fact that women have a lower share of resources such as education, information, mobility, good health, nutritious food, leisure and rest as compared to men. As a result, they cannot fully develop their capabilities and remain lower than men in the job market. It is further stated that due to gender socialisation factors, women are mostly associated with the secondary labour market. While analysing the reasons for gender stereotypes, it is explained that since computer science has the masculine connotations of technical and scientific work, it is found inhospitable to women. Therefore, gender stereotypes in computer work is not new, but it is a newly applied version of longer-standing images. The other reasons attributed to gender segregation are (i) women's own attitude to profession; (ii) employer's discrimination; (iii) interactions of labour market; (iv) and gender relations in society. Some studies have argued that human capital and the structural location of women in the society are the two important factors driving gender inequality through segregation. It is said that the gender segregation takes its root from the hiring practices of the employers.

POSITION OF WOMEN IN VARIOUS SEGMENTS OF THE SOFTWARE ACTIVITIES

An analysis of the gender situation in the stratified nature of the software development activities (high value added & low value added activities), shows that the largest segment of women are clustered in low-end jobs; while the smallest segment of women found at the higher end reflects to a larger extent the gender divide in the IT industry.

Table 5: Distribution of Women in various Segments of Software Activities

Sl. No.	*Segment of Activities*	*Companies*	*Contribution of Women*
1.	Development and marketing of software package	MNCs (Texas Instruments, Motorala)	Low
2.	Customization of software and development of software solutions (design projects)	Large firms and MNCs	Medium
3.	Software services (coding, programming and testing) either through body-shopping or off shore with extensive on-site work	Small and medium sized software firms	High

Though women are better represented in IT sector, they have not assumed significant role and status. Most of them have been concentrated in the lower status jobs, such as, coding and programming and only a minor percentage are noted in the development part of IT.

POSITION OF WOMEN IN ORGANISATIONAL HIERARCHY

With the growth in IT industry, there is a corresponding growth in job requirements in the areas of systems management, communications and network, systems development, technical support, operations and user support. Viewing the diversification and content of jobs, it is expected that the opportunities for women at different levels of hierarchies are expanding, but the existing studies have shown that this new and growing industry has been gendered. Evidences of low representation of women in most rewarding areas of computing work have signalled that gender inequalities are becoming even harder to ignore as an issue in this sector.

The Dataquest survey reveals that though women make up about 20% of IT workforce in India, only a few women reach the position of CEOs. As seniority rises, the number of women shrinks. In the career pyramid, women are clustered in the bottom hierarchy. Nevertheless, the oxymoron is that while women tend to rise faster up the corporate ladder, few reach the highest levels. Even few women who have struggled to reach the status of managers, have not been placed in the vital areas of work dealing with hardware and software-oriented jobs, but are found in administration. Similarly, women system workers are tied up with business-oriented analysis, which is typically considered as less technical and therefore less challenging. This may be because of lack of technical orientation among the women. Women are seen as a passive users rather than designers of technology. Most women use ICT as a tool of production for tasks such as data entry, word processing and programming and as a tool of communication. This might be the reason for women's under-representation in higher, decision-making positions. For example, in customer call centres, women predominate in lower positions and perform tasks such as data capture and verification, servicing of routine and account queries, order taking, referals, and after sales support. However, tasks that call for management authority, such as problem resolutions, were overwhelmingly performed by men.

REASONS FOR LOW PARTICIPATION OF WOMEN IN IT SECTOR

Low enrollment of women in science and technology impedes their ability to occupy higher positions in the IT organisations. According to 2001 census, female literacy is 54.16 % as against male literacy of 75.85 % in India. The enrollment of girls in educational institutions decreases as educational level goes higher. In particular, the percentage of girls enrolled to total enrollment is 43.6% in primary, 40.1% in middle, 37.1% in secondary level and 34.8 % in higher education according to the statistics of 1997. The enrollment of girls in Engineering/Technology/Architecture at Graduation level (in 1998) is 57968 as against 285137 boys. This imbalance is largely due to socio-economic reasons.

In addition, series of social and cultural norms constrain women's access to ICT, especially in common use facilities, such as cyber-cafes, tele-centres and phone shops. In many culturally conservative societies, women are often not allowed to go out, without supervision, to public venues where men are present or seek help from male users or staff. This is yet another reason for the low rate of participation of women professionals.

CHALLENGES FOR CARRIER DEVELOPMENT OF WOMEN IN IT SECTOR

There is not only restrictions at the entry point , but there are many barriers blocking women from moving up in the ladder of the organisational hierarchy. Studies have reported that women were not able to rise to the expected level of performance of IT employers.

With advancement in the levels of experience, the ratio of women drops steadily and at the senior levels, women constitute less than 6% of the workforce.

FACTORS RESTRICTING WOMEN'S CAREER CHOICES: MARRIAGE & FAMILY COMMITMENTS

The factors deterring women's carrier choices have been analysed and presented by Dataquest surveys. Marriage is found out as a point at which the shrinkage of women from the career pipeline has started. The first sharp drop in the number of women professionals is at 3+ years of experience.

It is because childcare and housework remain women's responsibilities, irrespective of her income, educational level or employment. This places a great burden on women and restricts women's choices in terms of better job opportunities. Though women employed in IT industry are relatively free from domestic drudgery, this is a class-specific phenomenon restricted to a few in high level jobs whose domestic responsibilities have been transferred to women of a lower economic class. The opportunities offered by IT have only benefited a privileged few. Table 5 shows that only a few women rule in the workplace well into marriage. Married women outnumber men in low-experience categories, but in 10+ years'—the stage at which serious seniority should come in—a large number of women either opt out of their careers, or accept less demanding roles.

FACTORS RESTRICTING WOMEN'S CHOICES: RELOCATION PREFERENCE

The demands of high responsibility may also play a role in keeping women from accepting such jobs. "Women have traditionally shied away from sales responsibilities," says Gita Dang, head of technology practice at Korn & Ferry, "because it involves a great deal of travel. The bulk of the important selling in the Indian software industry, for instance, happens overseas. "It is these business development people blossom into CXO roles. Women are left behind as team leaders only." The data about relocation preferences of both sexes shows that women are far less willing to relocate. The willingness to relocate is a major factor that drives the growth of IT professionals. It is one of the areas where men outscore women.

The other reasons that deter women from climbing up the carrier ladder includes mounting pressure at work place, work timings, time flexibility and travel.

FACTORS RESTRICTING WOMEN'S CARRIER CHOICES: UNCONVENTIONAL WORKING HOURS

BPO industry, which is a subset of IT industry, has its own unique conditions that pose impediments to achieve a good work-life balance for women. Offering a reason as to why women professionals tend not to rise above a certain level, Prakash Toppo, V-P, HR at Global Vantedge says, "Night shifts put an additional pressure on all employees in ITES sector. For women, it becomes even more challenging and hence the burnout is much higher. Marriage, more or less, forces women to quit night shift operations. For instance, the trend of more women employees in call centers is more visible in the North and Western part of the country. In the South, although there has been considerable increase in the number of women employees in call centers, yet it is quite low. This is attributed to unconventional working hours that call centers have.

OBSTACLES FOR CARRIER DEVELOPMENT IN IT SECTOR: GENDER DISCRIMINATION IN THE WORKPLACE

What is about gender discrimination in the workplace? A Survey among the HR managers reported that gender discrimination is not considered as an issue because the type of work done by software professionals, whether men or women, it is the same and they have equal opportunities of rising up the ladder, provided, they stay on in the job. In software, as the surveys in the project reveal, women enjoy preferences on a scale that they never experienced in any other field of engineering and science. In India, women occupy 19% of professional jobs in the software industry. In Kolkata and Bangalore, the figure is higher than average for India. In both of these cities, the proportion of women varied from company to company, and it is not unusual to find women occupying 20-25% of professional jobs. Neither in Bangalore nor in Kolkata did the researchers find any evidence of discrimination, either at the point of recruitment or in career progression. In some cases, companies prefer to recruit women as the attrition rate among women is lower than that among men.

Similarly, is the case of the media sector. However, the type and nature of problems that women face are different. In prevalence survey we conducted for this project, over 80% of the employers said that there is no discrimination and there is no gender preference. From 500 employers interviewed, about 80 employers said that there was gender preference in terms of sub contracting or outsourcing, out of which 47 stated their gender preference. Out of 47, 7 preferred women and 40 prefered men.

If there was no gender preference for outsourcing, one would imagine there would be no gender preference for employment. Software is the only sector, barring one or two instances, which said that they prefere women. As regards gender bias, nearly 40 out of 500 (8%) affirmed gender bias against women.

Moreover, access to jobs is more or less restricted to the urban based upper class youth. What are the advantages that women enjoy in new forms of work? It reduces the hard choices that women have to make. The strategies to draw more women lies in improving the manner in which work is conducted without jeopardising the quality of workers' lives.

Table 10: Barriers For Women's Progression in IT Carrier

Sl. No.	*Barriers/ Issue*	*Survey report*	*Employers remarks*
1.	Gender preference Or gender bias	Prevalence Survey	Out of 500 employers, 80 confirmed gendered preference in outsourcing or sub-contracting. No = 80%. Yes=20%
2.	Burnout Syndrome	Prevalence Survey	The routine nature of the job forced women to switch jobs (Airlines employees)
3.	Lack of confidence	IBM Survey	Women have the ability, education and experience to handle challenging jobs, but what they lack is confidence
4.	Differences in the way men and women approach technical subjects	IBM Survey	Women possess soft skills while men have technical skills
5.	Assignment of Priorities (family vs Profession) Padmaja Krishnan, Xansa	Dataquest Survey	Proportion of women in the IT workforce is 19%, but at senior position 6%. There is a smooth going from the fresher to the team leader and project leader stage. Growth of women IT professionals stop at the team leader stage
6.	Glass ceiling (H.R. Rajasekar VP Mistral Software)	Dataquest Survey	No discrimination towards women IT professionals

7.	Social factors (Mita Brahma, HR Head of Nucleus Software)	Dataquest Survey	Since many women manage to enter the workplace by rising above the social biases, they are strong and do well when given the opportunity
8.	Performance Robert F Danbeck V-P-HR at IBM India	Dataquest Survey	Indian women make better engineers; they have qualities like strong team playing abilities, the capacity to juggle a variety of issues, flexibility and creativity in abundance.

Source: Results of Prevalence/IBM Survey.

WHY THERE ARE JUST A FEW WOMEN AT THE TOP OF CORPORATE HIERARCHY?

A study of the entries getting into the Dataquest magazine reveals that there were no women CEOs getting into the Top 10 IT companies and this happened in an industry where women are supposed to stand shoulder to shoulder with the men. What is it that keeps Indian women from making it to the top rung of authority in the country's IT sector? Or is it IT sector that has not recognised and rewarded women well enough for their efforts? Or will maturity only come with age and experience, and it is because of the industry's nascent youth that women are yet to reach the top rung? Or is there a glass ceiling and despite whatever is said, it is not really a level playing field as far as women are concerned?

"The other perspective, for the lower status of women at the top of the corporate hierarchy, can be explained by the fact that the number of women entering IT industry has been lower than men", (Balu Doraisamy, president of HP India). It is argued that the lopsided gender ratio begins in academic institutes itself (Mita Brahma, HR Head of Nucleus Software). It is further stated that more than impediments at the workplace, it is women's personal choices and abilities to cope up with family and social pressures that decide whether they rise above the ordinary or quit the workplace prematurely. Some of the HR managers of the opinion that only a very few women IT professionals are passionate about their jobs as compared to men (M L Taneja, V-P, HR of HCL

Infosystems). Because men typically do not exit careers, so all of them are bound to stick to well over 10 years. "As against that, women exit the workforce, either by choice or because of their circumstances." (Mittal of Jobsahead).

HOW CAN THIS BE CHANGED?: ORGANISATIONAL PERSPECTIVE

It is clear that untimely exits, either due to circumstance or personal choice, are the biggest reason why the number of women in IT companies declines so sharply with a rise in experience. The IT companies should develop a definite strategy to curb those exits. The biggest challenge for organisations is to be sensitive to family and social pressures under which women have to work. Organisations should be sensitive to the needs of their women employees. They are wives, mothers and homemakers amongst other significant roles that they play. Various organisational policies must be drafted with these points in mind. Finally, despite all the good work that HR departments may put in to create truly women-sensitive work environments, it is the individual's own home support system, ambitions and career aspirations that determine whether a woman manager is able to balance her career and family.

14

Gender-based Differences in Information Technology with Special Reference to the National Informatics Center in India (NIC)

ABSTRACT

This paper attempts to present job opportunities created by IT sector for women both in the developed and developing economies. It further attempts to examine the socio-economic, educational, cultural and political factors that have motivated women.

Actually, there exists a shortage of IT work force in some western countries like Germany. Absence of women in IT sector is an added problem in this context. In countries like India, there is a good supply of IT labour force both sexes, so that they can even cover to some extent the urgent demand for qualified IT professionals in western countries. The aim of this paper is to present some of the results obtained from a study of gender based differences in the National Informatics Center (NIC) in India and to discuss these results in a cross national perspective.

INTRODUCTION

The dynamic growth of information technology (IT) industry and the increasing number of women in IT labour force, with the help of initiative from the government and employers in India, shows a very positive image of the position of women in this sector in this country. According to this general perspective, we could argue that the position of women and men in IT sector in this country is nearly balanced.

However, attending to the hierarchical positions that both sexes ocuppy in IT organisations, this picture does not seem to be optimistic. Only a few women reach the top positions in IT companies depending on the obstacles they have to face in the course of their professional careers.

A review of surveys related to the last few years in western countries suggests that there exists an unbalanced situation between both sexes regarding responsibilities, work allocation and promotional opportunities in IT companies. This situation has been attributed to several interacting factors— the organisational structure and the socio-economic and cultural context. In these contexts the image of IT and managerial positions are intrinsically linked to a male connotated culture that keeps women down in manufacturing and low level positions in IT industry.

According to the situation in developed countries regarding the participation and position of women in IT industry, enrolment of women in computer science education is very low and their lack of qualifications in technical fields hinder their entrance into IT labour market. In this context, a sharp decline of women (20%), in IT sector in 90´s has been noted in several studies (Adam, 1995; Grundy, 1996; Panteli, 1997; Ramsay et al. 1997).

This lack of participation of women in the IT sector has been interpreted from different perspectives (positivism, constructivism, post-modernism, etc.). Though they have illustrated a number of factors starting from women's biological differences to their lack of aptitude in computing as reasons for their lower representation (Suzarine, 1995), they have not given a complete picture of the problem.

The aim of this study is to identify obstacles that deter women from making progress in the IT sector based on an analysis of the situation in the National Informatics Center (NIC) in India. In a further discussion, we will refer to the situation in Germany regarding women's participation in this sector.

Taking into account the rapid growth of IT industry in a global perspective and shortage of manpower in this sector, an analysis of women´s position in this industry is a crucial and strategical issue for socio-economical development of the developing countries. On the other hand, the analysis of women's situation in this sector from a cross-national point of view can serve as a basis to propose measures for optimising women member in the labour force in IT industry.

The lack of studies exploring the problems and prospects for women IT professionals and about the factors shaping women's career in IT industry (Bruce and Adam, 1991) is incongruent to the optimistic picture that this sector shows for the career development of the women in India (Gaio, 1995).

THEORETICAL FRAMEWORK

The relationship between work and family life of IT professionals has been recognised in some studies. It is argued that women in IT field anticipate difficulties in balancing their career and family responsibilities, and then they attempt to minimise by remaining unmarried or childless (Igbaria, 1997).

The subordination of family lives of women in senior-management positions (Sonnentag, 1994) to the demands of a career has been documented. Often career progression polices and structures are designed to emphasize the period between the ages of 30 and 40 as the most important one for career development, which is infact the more intensive period for child rearing. Thus, especially women who wish to have both family and a career must juggle heavy responsabilities in both domains (Trauth, 1995). While programmes of maternity leave and parental or family-care leave, child and elder care facilities and services and flexible work arrangements often aim to attract and retain women, it has also been found necessary that male employees be encouraged to take up such options.

Since the ideology implicit in professionalism involves dedication to the job and career, one has to forgo private sphere demands in order to be successful in the profession. The traditional division of women in the private sphere, mostly tied to family responsibilities and men in the public one, hinder women presenting themselves as "serious" professionals or continuing technological education. Within the professional fields of science and technology these are the minimum requirements (Martin, 1999).

Parental educational background has also been recognised as an influencing factor in the professional advancement of individuals (Augustine, 1999).

Regarding the influence of gender in organisations, four main factors are considered:

1. Recruiting policy (Factors like: recuiting of women in part time or secondary level, the absence of jobs showing

preference for men in some vital positions, generating less promotional positions for women, exhibiting scepticism about women's capabilities and equal opportunities for individuals of both the sexes, are considered the main obstacles for the recruitment of women employees in IT organisations (Olde, 1991).

2. The structure of opportunities (the challenge available, the chances of learning new skills, the earning of organisational rewards).
3. The power or ability to get things done and the social composition of groups (average of women in working groups and departments).
4. Career options:
   - efforts taken to improve performance
   - organisational support/initiatives
   - rate of mobility across organisations and functional areas
   - access to training and career-related information

According to Kanter's theory on relative numbers, one would find less discrimination and better opportunities for women in organisations where there are many women employed than in those that are not used to employing women (Kanter, 1977).

Women with traditional work styles attributed to females, and women seeking consensus and team effort are looked upon as less confident and capable than men, while the women who emulate masculine behaviour are seen as aggressive and as being rejected by men for not conforming to feminine standards (Hemenway, 1995). Moreover, the reproduction of "mental roles" of success in the image of senior males may lead to the potential of female candidates being consequently devalued through such comparison. Male behaviour (such as "harmless" joking, "laddish" conversation, discussion of male interest and extreme forms of harassment) are shown as stressful and overtime can erode women's self-confidence and ability to present themselves successfully (Tierney, 1995).

The Computer Weekly Survey Report (Panteli et al., 1998) has established that the interest and aspiration of both men and women are equal in career development and one could find gender-equity in career choice and orientation.

Kanter (1984) also has argued that since women have been clustered in the lower levels of the organisational hierarchy, they have limited opportunities for mobility and, therefore, it would be unreasoneable to conclude that women limit their career aspirations due to their sex roles or family responsibilities.

Regarding gender differences and adoption of career building strategies, some studies have analysed both the gender patterns in the exploitation of career resources and is impact on their career advancement (Shapiro, 1994; Tierney, 1995; Baroudi et al., 1995). According to these studies, male IT professionals gain access to work related information with the help of their all male network and achieve organisational mobility. Women, on the other hand, have been excluded from the formal and informal networks of the corporation's primary operations and this lack of opportunities for extra- and intra-organisational interaction has seriously handicapped women in their career advancement.

Opportunities in an organisation vary with the differences in its structural factors. For instance, a public organisations with bureaucratic structure (fixed rules for advancement) offers women better opportunities. On the other hand, private organisations with more informal criteria and procedures in this respect, offer better opportunities for men than for women (McIlwee, 1992).

According to a study about women engineers in the USA, men have better opportunities than women in organisation where engineers have a powerful position, where growth and technical innovation are high and where authority relations are less bureaucratic. Moreover, women achieve equally with men, where engineers have a lower status and where the work place is most bureaucratic in structure. It is, therefore, concluded that women find better opportunities in traditional and large IT firms that have a stable environment and a bureaucratic structure. They also find better opportunities where there is an affirmative action programme that counters the preference for men in management (Robinson, 1989; Cockburn, 1991).

Especially the structure and culture of computing work is found to be quite incompatible with many women´s lives (Turkle, 1988). One of the reasons for this incompatibility is that in most of the computing work, separation between.working hours and leisure time disappears and the two become seamless (Avner and Gunnarsson, 1992). Moreover, computing profession favours those who have "single lifestyles". Cringely (1992) and Shapiro (1994) explained how women managers in the IT work environment tend to remain either single or if married not to have children to be able to compete with their male colleagues, while the male managers don't need to sacrifice their private sphere in order to promote in their occupation. Research into software development in Germany and Switzerland also reveals that a larger percentage of female team leaders remain childless to progress in their profession (Sonnentag, 1994).

Earlier studies have examined the image of masculinity in computing and its effect on women's work (Grundy, 1996; Henwood, 1993; Wright, 1996). Computing is considered as a male stereotyped work because of its requirement of aggresive display of technical self-confindence and hands-on ability for success (McIlwee, 1992). This masculine stereotyped computing culture hinders women's entrance into this professional field. Women drop out of the high-tech pipeline and the masculine stereotyped computer culture creates a "site of power struggle in which women are bound to lose" (Debare, 1987: 47).

OBJECTIVES

To analyse gender differences in manpower composition of the NIC and explore the extent of gender segregation across different types of occupational specialities (telecommunication, networking, multimedia, etc.) and job categories (project manager, system analysts, programmers, etc.).

To explore the human capital variation (educational attainments, experience, in-service training and access to the latest developments) among the male and female IT workers in NIC and identify its impact on their career achievement.

To analyse the impact of socio-economic and organisational factors on career development of both sexes in NIC.

To explore the degree of gender development and identify organisational intiatives to improve the status of women.

To suggest suitable strategies and policy frameworks for gender development in software related organisations.

HYPOTHESIS

There exists a significant relationship between gender and occupational status of IT professionals in the NIC.

There is no relationship between human capital attributes and the occupational distribution of IT professionals in NIC.

Socio-economic, family and organisational factors influence significantly the gender based differences in NIC.

There is a close association between the national culture and occupational culture of NIC.

METHODOLOGY

Data Collection

Questionnaire collects data regarding:

— educational and employment status

— family background

— organisational environment of the respondents

- climate (hiring practices, level of autonomy in the workplace, employers´ treatment, treatment from colleagues and superiors)
- career opportunities (facilities for training, delegation to higher studies, chances for career mobility, avenues for promotion)
- structure (formal and informal career practices, career reward structures)
- prevalence of gender neutrality

were collected from a sample of 603 employees (452 male and 151 female) in thirteen state capitals and two union territories in India.

Analysis of the data

Gender gap is measured in terms of the ratio of differences between male and female to the total (M-F/T). To measure the magnitude of response of the factors selected for the study, weightage index (WI)[1] has been used.

Percentage analysis has been used to estimate the level of representation of male and female respondents across various socio-economic and organisational environments.

Analysis of variance (one-way) has been applied to examine gender gap in the human capital and characteristics of the respondents.

Spearman's Rank correlation coefficient is used to examine the differences in the motivational factors of male and female respondents[2].

Profile of the Sample Institution

National Informatics Centre (NIC) is a premier Information Technology Organisation in India, committed to provide state-of-the art solutions for IT needs of the Government of India at all levels. It carries the distinction of being the largest IT organisation in the country and offers a wide range of services from Consultancy, Software Design and Development, Office Automation and Networking Services to Training, Video Conferencing, CAD, E-Commerce, Multimedia and Internet Services including Web Site Development and Hosting.

Organisational Structure

The organisational set up of NIC encompasses its Headquarters at New Delhi; State Units in all the 25 State capitals and 7 Union Territory Headquarters and District Centres in more than 540 Districts in India.

At the NIC Headquarters, a large number of Application Divisions exist which provide total informatics support to the Ministries and Departments of the Central Government. NIC computer cells are located in almost all the Ministry Bhawans of the central Government and Apex Offices including the Prime Minister's Office, the Rashtrapati Bhawan and the Parlamient House. Apart from this, NIC has some Resource Divisions.

Since the supremacy of the NIC in the software industry depends to a large extent on its manpower composition, it is felt necessary to analyse the manpower profile of the various sections of this institution.

RESULTS

Regarding personal characteristics of the respondents, the results of the analysis of variance (one-way) reveals gender differences in respect of age and parental education. Regarding marital status and number of children there are no significant differences between both the sexes.

The educational status of the respondents (research qualification: Male=12,38%; Female=12,02%; Post graduate qualification: Male=54,43%; Female=52,98%; Graduation: Male=26,78%; Female=30,46%) indicates parallelism existing between the educational level of men and women in NIC. It also exhibits the recruitment policy of the organisation is in conformity with the general tradition of IT industry, that favours those with adequate skills and where gender doesn´t represent a recruitment criterion.

It is generally seen that the larger the organisational and job tenures, the higher will be the career development of the professionals. But in the case of IT, there is no correlation between these two variables. What is more important is the skill and efficiency of the employee. Neither age, nor experience has a role in the promotion or career advancement of the professionals. Our results support this trend. For instance, nearly 50% of the NIC professionals have less than 6 years of experience (Male=50,43%; Female=45,69%); nearly 39% has less than 12 years of experience (Male=37,84; Female=42,39%); and 11% has more than 12 years of experience (Male=11,73%; Female=11,88%). There doesn't seem to be any gender difference with respect to the tenure of the male and female employees in NIC.

Among the selected human variables (Education level of the respondents, years of experience and engagement in training programms and access to information) only in relation to the access to information significant differences between men and women in NIC were found. Male members´ average of access to the print media is higher (40.07%) than those of their female collegues (29.24%) while a balanced average of male and female professionals (Male=24.34%; Female=25.17%) have shown preference for the Internet and E-mail correspondence. On the other hand, the female respondents´ access to peer groups (Female=16.56%; Male=11.95%) and conferences and seminars information (Female=14.57%; Male=11.28%) is found to be higher than their counterparts.

Regarding the recruitment policy of the organisation, nearly three-fourth of the respondents have opined that educational qualification is given more consideration in the choice of the candidates and only a limited importance is attributed to other characteristics like professional qualifications and skills. The personal characteristics of the respondents and their gender character have no relevance in the selection policy of the organisation.

A comparative analysis between men´s and women´s opinion regarding NIC recruitment policy reveals that the ranking order of the selection criteria seems to be balanced though there remains variation in the degree of their acceptance by male and female respondents. Nearly 84.77% of the female and 69.69% of the male respondents felt that educational qualification is the basic criterion for getting into NIC. Similarly, 27,21% of the male and 13,24% of the female respondents felt that next to academic qualification, professional experience and skills have been considered for the selection of the candidates to NIC. It is quite heartening to note that both sexes have acknowledged that there exists no gender or personal bias in the reruitment practices of the organisation.

Though women are distributed across various categories, there is no equal representation of men and women in NIC. The strength of women´s representation is only 25% in the high, middle and lower levels of the organisational hierarchy. Among the thirteen different job categories, women's absence is felt in the higher positions. However, the average of women is found to be higher in categories such as Technical Director, System Analyst, Programmer and Data Entry Operator. The percentage distribution of both sexes is almost equal in the Senior System Analyst and Scientist categories.

As far as the percentage distribution of the male and female respondents are concerned, female respondents have been mostly dominating the "soft" area of computing: customers services, human resources development units, personnel department, commercial information provision division, bibliographic information division, etc. On the contrary, male respondents dominate in the "hard" area of computing: computes aided designing, database and software designing, industry information system design, infrastructure building, engineering support, etc.

Regarding professional mobility, the percentage of female respondents receiving promotions in the higher (Technical

Director: Male=1,55%; Female=3,97%) and the middle level (Senior System Analyst/System Analyst: Male=6,41%; Female=9,26%) cadres are slightly higher than their male colleagues. Even in the "scientist" category the percentage of female respondents receiving more than two promotions is higher than the male.

There seems to be no difference between married and unmarried respondents with respect to their professional mobility in NIC. Regarding career orientation there seems to be no difference between men and women in NIC. The level of importance attached to the various factors associated with career orientation (task orientation, perseverance, fear of failure, social acceptance, reaction to success and failure, future orientation, competitiveness, independence, rigidity, etc.) remains the same among the male and female respondents.

Among the various organisational factors that have affected the career development of the respondents, nearly one-fifth of the respondents suffered due to promotion denial. The majority of the male respondents (56,83%) found fault with the norms fixed by the organisation and the government for promotion. But a large percentage of female respondents that in addition to the discrepancies in the promotional policies, personal prejudice also has contributed to the denial of promotion in the organisation. However, both men and women feel that other factors like gender and community bias, want of promotional avenues in certain categories of jobs are only minimal for promotion denial. One fifth of the respondents have felt that discrimination based on gender, nativity, religion, caste/community, professionals vs. non professionals existed in the organisation. Among these areas, one pertaining to professionals vs non-professionals seems to dominate (5,21%) followed by gender bias (4,2%). There seems to be no gender variation in the order of identification of the discrimination areas, but in the magnitude of perception.

The order of priority of the factors that have attracted a majority of respondents into NIC include travel and leave facilities, incentives, the work place autonomy and the challenging work environment. A vast majority of men have given importance to fringe benefits (Male = 58.41%; Female=27.81%), while female respondents have given preference to the facilities available for professional development (Male = 30.74%; Female=42.38%) and personal development (Male= 10.84%; Female = 29.81%). Factors like workplace autonomy and opportunity for professional achievement have motivated both sexes equally.

Among factors that have contributed to the satisfaction of the employees, more than 62% of the female respondents and 41% of the males felt that they were more satisfied with the organisation due to its friendly environment. Men gave preference to the support that they have received from their supervisors (Male=17.04%; Female= 5.3%); on the other hand, the female respondents gave priority to the assistance that they get from their colleagues in improving their performance (Male=7.5%; Female=17.9%) and in setting their goals (Male= 4.2%; Female=16.6%). Nearly 29% of the men and 20% of the women felt that they prefer working in NIC because of autonomy given to them in the work-related activities.

DISCUSSION

The results of this case study reveal that there doesn´t exist evidence of gender segregation in the NIC in India. The respondents don´t feel discriminated in the recruiment process of the organisation. Regarding the work specialisation, it has been noted that women tend to work in the "soft" area of computing, while men are mostly located in the "hard" area.

In IT professions in Germany, the average of women in this sector accounts for 23% (21% in West Germany and 41% in East Germany)[3], and it is similar to the corruption in NIC. According to official data from the Ministry of Labour 40% of the specialists in application software are women[4]. A survey with a sample of 42 women IT specialists in Germany reveals also this pattern: the majority of the respondents were working in application fields[5]. Another survey also supports these results and indicates that almost no women were working in hardware related fields[6]. Regarding this aspect, the pattern in both countries seems to be similar: women tend to prefer software computing areas as hardware as a professional perspective.

The absence of women in the high levels of the organisation´s hierarchy in NIC in India is noted in this survey, though their average is higher in the category of Technical Director or System Analyst. In Germany, only 11% of Technical Directors in IT field are women and 12% of the System Analysts[7]. Social and organisational as well as cultural factors linked to traditional social male roles implicit in IT field explained the distance of women to computing in Germany.

Although women are not in the highest positions in IT sector in India, their presence in the field is wide. In the case of NIC, the employees feel satisfied with the work atmosphere and incentives in the organisation. Both men and women found workplace autonomy and challenges in NIC very important.

Though there exists good prospect for IT professionals in Germany, especially at the present moment, according to the urgent demand of work force in this sector in Germany as we have already mentioned, unemployment among women in computing is twice higher than among men (6,8% female and 3,4% male, Schreyer, 1999). Since the average of women in IT studies (mostly in those that have an image directly related to technik or engineering) in Germany is very low, there is absence of women in IT professions. Also in new short term studies like "Fachinformatiker/-in" created in 1997 the average of women accounts for only 12%[8].

The relationship between work and family life of IT professionals has been emphasized as a structural obstacle for women in this professional field in Germany. It is argued that women in the IT field anticipate difficulties in balancing their career and family responsabilities, which they attempt to minimise by remaining unmarried or childless (Igbaria, 1997). In the NIC in India there was no evidence of differences between the professional mobility of married and unmarried women. Compared with men, the average of women receiving promotions is slightly higher in the higher and middle level.

The positive results of the government initiatives in India regarding the development of IT industry and the support of women in this sector should be considered in more detail to create a successful framework for this sector in other countries.

REFERENCES

1. WI=total score value (TS)/num. of respondents (N)* 100, where:
   TS = N(wlrl + W2r2 + W3r3)/R, where:
   R = r1+r2+r3,where:

r = number of respondents in each level
W = weightage assigned to each level

2. the lower the value of "R" is, the higher is the difference between male and female motivational factors.

3. Schreyer, F. (1999). Studienfachwahl und Arbeitslosigkeit: Frauen sind häufiger arbeitslos – gerade wenn sie ein "Männerfach" studiert haben. In: *IAB Kurzbericht.* 14, Nürnberg.

4. Tischer, U. (1999). "Thesen und Chancen für Frauen in der Informationsgesellschaft". In: *Bundesanstalt für Arbeit: Frauen in der Informationsgesellschaft.* Num. 13. p. 966.

5. Erb, U. (1992). "Was forschen Frauen in der Informatik?". In: *Frauenarbeit und Informatik.* März, S. 52-61.

6. Behnke et al. (1993). "Umfrage zur Arbeitswelt von Frauen in der EDV." In: *Frauenarbeit in der Informatik.* Juni. S. pp. 57-71.

7. Tischer, U. (1999). "Thesen und Chancen für Frauen in der Informationsgesellschaft. In: *Bundesanstalt für Arbeit: Frauen in der Informationsgesellschaft.* Num. 13, p. 966.

8. Tischer, U. (1998) *Neue Beschäftigungsfelder und weibliche Qualifikationspotentiale.* In: "Oechterring, V. & Winker, G. *Computernetze", Frauenplätze. Frauen in der Informationsgesellschaft,* Opladen. Leske+Budrich. pp. 33-57.

9. Adam, A. "Women and Computing in the U.K." *Communications of the ACM.* Jan. 38 (1). (1995).

10. Augustine, D. "The socialist 'silicon ceiling': East German Women in Computer Science. In: *Proceedings of the International Symposium on Society, Women and Technology: Historical, societal and professional perspectives.* New Brunswick. New Iersey. pp. 347-355. (1999).

11. Baroudi, J. & Igbaria, M. "An examination of gender effects on career success of information systems employees". In: *Journal of Management Information Systems.* Winter. Vol. 11 (3). pp. 181-201.(1995).

12. Bruce, M. & Adam, A. "Women´s career paths in artificial intelligence". In: M. Bruce & A. Adam (Eds.): *Women into Computing: Selected Papers.* London. Springer Verl. (Chap. 44. pp. 294-300). (1991).

13. Cringely, R.X. "Accidental Empires: How the boys of Silicon Valley make their millions, battle foreign competition, and still can´t get a date". Harmongsworth: Penguin (1992).

14. Gaio, F.J. "Women in software programming: The experience of Brazil", In: F.J. Gaio (Ed.): *Women Encounter Technology: charging patterns of employment in the third world.* London. Routledge. pp. 205-232. (1995).

15. Grundy, F. "Women and Computers". *Exeter,* Intellect Books (1996).

16. Hemenway, K. "Human nature and the glass ceiling in industry". In: *Communications of the ACM*. Vol. 38. (1). pp. 55-62. (1995).
17. Henwood, F. "Establishing gender perspectives on Information Technology". In: E. Green & J. Owen: *Office Systems*, London, Taylor and Francis (1993).
18. Igbaria, M.; Parasuraman, B.; Greenhaus, J.H. "Status Report on women and men in the IT work place". *Information Systems Management*. Summer. 14 (3). pp. 44-53 (1997).
19. Kanter, R.M. "Variations of Managerial Career Structures in High Technology Firms: The impact of organisational characteristics on international labour market patterns". In: Offerman, P. *International Labour Markets*. Boston. MIT Press. pp. 102-189 (1984).
20. Martin, S. Gender. "Technology and Work: Understanding Patterns in Women´s employment in Science and Technology Occupations". In: *Proceedings of the International Symposium on Society, Women and Technology: Historical, societal and professional perspectives*. New Bruenswick. New Jersey. pp. 118-129. (1999).
21. Olde, C. de et al. "Positions of women in information technogy in the Netherlands: Education, Job characteristics and proposals for an equal opportunity policy". In: Erikssan, J. et al. (Ed.) *Women, work and computerisation: Understanding and Overcoming bias in Work and Education*. London. Elsevier. pp. 347-362. (1991).
22. Pentali, A. et al. "Women in the U.K. Software Industry. How much do you know?" In: Lander, R. & And, A. (Eds.) *Women in Computing*, London, Intellect Ltd., pp. 94-101. (1997).
23. Ramsay, H. et al. "Empowerment and Disempowerment: Active Agency, structural Constant and Women Computer Uses". in: Lander, A. & And, A. (Eds.) *Women in Computing*. London. Intellect Ltd. pp. 73-83. (1997).

15

Gender Democracy in Digital Economy: An Indian Experience

ABSTRACT

The spurt in the growth of knowledge economy or e- economy in the last two decades have enforced the developing nations including India to concentrate more on the human resource development. As these countries have skipped the agricultural and industrial revolution, they worked hard to catch up with IT revolution by building their manpower and network infrastructure. Though India has a large talent pool with 1.67 million engineering and 1.54 millions of non-engineering graduates passing out of India's educational institutions annually, there remains a shortage of skilled labour force. It is also estimated that the demand for IT trained manpower in India will grow up to 370,000 in the year 2008 (The Asia week May 18, 2001). The question here is how these skill shortages are to be managed and what is the share of women in the manpower development process in the Indian sub-continent. This implies that in order to achieve genderdemocracy in the e-society, equitable participation of the gender groups in IT education and IT employment is considered as an essential input factor.

Keywords: *Knowledge economy; gender democracy; women in IT labour market; gender equity*

INTRODUCTION

One of the parameters for participating in the e-society is the capability to build technical manpower. The spurt in the growth of knowledge economy or e-economy in the last two decades have enforced the developing nations including India to concentrate more on the human resource development. As these countries have skipped the agricultural and industrial revolution, they worked hard to catch up with IT revolution by building their manpower and network infrastructure. India, a country freed from foreign yoke 55 years back, is emerging as one of the world class leaders in IT with 220,000 world class IT professionals rolling out annually. According to the NASSCOM annual survey, IT industry has employed 650,000 IT professionals in 2003 representing an increase of 24.4% over the previous year. The demand for the skilled manpower in IT sector is projected to be 235,000 by 2008. Though India has a large talent pool with 167,000 engineering and 1.54 millions of non-engineering graduates passing out of India's educational institutions annually, there remains a shortage of skilled labour force. It is also estimated that the demand for IT trained manpower in India will grow up to 370,000 in the year 2008 (The Asia week May 18, 2001). The question here is how these skill shortages are to be managed and what is the share of women in the manpower development process in the Indian sub-continent. This implies that in order to achieve gender democracy in the e-society, equitable participation of the gender groups in IT education and IT employment is considered as an essential input factor.

STATEMENT OF THE PROBLEM

It is generally believed that IT is one of the best – equal opportunity areas 'that provide wider opportunities for women to enter and succeed in the computer industry'. Nevertheless, the validity of these claims is yet to be established through empirical analysis. For such a transition in attitudes toward gender to take place, certain prerequisites have to be met. First, there should be an adequate proportion of technically trained female labour force. Second, for the permeation of an alternate gender culture, there needs to be a process of de-learning and re-learning from the new work environment for both men and women. In essence, the family life of a woman and her professional commitments adapt to one another. To illustrate the gender situation in IT, one has to view 'the women in technology approach' and 'the women and technology approach'. The former approach tries to involve more women via equal access to education and employment; while the latter has a broader focus on the nature of technological work.

OBJECTIVES OF THE STUDY

This study attempts to find answers to such questions as: (i) Where are women in IT industry? How do they benefit? (ii) How has IT industry changed women's position? Is there any change in the gender division of labour as a result of women's employment in IT industry? Is there any change in women's mobility due to IT industry? (Mobility is a measure of gender relations). The findings of this study would throw light on the distribution of women's work in IT sector and illustrate the (i) position of women in various service sectors; (ii) opportunities for women in the new economy; (iii) and the impact of changing organisational structures on women's work. The gender situation is measured by adopting various common indicators like (i) the proportion of women in the various subsets of IT industry; (ii) segregation of women across the high, medium and low end jobs; (iii) types of jobs undertaken; (iv) working condition of the organisation; and the (v) facilities to learning and career progression.

TRENDS IN THE PARTICIPATION OF WOMEN IN IT INDUSTRIES

Women's position in IT sector has seen both positive and negative trends in the last decade in the Indian sub-continent. There are studies that have highlighted the fast track that women have made in IT related industries. Women's composition in IT workforce has risen from 10% in 1993 to 18% in 1998 which is much higher than the national average of 12 percent (NASSCOM 1999). To a great surprise, the entry of women has shot upto 21 percent in 2002 (NASSCOM, 2002) and it is expected to go up to 35 percent by 2005. The following table illustrates the wide spread participation of women in the various segments of IT industries.

The high rate of women employees in ITES and BPO sectors is a welcome change from the low 12.5 percent women being employed in IT industry. According to a Dataquest-IDC survey in October 2002, the highest number of women was employed by NIIT at 29 percent while Rolta India employed the lowest number of women at four percent. Top software companies like Infosys employs 17 percent women, TCS employs 20 percent and Wipro employs 19 percent women. The massive incorporation of women into paid work and their positions of authority in IT industry have improved their social status.

Table 1. Distribution of women among the subsets of IT

Sl.No.	*IT Sector*	*F/M Ratio*	*Type of Work and skill requirements*
1.	Software industry	19:81	Software development not just design, customisation and adaptation of software
2.	Telecom Industry*	40:60	Technical and creative work. Required highly qualified engineers
3.	Airlines	80:20	Customer service. Required Communication, Language and Software Skills
4.	IT-Enabled service sector	45:55	Demands linguistics and domain skill
5.	BPO**	49:51	Indian BPO is predominantly voice-based (outbound calls)

Source: DATAQUEST, April 22, 2003.

Though the above statistics has shown a rosy picture of women in this sector, a further investigation is required to know the existing situation in the various regions of the IT related sector in the country.

GENDER COMPOSITION OF IT WORKFORCE IN FIRMS OF DIFFERENT SIZES

The composition of male and female IT workers in the firms of different sizes and activities needs to be analysed in order to identify their levels of participation. State-level survey reports indicated that the employment opportunities opened for women are relatively higher in the IT sector when compared to other industries. Out of 28,109 employees surveyed from 156 firms in Mumbai, it was noticed that the percentages of female workers were 32.1 percent in the IT firms and 12 percent in other firms. Not only in terms of numbers but also in positions of power and authority, women's status is higher in IT related industries than in non-IT sectors. It is evident that IT industries have opened a gateway for women's entry as well as for their career progression compared to other non-IT sectors. Figure 1 is illustrative of advantageous situation that women have experienced in software sector than in other traditional banking and media sectors.

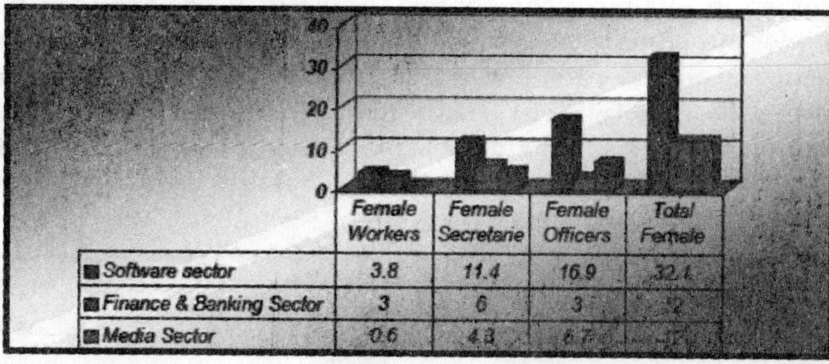

Source: Teleworking, Economic and Political Weekly, 2002.

Fig. 1 : Distribution of Women Workers among IT and Non-IT Sectors

The next issue that needs to be addressed is whether IT sector offers equality of opportunities for both men and women in their roles and responsibilities. Before investing the response of the industries to the gender factor, it is necessary to find out the transformation that has taken place in the areas of gender technology relations, traditional gender roles in the society, attitudinal changes in the gender groups with respect to their professional choices, social, political and economic pressures on gender participation in the national economy etc. For centuries together women were allowed to play a secondary role both in the domestic and public spheres. But the sudden changes that have taken place in the areas of globalisation, media, knowledge management and the compulsion on the part of the individual nations to response to the changing situation directly and indirectly enforce them to develop their human capital irrespective of gender, caste or creed. Now the question before us is, does this changing global situation have brought any positive change on women's situation in this new economy? Since the key pillars of this new economy (knowledge based industries) is based on expertise in infostructure, corporate intelligence, high-tech infrastructure etc. it is interesting to find out—Where do women figure into this competitive industry? Have they been able to participate on equal plane with their male counter parts in all spheres of IT based industries? What were the factors both contributing and deterring their progress in this sunrise industry? ILO has recently undertaken a survey to identify—Where are women in this most competitive industry? It has analysed the gender structure in more than 100 IT firms located at the major metros in the country. The main purpose of this survey was to find out the type of firms where women are mostly accommodated and the kind of activities that women are involved in the software development. Fig. 2 explains the areas where women have dominated in IT sector.

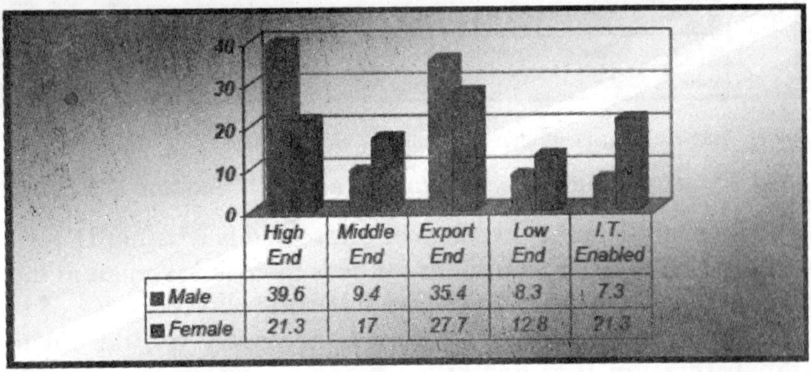

Source: International Labour organisation, New Delhi, 2001.

Fig. 2 : Distribution of Women in IT Firms of various Types and Sizes

It is noted that a major segment of women are clustered in the low-end jobs; while a minor segment of women are found at the high end jobs reflecting the gender divide in IT industry. Though women are better represented in IT sector, they have not assumed significant role and status. Most of them have been concentrated in the lower strata of job categories such as coding and programming; and only a minor percentage is presented in the development part of IT. ILO report clearly indicated that the high end firms that undertake software products, R&D, turnkey solutions and strategic technical alliances prefer to employ more men than women. The professional demands in this area of work are mostly engineering graduates, PhDs and post-graduates with technical multi-skilling. The proportion of women with such professional background is less and, therefore, they are relegated to the less prestigious and low-paid jobs. For instance, IT enabled and domestic end firms that perform low skilled, routinised and back-office jobs employed more women, since they require only certificate holders with pure technical, coding and maintenance, skills. Women's representations outnumber their male counterparts in these low-skilled and low-paid jobs. The male and female ratio of IT workers in the organisational hierarchy is diagrammatically shown below: The above situation supports the hypothesis that IT industry is not in any way different from the other industries and women have not enjoyed any special status or privilege in this industry. It is noted from the above diagram that higher the hierarchy, the lower will be the number of women and *vice-versa*.

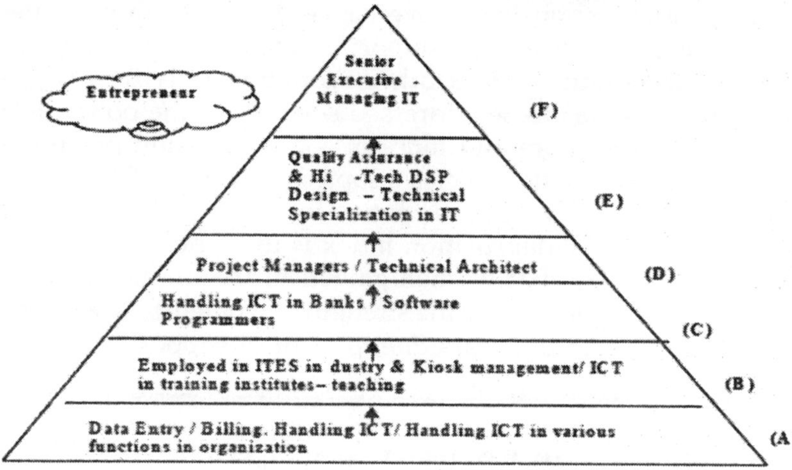

Source: WICT in India and China.htm

Fig. 3 : Women in IT Pyramidal growth and presence from the grass root level of ICT

The reasons for this under-representation may be owing to various educational, social, political, cultural and individual factors and, therefore, efforts should be made to analyse the gender technology variables such as the status of (i) gender socialisation, (ii) gender bias in access to ICT, (iii) gender preference to technical education, (iv) parental encouragement, (v) availability of role models, (vi) support from family and institutions and the (vii) cost of high-tech education etc. Among these various factors that deter women from occupying positions of authority and power, let us give priority to the educational factors at the first instance.

STATUS OF NATIONAL AND STATE-LEVEL IT POLICIES ON GENDER ISSUES

Policies formulated in this direction are also silent on gender issues. For instance, in 2000, the Indian government created a 'Working Group on Information Technology for Masses'. However, the working group's report with recommendations for how to broaden access to "the common man" does not specifically mention women. The recommendations call for activities related to access, education, and awareness raising of the importance and benefits of IT opportunities that if implemented, which will also benefit women, however, targeted strategies for ensuring female access and training are not discussed. To close the gender divide, gender responsive e-governance should be implemented. Funds should be raised to support women's initiatives in ICT base entrepreneurship and other economic activities. Digital marginalisation has to be addressed squarely at the policy level. This necessitates more and more of social inclusion process by way of conscious state policies adopted in favour of promoting women's education and participation in IT sector. Digital divide distribution and IT deprivation index is to be developed to see the level of access that women gained in the digital economy. The following explains how the strength of women gets decreased in the IT field over the years due to want of support system.

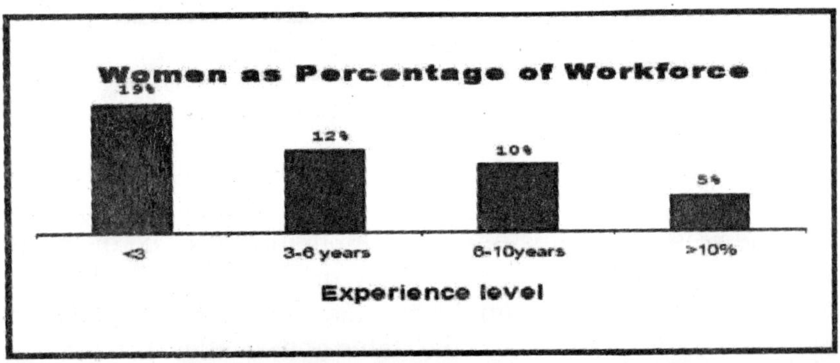

Fig. 4 : Women as percentage of workforce

However, it needs to be realised that training in ICT by itself cannot be an answer and elixir to all problems facing women development, but it does bring new information resources and can open new communication channels for the marginalised communities.

IMPACT OF SOCIAL AND CULTURAL FACTORS

Vittal (2003) observed that in order to empower women in IT

sector in the real sense, it is necessary to investigate the social impact of IT sector on the women's community. Empowering women in the real sense implies that their positions should be strengthened in the family and in the society; adequate support system is to be built up both at the private and in the public spheres. This requires a lot of cultural and attitudinal change in the mind-set of the people to accept women's progression In this context, Mr.Vittal has indicated the emergence of 'metro-sexual men', men who are sharing the responsibility of the family which might help women to be an active agent in the IT workforce. It is also observed that the drop-out rates of women gets increased with their marriage and childbirth. It is because childcare and housework remain women's responsibilities, irrespective of her income, educational level or employment. This places a great burden on women and restricts women's choices in terms of better job opportunities. The Jobs-ahead survey substantiates the fact that the drop-out rate of women increases with their advancement in experience. There seems to be a negative correlation that exists between women's presence in the IT workforce and their years of experience. Lesser the year of experience, larger will be the proportion of women and vice-versa. Women were not able to continue their job with sustained interest due to various interruptions that happened in their life which forced them to drop out from their aspiration of building a better career in IT. It is also observed that the social barriers are so strong and women who manage to enter workplaces by rising above societal biases are probably very strong and, therefore, do well when given the opportunity.

WHY THERE ARE JUST A FEW WOMEN AT THE TOP OF THE CORPORATE HIERARCHY?

A study of the entries getting into Dataquest magazine reveals that there were no women CEOs getting into the Top 10 IT companies and this happened in an industry where women are supposed to stand shoulder to shoulder with the men (Figure-5). What is it that keeps Indian women from making it to the top rung of authority in the country's IT sector? Or is it IT sector that has not recognised and rewarded women well enough for their efforts? Or will maturity only come with age and experience, and it is because of the industry's nascent youth that women are yet to reach the top rung? Or is there a glass ceiling. Despite whatever is said, it is not really a level playing field as far as women are concerned?

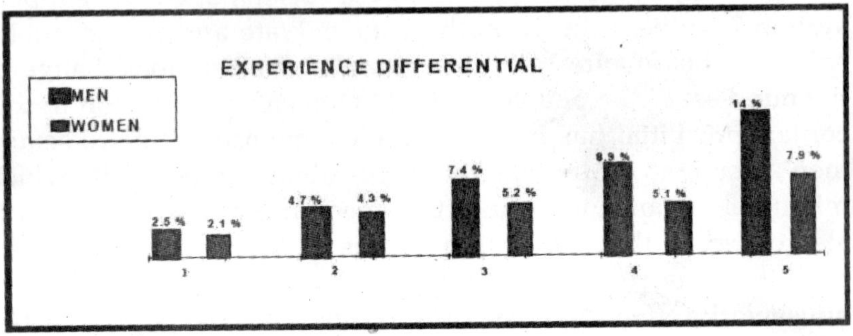

Fig. 5 : Status of Women in the Organisational Hierarchy

1- Software Engineer, 2-Team Leader, 3-Project Manager, 4-Programme Manager, 5-Vice-President

"The other perspective for the lower status of women at the top of the corporate hierarchy can be explained by the fact that the number of women entering IT industry has been lower than men," (Balu Doraisamy, president of HP India). It is argued that the lopsided gender ratio begins in academic institutes itself (Mita Brahma, HR Head of Nucleus Software). It is further stated that more than impediments at the workplace, it is women's personal choices and abilities to cope up with family and social pressures that decide whether they rise above the ordinary or quit the workplace prematurely. Some of the HR managers are of the opinion that only a very few women IT professionals are passionate about their jobs as compared to men (M L Taneja, VP, HR of HCL Infosystems). Because men typically do not exit careers, so all of them are bound to stick on well over 10 years. "As against that, women exit the workforce, either by choice or because of their circumstances" (Mittal of Jobs-ahead).

OBSTACLES FOR CARRIER DEVELOPMENT IN THE IT SECTOR

Several surveys have been undertaken to take stock of the common problems that women have encountered in their workplace in order to sort out the remedial measures. Prevalence survey and IBM survey have identified the following reasons for the representation of women in IT industry.

Table 2 : Barriers for Women's Progression in IT Carrier

Sl.No.	*Barriers/Issue*	*Survey report*	*Employer's remarks*
1.	Gender preference Or gender bias	Prevalence Survey	Out of 500 employers, 80 confirmed gendered preference in outsourcing or sub-contracting No =80% Yes=20%
2.	Burnout Syndrome	Prevalence Survey	The routine nature of the job forced women to switch jobs (Airlines employees)
3.	Lack of confidence	IBM Survey	Women have the ability, education and experience to handle challenging jobs, but what they lack is confidence
4.	Differences in the way men and women approach technical subjects	IBM Survey	Women possess soft skills while men have technical skills
5.	Assignment of Priorities (family Vs Prófession) Padmaja Krishnan, Xansa	Dataquest Survey	Proportion of women in IT workforce is 19%, but in senior position 6%. There is a smooth going from the fresher to the team leader and project leader stage. Growth of women IT professionals stop at the team leader stage
6.	Glass ceiling (H.R. Rajasekar VP Mistral Software)	Dataquest Survey	No discrimination towards women IT professionals
7.	Social factors (Mita Brahma, HR Head of Nucleus Software)	Dataquest Survey	Since many women manage to enter the workplace by rising above the social biases, they are strong and do well when given the opportunity
8.	Performance Robert F Danbeck V-PHR at IBM India	Dataquest Survey	Indian women make better engineers; they have qualities like strong team playing abilities, the capacity to juggle a variety of issues, flexibility and creativity in abundance.

Source: Results of the Prevalence/IBM Survey.

CONCLUSION

While technology has the potential for leveling the playing field on a global scale, it is also responsible for contributing to the digital divide. Despite modernisation and technological developments, the traditional gender roles remain firmly entrenched in all levels of the Indian society. The research question is what is the impact of the socially constructed traits on women's participation in information technology sector. As gender roles are firmly enriched into society, how women in India moved into IT labour force, and how do they navigate between these spheres? These are the serious issues which needs further nvestigations. The goal of empowerment of women however, can be achieved only if the countries and states implement some adequate policies, which emphasise on enhanced female participation in education sector to get benefited from ICT. It is saddened to note that "women constitute 50% of the population but do 60% of works, earn one-tenth of the income and own 1/100 of the assets" (http://www.uneca.org/aisi/aisi.htm#gender). The question before the entire nation is how to close the digital divide among the gender groups, caused due to various factors, including lack of resources, illiteracy and low levels of education, (APC.ORG)

REFERENCES

- Artee Aggrawal. "State initiatives in Gender Empowerment through Information and Communication Technologies-With special reference to Uttarpradesh." Giri Institute of Development Studies. Lucknow. Uttar Pradesh. 1st i4d Seminar.
- 14th October, 2003. Putra World Trade Centre. Kula Lumpur. Malaysia.
- Balaka Baruah Aggarwal. "IT Women Come to the Fore". *DATAQUEST*, Tuesday. April 22, 2003.
- Elango, R (2003). "Empowering women in Information Technology". In: The International Conference on women in the digital era: opportunities and challenges. December 10-12. Annamalai University. India.
- "Gender and ICTs: What difference does it make?" Apc.org
- Manjiri Kalghatgi and Rishiseth (2003). "Why just a few women on top?" *DATAQUEST*. Monday. June 30. 2003
- Mitter, S. 2000. "Teleworking and Teletrade in India". *Economic and Political Weekly*. 35. 26. 2241-2252.

- Rajalakshmi, R (2003). "The Emerging Trends of Women in Information Technology". In: *Women, Information and Communication Technology in India and China*. The Hawke Research Institute. Adelaide. South Australia. November 5-7. 2003.
- Rothboeck, S; Vijayabaskar, M; & Gayathri, V (2001). "Labour in the New Economy: The Case of the Indian Software Labour Market." *International Labour Organisation*, New Delhi. 2001. p. 34.
- Vittal (2003). "Strategies to empower women in the IT sector". In: The International Conference on women in the digital era: opportunities and challenges, December 10-12, Annamalai University, India.

16

Dismantling the Barriers for Women in Computing: An Indian Perspective

INTRODUCTION

The last two decades have witnessed a tremendous growth in the knowledge economy or digital economy in the developing countries including India. As these countries have skipped the agricultural and industrial revolution, they worked hard to catch up with IT revolution by building their manpower and structural infrastructure. India, a country freed from foreign yoke 55 years back, is emerging as one of the world class leaders in IT with 220,000 world class IT professionals rolling out annually. According to NASSCOM annual survey, IT industry has employed 650,000 IT professionals in 2003 representing an increase of 24.4% over the previous year. The demand for skilled manpower in IT sector is projected to be 235,000 by 2008. Though India has a large talent pool with 167,000 engineering and 1.54 millions of nonengineering graduates passing out of India' s educational institutions annually, there remains a shortage of skilled labour force. It is also estimated that the demand for IT trained manpower in India will grow up to 370,000 in the year 2008 (The Asia week May 18, 2001). The question here is. How these skill shortages are to be managed and what is the share of women in the manpower development process in the Indian sub-continent?

STATEMENT OF THE PROBLEM

It is generally believed that IT is one of the best–equal opportunity areas 'that provide wider opportunities for women to enter and succeed in this industry'. Nevertheless, the validity of these claims is yet to be established through empirical analysis. For such a transition in attitudes toward gender to take place, certain prerequisites have to be met. First, there should be an adequate proportion of technically trained female labour force.

Second, for the permeation of an alternate gender culture, there needs to be a process of de-learning and re-learning from the new work environment for both men and women. In essence, the family life of a woman and her professional commitments adapt to one another. To illustrate the gender situation in IT, one has to view 'the women in technology approach' and 'the women and technology approach'. The former approach tries to involve more women via equal access to education and employment; while the latter has a broader focus on the nature of technological work.

OBJECTIVES OF THE STUDY

This study attempts to find answers to such questions as: (i) Where are women in IT industry? How do they benefit? (ii) How has IT industry changed women's position? Is there any change in the gender division of labour as a result of women's employment in IT industry? Is there any change in women's mobility due to IT industry? (Mobility is a measure of gender relations). The findings of this study would throw light on the distribution of women's work in IT sector and illustrate the (i) position of women in various service sectors; (ii) opportunities for women in the new economy; (iii) and the impact of changing organizational structures on women's work. The gender situation is measured by adopting various common indicators like (i) the proportion of women in the various subsets of IT industry; (ii) segregation of women across the high, medium and low end jobs; (iii) types of jobs undertaken; (iv) working condition of the organisation; and the (v) facilities to learning and career progression.

TRENDS IN THE PARTICIPATION OF WOMEN IN IT INDUSTRIES

Women's position in IT sector has seen both the positive and negative trends in the last decade in the Indian sub-continent. There are studies that have highlighted the fast track that women have made in IT related industries. Women's composition in IT workforce has risen from 10% in 1993 to 18% in 1998 which is much higher than the national average of 12 percent (NASSCOM 1999). To a great surprise, the entry of women has shot upto 21 percent in 2002 (NASSCOM, 2002) and it is expected to go up to 35 percent by 2005. The following table illustrates the wide spread participation of women in the various segments of IT industries.

Table 1 : Distribution of women among the subsets of IT

Sl. No.	*IT Sector*	*F/M Ratio*	*Type of Work & Skill requirements*
1.	Software Industry	19:81	Software development not just design, customisation and adaptation of software
2.	Telecom Industry*	40:60	Technical and creative work. Required highly qualified engineers
3.	Airlines	80:20	Customer service. Required Communication, language & software skills
4.	IT-Enabled service sector	45:55	Demands linguistics and domain skill
5.	BPO**	49:51	Indian BPO is predominantly voicebased (outbound calls)

Source: DATAQUEST, April 22, 2003.

The high rate of women employees in ITES and BPO sector is a welcome change from the low 12.5 percent women being employed in IT industry. According to Dataquest-IDC survey in October 2002, the highest number of women was employed by NIIT at 29 percent while Rolta India employed the lowest number of women at four percent. Top software companies like Infosys employs 17 percent women, TCS employs 20 percent and Wipro employs 19 percent women. The massive incorporation of women into paid work and their positions of authority in IT industry have improved their social status. Though the above statistics has shown a rosy picture of women in this sector, a further investigation is required to know the existing situation in various regions of IT related sector in the country.

GENDER COMPOSITION OF IT WORKFORCE IN FIRMS OF DIFFERENT SIZE

The composition of male and female IT workers in firms of different size and activities needs to be analyzed in order to identify their level of participation. State-level survey reports indicated that the employment opportunities opened for women are relatively higher in the IT sector when compared to the other industries. Out of the 28,109 employees surveyed from 156 firms in Mumbai, it was noticed that the percentage of female workers were 32.1 percent in IT firms and 12 percent in other firms. Not only in terms of numbers but also in positions of power and authority, women' s status is higher in IT related industries than in the non-IT sectors. It is evident that IT industries have opened a gateway for women's entry as well as for their career progression compared to other non-IT sectors. Figure-1 is illustrative of the advantageous situation that women have experienced in the software sector than in other traditional banking and media sectors.

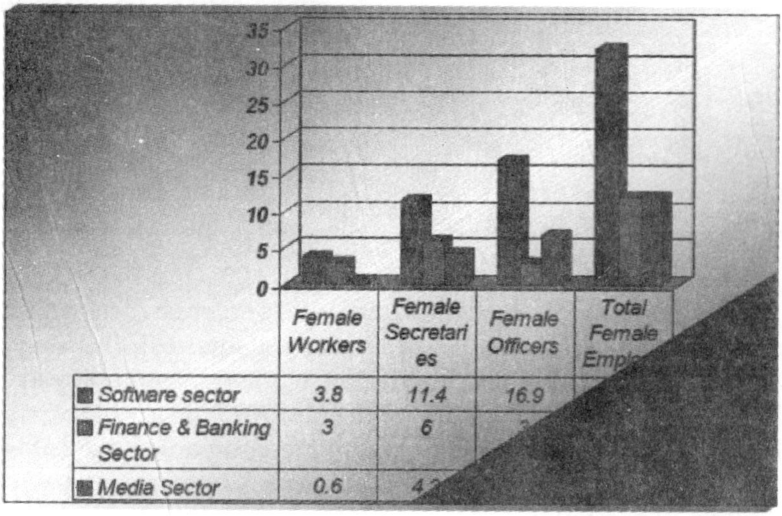

Source: Teleworking, Economic and Political Weekly, 2002

Fig. 1 : Distribution of Women Workers among IT and Non-IT Sectors

The next issue that needs to be addressed is whether IT sector offers equality of opportunities for both men and women in their roles and responsibilities. Before investing the response of the industries to the gender factor, it is necessary to find out the transformation that has taken place in the areas of gender technology relations, traditional gender roles in the society, attitudinal changes in the gender groups with respect to their professional choices, social, political and economic pressures on gender participation in the national economy etc. For centuries together women were allowed to play a secondary role both in the domestic and public spheres. But the sudden changes that have taken place in the areas of globalisation, media, knowledge management and the compulsion on the part of the individual nations to response to the changing situation directly and indirectly enforce them to develop their human capital irrespective of gender, caste or creed. Now the question before us is, does this changing global situation have brought any positive change on women's situation in this new economy. Since the key pillars of this new economy (knowledge based industries) is based on expertise in infostructure, corporate intelligence, high-tech infrastructure etc, it is interesting to find out: Where do women figure into this competitive industry? Have they been able to participate on equal plane with their male counter parts in all spheres of IT based industries? What were the factors both contributing and deterring their progress in this 'sunrise industry'.

ILO has recently undertaken a survey to identify where are women in this most competitive industry. It has analysed the gender structure in more than 100 IT firms located at the major metros in the country. The main purpose of this survey was to find out the type of firms where women are mostly accommodated and the kind of activities that women are involved in the software development. Figure-2 explains the areas where women have dominated in IT sector.

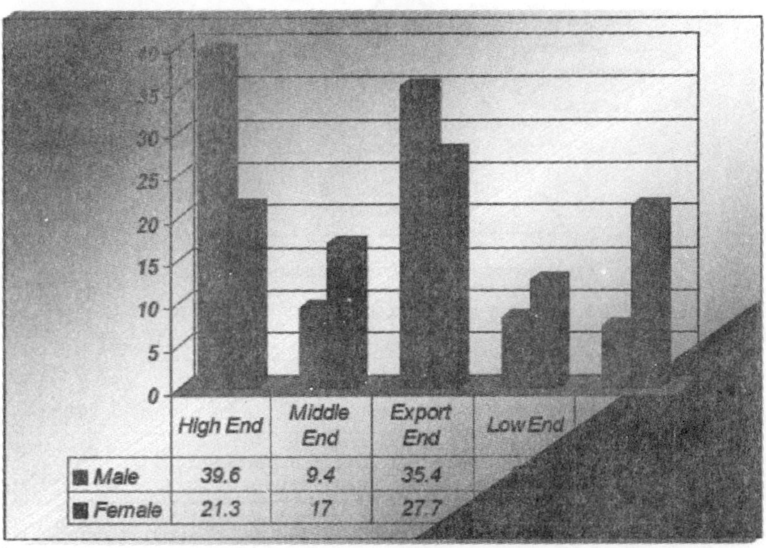

Source: International Labour organisation, New Delhi, 2001.

Fig. 2 : Distribution of Women in IT Firms of Various Types and Size.

It is noted that a major segment of women are clustered in the low-end jobs; while a minor segment of women are found at the high end jobs reflecting the gender divide in IT industry. Though women are better represented in IT sector, they have not assumed significant role and status. Most of them have been concentrated in the lower strata of job categories such as coding and programming; and only a minor percentage are presented in the development part of IT. ILO report clearly indicated that the high end firms that undertake software products, R&D, turnkey solutions and strategic technical alliances prefer to employ more men than women. The professional demands in this area of work are mostly engineering graduates, Ph.Ds and post-graduates with technical multi-skilling. The proportion of women with such professional background are less and, therefore, they are relegated to the less prestigious and low-paid jobs. For instance Figure, IT enabled and domestic end firms that perform low skilled, routinised and back-office jobs employed more women, since they require only certificate holders with pure technical, coding and maintenance skills. Women's representations outnumber their male counterparts in these low-skilled and low-paid jobs. The male and female ratio of IT workers in the organisational hierarchy is diagrammatically shown below:

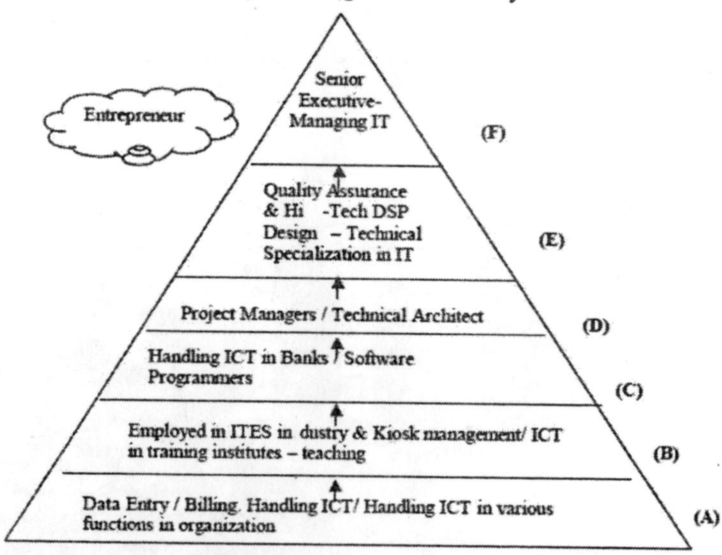

Source: WICT in India and China.htm.

Fig. 3 : Women in IT Pyramidal growth and presence from grass-root level of ICT.

The above situation supports the hypothesis that IT industry is not in any way different from other industries and women have not enjoyed any special status or privilege in this industry. It is noted from the above diagram that the higher the hierarchy, the lower will be the number of women and vice-versa. The reasons for this under-representation may be owing to various educational, social, political, cultural and individual factors and, therefore, efforts should be made to analyse the gender technology variables such as the status of (i) gender socialisation, (ii) gender bias in access to ICT, (iii) gender preference to technical education, (iv) parental encouragement, (v) availability of role models, (vi) support from family and institutions and the (vii) cost of high-tech education etc. Among these various factors that deter women from occupying positions of authority and power, let us give priority to the educational factors at the first instance.

TRENDS IN THE PARTICIPATION OF WOMEN IN THE TECHNICAL EDUCATION

Literacy Level of Girls and Women in India

It is widely observed that lack of access to basic education and literacy for girls and women in India is the foremost obstacle to their access to IT job opportunities. Education and literacy are low for both men and women, with women's literacy rate at only 51.4%, compared to men's 74.5%. While enrollment rates have increased at the primary level for boys and girls, upper primary enrollment drops off, particularly for girls. Moreover, only 48% of girls stay in the system until the secondary level. These statistics also vary widely between specific states within the country, where

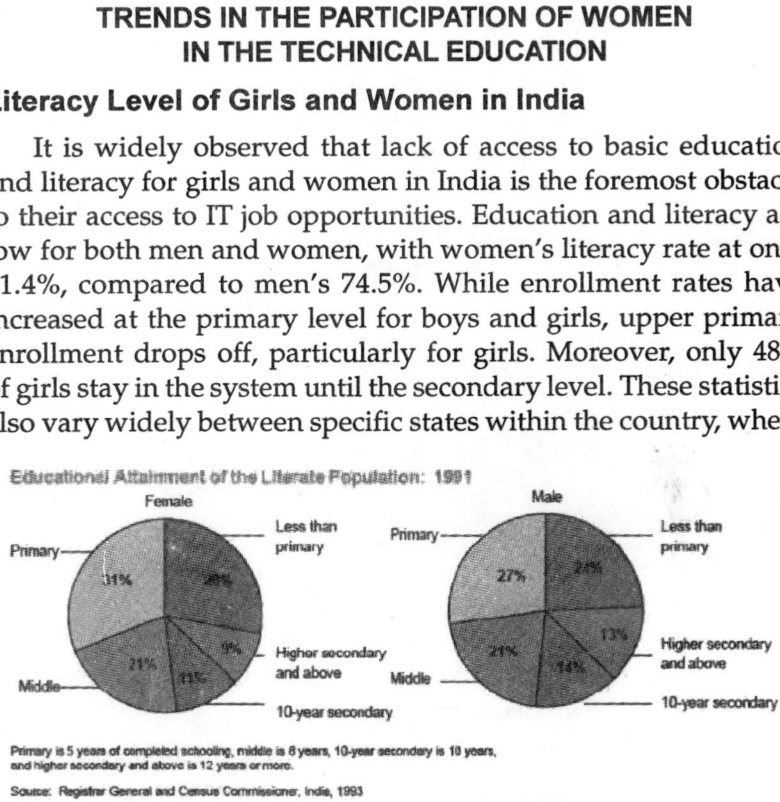

Fig. 4 : Literacy level of Indian Women According to 1991 Census.

particularly the Northern and Eastern states have the lowest health and education indicators. The following census substantiates this statement.

Computer and Media Literacy Level of Women in India

As most Indian women lack literacy and basic education, more advanced or specialised IT education is out of the reach of the poorer women and only realistic for those middle class women and elite who can afford it in some form. Currently, IT education and training is available in degree programs in engineering colleges and universities and in diploma and certificate courses at polytechnics, and commercial and government training centers. Due to cost and selectivity of admissions at the universities and engineering colleges, most Indian women are able to access IT training through training centers or women's polytechnics. However, not surprisingly, the quality of the training varies with each option. As the job market has become more competitive, certificates from training centers, or even diplomas in IT subjects from polytechnics, often do not equip job seekers with the competitive skills to guarantee a job, not to mention a well-paid job. Moreover, the majority of women pursue their studies in the

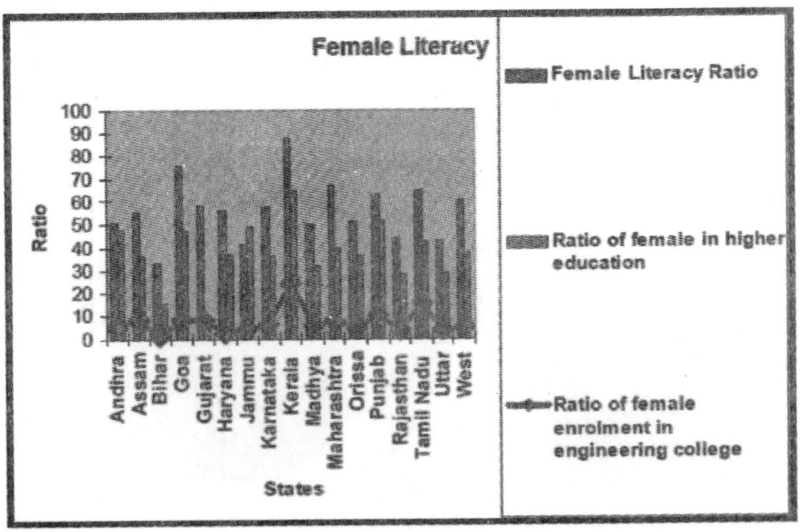

Source: i4donline Events.htm.

Fig. 5 : Proportion of Women' s Participation in IT Education.

humanities and business rather than IT related fields. Women make up 88% of the students in the arts, science and commerce, while education and law account for 4% of women students, and engineering accounts only for 1%. Figure-4 illustrates the status of women' s education in general and engineering education in particular.

A close examination of the graph clearly indicates that the states like Kerala (24.19%), Tamil Nadu (15.35%), Punjab (10.36%), Andhra Pradesh, and Maharashtra are marching ahead in the field of ICT while the states like Bihar, Uttar Pradesh, Orissa are lagging behind. Uttar Pradesh, with a low female literacy level, low female enrolment in higher education, and low female enrolment in technical colleges is still lacking behind in providing basic infrastructure to utilise full potentials of ICT. The lopsided gender ratio in IT industry begins in academic institutes itself, as "there are far fewer women candidates as compared to men in engineering and management institutes". (Dataquest, 2002)

NATIONAL LEVEL INITIATIES TO INVOLVE MORE WOMEN IN IT SECTOR

The marginalisation of Women in IT Education and IT employment in India is a major concern among the Indian administrators. To stay in the global competition, human resource development becomes the area of top priority. State-level programmes have been launched to train and develop IT skills among the women community based on the market demand. For instance, Government of India through its "National Programme for Education of Girls in Elementary Level (NPEGEL) with an outlay of US$ 230 Million and reach in 21 States has created enough synergy to improve rural female literacy and gender gap in the educationally backward blocks. Institutions like NIIT through its "SWIFT JYOTHI FOR WOMEN" programme target one million non-computer literate women in India and educate them on ICT. The efforts of CISCO, HP, IBM and Datamation can't be under-estimated in this regard. Internet-enabled "cyber incubators" are emerging to provide counseling and training support to larger numbers of small businesses over long distances from multiple sources. The encouragement from the government sector; the financial support from the nationalised banks; and the scholarships programmes introduced by leading IT industries serve as an impetus for both men and women to enter into this course in large numbers. For instance, in the year 2001, nearly 7929 colleges for general education and 2223 engineering and professional colleges were enrolling 36.9% of women in higher education (degree and above level). Fig. 4 indicates the increase in the enrollment of girls for higher education.

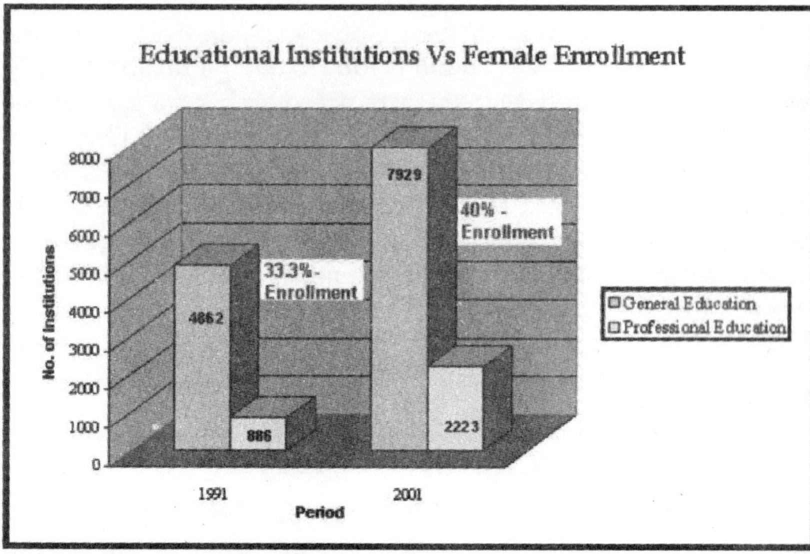

Fig. 6 : Growth Pattern of Women in Higher Education.

One of the major problems faced by women is access to IT education. It is seen that access to IT is limited to a certain class of women only. Access to IT education and training is highly skewed towards urban centered, English speaking masses with a high socio-economic status. The central government plans, to upgrade the higher education institutions providing IT education and training, will establish more IITs throughout the country and improve the regional engineering colleges. These efforts should strengthen the caliber of IT training available to Indian elites, but will have little impact on the majority of women. The major criticism is that while women form the majority among the deprived community, the government has not taken concrete efforts to uplift their status in technology. The way things are moving would only widen the gender based digital divide and it is a serious concern which calls for attention of the policy makers. As rightly observed by Kofi Annan the Secretary-General of the

UN at the first world submit on information society that the so called digital divide is actually several divides: a technological divide in infrastructure, a language divide with much of the content in English, a gender divide for women in many nations, a commercial divide where e-commerce reaches only some. Indeed the digital divide is the biggest non-tariff barrier to world trade today. It is difficult to captivate the digital divide precisely. From a policy angle, a specific absolute cut off line may be drawn up to denote the minimum level of IT knowledge required for any individual, especially the women, the most suppressed and deprived community. Any shortfall denotes the distance to be covered by the individual suggesting that the state should initiate suitable steps to rectify the situation. This perhaps opens up a new area of further research (Elango, 2003).

Status of National and State-Level IT Policies on Gender Issues

Policies formulated in this direction are also silent on gender issues. For instance, in 2000, the Indian government created a 'Working Group on Information Technology for Masses'. However, the working group's report with recommendations for how to broaden access to "the common man" does not specifically mention women. The recommendations call for activities related to access, education, and awareness raising of the importance and benefits of IT opportunities that if implemented, which will also benefit women, however, targeted strategies for ensuring female access and training are not discussed. To close the gender

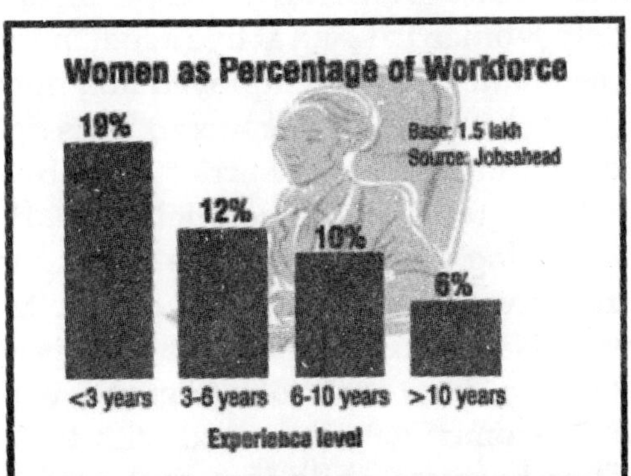

Fig. 7.

divide, gender responsive e-governance should be implemented. Funds should be raised to support women's initiatives in ICT base entrepreneurship and other economic activities. Digital marginalisation has to be addressed squarely at the policy level. This necessitates more and more of social inclusion process by way of conscious state policies adopted in favour of promoting women' s education and participation in IT sector. Digital divide distribution and IT deprivation index is to be developed to see the level of access that women gained in the digital economy. The following explains how the strength of women gets decreased in the IT field over the years due to want of support system.

However, it needs to be realised that training in ICT by itself cannot be an answer and elixir to all problems facing women development but it does bring new information resources and can open new communication channels for the marginalised communities.

IMPACT OF SOCIAL AND CULTURAL FACTORS

Vittal (2003) observed that in order to empower women in IT sector in the real sense, it is necessary to investigate the social impact of IT sector on the women's community. Empowering women in the real sense implies that their position should be strengthened in the family and in the society; adequate support system is to be built up both at the private and in the public spheres. This requires a lot of cultural and attitudinal changes in the mind-set of the people to accept women's progression. In this context, Mr.Vittal has indicated the emergence of 'metro-sexual men', men who are sharing the responsibility of the family which might help women to be an active agent in the IT workforce. The drop-out level after getting employed and not able to sustain employment has been a matter of concern. This drop-out effect is because of the cultural and social barrier faced by even educated women today. It is a fact that women deliver 100% both at work and at home. Entering a marriage phase or encountering a child birth forces many women to drop out of IT. "Marriage-Baby" phase for women is the most crucial part of their work life which forced them to drop from their jobs. Figure-5 explains how the drop-out rates of women gets increased with their marriage and child-birth. It is because childcare and housework remain women's responsibilities, irrespective of her income, educational level or employment. This places a great burden on women and restricts women's choices in terms of better job opportunities. Though women employed in the IT industry are relatively free from domestic drudgery, this is a class-specific phenomenon restricted to a few in high level jobs whose domestic responsibilities have been transferred to women of a lower economic class. The opportunities offered by IT have only benefited a privileged few. The above table shows that only a few women rule in the workplace well into marriage. Married women outnumber men in low-experience categories, but in 10+ years' —the stage at which serious seniority should come in —a large number of women either opt out of their careers, or accept less demanding roles. The Jobs-ahead survey also substantiates the fact that the drop-out rate of women increases with their advancement in experience. There seems to be a negative correlation that exists between the women's presence in IT workforce and their years of experience. Lesser the year of experience, larger will be the proportion of women and vice-versa. Women were not able to continue their job with sustained interest due to various interruptions that happened in their life which force them to drop out from their aspiration of building a better career in IT.

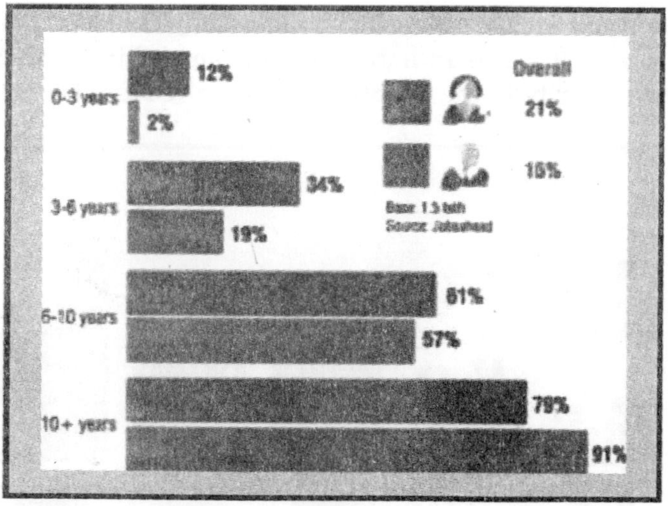

Source: Dataquest Jobs-ahead Survey.

Fig. 8 : Socio-cultural Factors Depriving Women From IT Workforce.

To overcome this, the society at large should bring about proper understanding in family life and support work-going women in shouldering some of her burdens. In nuclear families, husband has to support this cause. Organisations have to bring about more pronounced flexi timing at work, even to the extent of supporting women to "work from Home", with investment in ICT infrastructure and flexible compensation packages. This trend is already noticed to tap the vast potential that experienced women would have which otherwise could go untapped, if they drop out due to cultural and social pressure. This emerging trend shall certainly bring about a substantial decline in women being unemployed and getting back to household chores.

The social barriers are so strong and women, who manage to enter workplaces by rising above societal biases, are probably very strong and, therefore, do well when given the opportunity. (Data Quest, 2002)

WHY THERE ARE JUST A FEW WOMEN AT THE TOP OF THE CORPORATE HIERARCHY?

A study of the entries getting into Dataquest magazine reveals that there were no women CEOs getting into the Top 10 IT companies and this happened in an industry where women are supposed to stand shoulder to shoulder with the men (Figure-6). What is it that keeps Indian women from making it to the top rung of authority in the country's IT sector? Or is it IT sector that

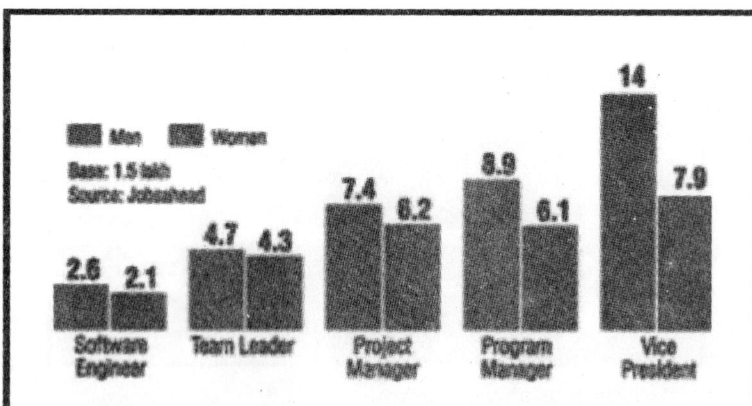

Fig. 9. Status of Women in the Organisational Hierarchy.

has not recognised and rewarded women well enough for their efforts? Or will maturity only come with age and experience, and it is because of the industry's nascent youth that women are yet to reach the top rung? Or is there a glass ceiling and despite whatever is said, is it not really a level playing field as far as women are concerned?

The other perspective for the lower status of women at the top of the corporate hierarchy can be explained by the fact that the number of women entering IT industry has been lower than men," (Balu Doraisamy, president of HP India). It is argued that the lopsided gender ratio begins in academic institutes itself (Mita Brahma, HR Head of Nucleus Software). It is further stated that more than impediments at the workplace, it is women's personal choices and abilities to cope up with family and social pressures that decide whether they rise above the ordinary or quit the workplace prematurely. Some of the HR managers of the opinion that only a very few women IT professionals are passionate about their jobs as compared to men (M L Taneja, V-P, HR of HCL Infosystems). Because men typically do not exit careers, so all of them are bound to stick on well over 10 years. "As against that, women exit the workforce, either by choice or because of their circumstances" (Mittal of Jobsahead).

OBSTACLES FOR CARRIER DEVELOPMENT IN IT SECTOR

Several surverys have been undertaken to take stock of the common problems that women have encountered in their workplace in order to sort out the remedial measures. According to the 'prevalence survey' over 80% of the employers said that there is no discrimination and there is no gender preference. Another survey reported that out of the 500 employers interviewed, about 80 employers said that there was gender preference in terms of sub-contracting or outsourcing, out of which 47 stated their gender preference. Out of 47, 7 preferred women and 40 prefered men. If there was no gender preference for outsourcing, one would imagine there would be no gender preference for employment. Software is the only sector, barring one or two instances, which said that they prefere women. As regards gender bias, nearly 40 out of 500 (8%) affirmed gender bias against women.

Table: 10: Barriers for Women's Progression in IT Carrier

Sl.No.	*Barriers/Issue*	*Survey report*	*Employers remarks*
1.	Gender preference Or gender bias	Prevalence Survey	Out of 500 employers, 80 confirmed gendered preference in outsourcing or subcontracting No = 80% Yes=20%
2.	Burnout Syndrome	Prevalence Survey	The routine nature of the job forced women to switch jobs (Airlines employees)
3.	Lack of confidence	IBM Survey	Women have the ability, education and experience to handle challenging jobs, but what they lack is confidence
4.	Differences in the way men and women approach technical subjects	IBM Survey	Women possess soft skills while men have technical skills
5.	Assignment of Priorities (family Vs Profession) PadmajaKrishnan, Xansa	Dataquest Survey	Proportion of women in the IT workforce is 19%, but at senior position 6%. There is a smooth going from the fresher to the team leader and project leader stage. Growth of women IT professionals stop at the team leader stage
6.	Glass ceiling (H.R. Rajasekar VP Mistral Software)	Dataquest Survey	No discrimination towards women IT professionals
7.	Social factors (Mita Brahma, HR Head of Nucleus Software)	Dataquest Survey	Since many women manage to enter the workplace by rising above the social biases, they are strong and do well when given the opportunity
8.	Performance Robert F Danbeck VP-HR at IBM India	Dataquest Survey	Indian women make better engineers; they have qualities like strong team playing abilities, the capacity to juggle a variety of issues, flexibility and creativity in abundance.

Source: Results of the Prevalence/IBMSurvey.

Moreover, access to jobs is more or less restricted to the urban based upper class youth. What are the advantages that women enjoy in the new forms of work? It reduces the hard choices that women have to make. The strategies to draw more women lies in improving the manner in which work is conducted without jeopardising the quality of workers' lives. The following table illustrates the barriers that women have encountered in their efforts to progress in their career in IT sector

CONCLUSION

While technology has the potential for leveling the playing field on a global scale, it is also responsible for contributing to the digital divide. Despite modernisation and technological developments, the traditional gender roles remain firmly entrenched in all levels of the Indian society. The research question is what is the impact of the socially constructed traits on women's participation in information technology sector. As gender roles are firmly enriched into the society, how women in India moved into IT labour force, and how do they navigate between these spheres? These are the serious issues which needs further investigations. The goal of empowerment of women however, can be achieved only if the countries and states implement some adequate policies, which emphasize on enhanced female participation in education sector to get benefited from ICT. It is saddened to note that "women constitute 50% of the population but do 60% of works, earn one-tenth of the income and own 1/100 of the assets" (http://www.uneca.org/aisi/aisi.htm#gender). The question before the entire nation is how to close the digital divide among the gender groups which caused due to various factors including lack of resources, illiteracy and low levels of education. (APC.ORG).

REFERENCES

- Balaka Baruah Aggarwal, " IT Women Come to the Fore". *DATAQUEST*, Tuesday. April 22, 2003.
- "Teleworking in India" "Economic and Political Weekly, 2002".
- Rothboeck, S; Vijayabaskar, M; & Gayathri, V (2001). "Labour in the New Economy: The Case of the Indian Software Labour Market". International Labour Organisation. New Delhi. 2001, p. 34.

- Rajalakshmi, R. (2003), "The Emerging Trends of Women in Information Technology". In: *Women, Information and Communication Technology in India and China*. The Hawke Research Institute. Adelaide. South Australia. November 5-7, 2003.
- "Gender and ICTs: What difference does it make?" Apc.org.
- Artee Aggrawal. "State initiatives in Gender Empowerment through Information and Communication Technologies - With special reference to Uttarpradesh Giri Institute of Development Studies", Lucknow. Uttar Pradesh. 1st i4d Seminar. 14th October, 2003. Putra World Trade Centre. Kula Lumpur. Malaysia.
- Elango, R (2003). "Empowering women in Information Technology". In: The International Conference on women in the digital era: opportunities and challenges. December 10-12. Annamalai University. India.
- Vittal (2003). "Strategies to empower women in the IT sector". In: The International Conference on women in the digital era: opportunities and challenges. December 10-12. Annamalai University. India.
- Manjiri Kalghatgi and Rishiseth (2003). "Why just a few women on top? *DATAQUEST*. Monday. June 30. 2003.

17

An Overview of E-governance in the Educational Sector: A Gender Perspective

ABSTRACT

As the importance for e-governance has heightened with the spread of internet usage for the past two decades, concerns for information poverty for women as it is widely observed that women are at the bottom of the digital divide due to the existing socio-economic variables that are unfavourable for women. The paper sheds light into such phenomenon and introduces various women-friendly e-governance initiatives in the education sector, including government initiatives for imparting basic computer literacy and for improving women's education in ICT, NGOs' initiatives toward educating women in ICT and efforts of the IT companies in improving ICT education of girls and women.

Key words: *e-governance. digital divide, information poverty, gender, ICT, computer literacy*

INTRODUCTION

E-governance has been in the global agenda for about two decades. International conferences, workshops, projects and programmes are centering around this phenomena invariably in all the countries of the world. The common concern is (i) how to make this 'knowledge society' or 'information society' a place for all; (ii) how to balance the 'information haves[1] and 'information have-nots'; (iii) how to close the digital divide caused by the technological revolution? As rightly stated by the UN's Administrative Committee, 'we are profoundly concerned at the deepening maldistribution of access to resources, and opportunities in the information society. This widening inequalities leads to a new type of poverty called information poverty that leads to a new form of electronic feudalism. The question before us is: (i) what should we do to realise the desirable scenario? (ii) how can we help the millions of deprived in the country? (iii) how can we use digital technologies to improve their livelihood? At the same time, we must be conscious that the new technologies are going to stay; no one can wipe them away. We must also realise that, it would be impossible to provide the same level of access to ICT tools for all the people. The slogans like 'information for all', 'IT for all' will remain only a slogan as long as the other socio-economic variables remains same. How are we going to deal with this skeptical situation? The cyber-optimists say that e-governance is one of the best models to bridge the digital divide and to establish the real democracy. Yet another critical issue among the promoters of e-governance is: "Is e-governance a gender issue or a women's issue.'

There is a growing concern that women are at the bottom of the digital divide and the question is how to leverage them and to make them be equal partners in this knowledge society. The major concerns related to gender issues are:

(i) What are the gender specific antecedents that impede women's access to government information and public services (literacy and education, language, time, cost, geographical location of facilities, social and cultural norms, women's IT skills etc.)?

(ii) What strategies could be adopted to give access to government schemes and making woman aware of their rights? And how to create political awareness among the woman along with IT skills and to make them participate in e-administration?

(iii) What efforts have been made to incorporate women in e-governance initiatives undertaken by the government, private and corporate sectors?

(iv) What kind of women-targeted technologies, programmes and training modules have been initiated, to increase women's access to government services?

PROBLEM STATEMENT

In the last couple of years, e-governance has become a priority area of many Asian governments resulting in the implementation of various programs that apply ICT in delivering government services and promoting transparency and accountability. Beyond these goals however, e-governance is being more closely defined along the concepts of governance. The delivery of government services and information to the public, using electronic means, is differentiated as e-government. e-governance, on the other hand, is defined as the transformation of (governance) processes (resulting from) the continual and exponential introduction into the society of more advanced digital technologies. e-governance focuses on how these new technologies can be used to strengthen the public's voice as a force to reshape the democratic processes, and refocus the management, structure, and oversight of government to better serve the public interest.

Defined in this way, e-governance becomes significant in the exercise of citizenship and direct public participation in government activities. Both are key elements in women's empowerment and achievement of gender equality. It can potentially bring forth new concepts of citizenship, both in terms of needs and responsibilities. For many governments in Asia, however, allowing e-governance to make it possible for their citizens to truly communicate with government, participate in policy-making and strengthen democratic processes remain a huge challenge. Three barriers immediately come to mind. First, the serious gaps in universal access to ICT as a means of participation; second, the complete absence of gender equality consideration in e-governance plans of governments and; third, the restrictions on civil liberties and freedom of expression imposed by undemocratic and fundamentalist states that seriously put into question citizen's access to information and participation in political processes. e-governance policy of Indian sub-continent is a good case study that illustrates the first two barriers. Though e-governance plan has been in vogue for more than 2 decades in the government administration, a paradigm shift in the focus of e-governance plan takes place in the early part of the 20th century.

The e-governance plan of India has set the enabling policy, institutional infrastructure and environment, direction, priorities and benchmarks for computerisation of key government operations and activities over the next five to ten years. It is envisioned as the blueprint for an electronic bureaucracy that is widely and readily accessible to its constituency. However, like in any other developing counties, it also remains silent on the gender factor. In other words, e-governance policy framework is gender blind and totally devoid of any provisions that address gender gaps in access, education, government services and political processes. Policy-makers have not thought of factoring in gender in their e-governance projects at all. There was very little understanding that e-services may entail specific planning requirements that take into consideration women's and men's access, knowhow and control over ICT. It is to be noted that without explicit attention to gender-based inequalities, men and women will not have equal opportunities to enter the information age. Without explicit gender analysis and incorporation of the results into policies, programmes and projects, it is unlikely that the results will have positive impact on women. The benefits of ICT may bypass women even if their countries develop adequate information infrastructure and service delivery (Marcelle, 2000). Without direct intervention, gender equality will not occur. This study is an attempt to examine the gender sensitiveness of e-government programmes and projects in India with special reference to the educational sector. We must realise that developing and implementing gender sensitive ICT policies, along with gender sensitive ICT capacity building programmes represents the best and the quickest route for women to participate in the digital economy.

e-GOVERNANCE AND GENDER

e-governance in particular is seen as important for women and as one way to empower them (Hafkin and Taggart 2001). Gender responsive governance is the active and meaningful participation of women in all levels of decision-making and ensuring greater transparency and accountability in government. e-governance ensures equality in ICT access, knowledge and use cutting across all races, sexes and classes. It also offers the basic ingredients required to participate in the information society viz: (i) technology fluency; (ii) mastery of analytical skills; (iii) ability to use technology innovatively; and (iv) ability to develop, find and use information and knowledge to improve one's life and expand one's choices. The Geneva Declaration of Principles acknowledges women as important stakeholders of e-governance and information society. It states: "We affirm that development of ICTs provides enormous opportunities for women, who should be an integral part of, and key actors, in the Information Society. We are committed to ensuring that the Information Society enables women's empowerment and their full participation on the basis on [sic] equality in all spheres of the society and in all decision-making processes. To this end, we should mainstream a gender equality perspective and use ICTs as a tool to that end." However, studies have reported that achieving gender equality in e-governance will be remote in the absence of social re-engineering and changes in the social structures. Currently, women's dealings with the State, at the local or higher levels, as well as their participation in it, are hampered by many factors, including time constraints, low literacy levels, low awareness and social norms (Agarwal 1994).

A gendered division of labour ensures that household duties have to be fulfilled by women, limiting the time they can devote to activities outside the domestic sphere. Low literacy levels restrict the information that women can access and use. The gendered segregation of community spaces and restricted freedom of movement ensure that public interactions, and awareness of public affairs, is limited. Gendered behaviour patterns in most communities stress that women be subservient and not assertive, adversely affecting their ability to participate in decision-making, to voice their dissent and to control their lives. The involvement of women in local bodies is very low and, even when they are a part of these bodies, women's participation in decision-making is much less than that of the men. Women, especially from communities where male-female interaction is restricted, require male mediation to interact with government officials, the majority of whom are male. The other critical factors that retard promotion of women friendly e-Governance are: poor access of women to education and economic opportunities, inadequate number of women IT professionals, and inadequate political willingness for implementing gender sensitive concepts. There has been very little research done to understand the information needs of women in terms of the strategic information they wish to receive or produce. It is to be remembered that only a knowledge-sharing model which puts women in a greater control over the kind of information they need and produce should be considered in order to empower women. A vast majority of the e-governance initiatives place greater emphasis on ICT rather than on gender which gives the impression that only citizens with technological competence would take part in this new form of governance. Adequate measures are to be taken to educate the citizens on the use of technology effectively. "The use of ICT cannot grow in a vacuum. It needs complementary policies and programs in education, business, regulatory framework that can foster the growth of ICT. Without holistic and global strategies, the use of ICT will remain in the hands of ajjtlyileged few". In an interview with an IT Minister of India, Ric-rfard Heeks, an e-governance expert based at Britan's Manchester Versity, remarked "At present, IT is reinforcing more than attacking inequality; men are benefiting more than women; the rich are benefiting more than the poor. The challenge is to create conditions for reversing the polarities; but this is a task for social movements more than computers." The implication is that gender factor in e-governance should be given adequate attention in order to achieve social cohesion. The other factors that need to be considered in planning the e-governance initiatives are the (i) gender specific barriers that restricted access to ICT (high access costs); (ii) limited access to learn new skills (lack of information and encouragement to apply for ICT training: (iii) insufficient networks and perception of ICT as a male sector; (iv) differences among women in access to ICT as determined by geographical factor (urban-rural areas), family status and age; (v) absence of sex-segregated data for more comprehensive evaluation of the gender digital divide; (vi) want of women-related information/absence of women centered knowledge repositories and (vii) adoption of appropriate technologies.

The following approaches are required to facilitate women to be active in the new society:

(i) creating an enabling environment (telecom regulation; ICT delivery);

(ii) developing content which speaks of women's concerns and reflects their local knowledge;

(iii) education of girls and women in STEM;

(iv) promoting increased employment in IT sector and use of ICTs for women's SME;

(v) implementing e-governance strategies which are accessible to women and promoting women's lobbying advocacy activities.

e-GOVERNANCE INITIATIVES IN THE ACADEMIA FROM GENDER PERSPECTIVES

The e-governance initiatives in the educational sector could be seen from the following two approaches viz: (i) ICT Development in the academia and (ii) ICT for Development in the community. Both these approaches are seen from gender perspective.

ICT Development in the academia refers to building media and digital facilities to support institutional functions, along with an academic and research programmes that prepare students to function effectively in an information society - in both the public and the private sectors;

ICT for Development refers to the educational institution applying ICT in programmes outside its walls in the service of communities and the nation. It means extending their knowledge and learning resources to the surrounding communities and to other populations in the region. This includes translating, adapting, localising and re-packaging information from external sources to fit the agronomic and cultural characteristics of those local communities. This function is especially vital to the worldwide priorities identified in the Millennium Development Goals.

For instance, Indira Gandhi National Open University (IGNOU) has made a landmark in adopting the high level information and communication technology for networking and sharing information among women groups. Under the Satellite Instructional Television and Experiment (SITE) programme which was considered to be the first application of ICT for education and development programme (1970s)-IGNOU has telecasted its primary education and training programme to 2,330 villages in economically disadvantaged regions in India. It has also offered women-specific contents and information which were mostly concerned with agriculture, health, hygiene and family planning practices. Some satellite-based one-way video and two-way audio experiment was started in support of education, mass literacy and human resource development during the 1990s. These applications included distance education programmes ranging from engineering to maternal health, rural development programmes covering such topics as the role of women in afforestation, programmes for women and children, programmes supporting panchayat raj (local community self-government) and industrial training. The IGNOU's training Certificate Programme "Empowering Women through Self Help Groups" prepare a cadre/network of master trainers for the sustainability of the grassroot/low literacy women groups. The objective of the programme is to empower the change agents to function more effectively as trainers and community organisers in helping set up SHGs and addressing gender issues. A unique feature of this project is the establishment of the Direct Satellite Receiving System at 150 centres all over the country for regular teleconferencing with this disadvantaged section of society.

GOVERNMENT INITIATIVES FOR IMPARTING BASIC COMPUTER LITERACY

Most of the countries in the world are rapidly moving into the information society with varying degrees of e-readiness. India has initiated some catalytic, pro-active and enabling steps to spread computer literacy by undertaking such programmes as (i) enabling literacy and education for the masses; (ii) fulfilling local information needs of the people; (iii) educating citizens about their duties; and (iv) enabling women in technology. The first programme aims at spreading computer literacy to the school teachers and students besides equipping the schools with computer labs. The second programme aims at establishing networking and knowledge sharing centers such as 'citizen service points[1], cyber cafes and information kiosks in order to establish the linkages between the government and the citizens using the internet facility. The third one aims at educating the citizens on various welfare programmes. In addition to these generic programmes, the Indian government also has come out with a large programme for promoting women's literacy. For instance, an IT literacy programme specially directed towards spreading literacy among women was launched by the year 2001. Government also has encouraged the NGOs to set up B2C (business to consumer) and B2B (business to business) websites to promote interest of the women doing business in the state.

GOVERNMENT INITATIVES FOR IMPROVING WOMEN'S EDUCATION IN ICT

The UN World Conference on Women, Beijing and Beijing +5, Gender Caucus of WSIS 2003 and many other national and international forums have reaffirmed the need to focus on gender equality issues through ICT use, since the lack of access to ICT is considered as one of the major impediments towards achieving an information society. It is also recommended that 'government and other stakeholders should provide the necessary conditions to ensure women's equal access to information and knowledge as well as ensuring their equal role as producers and decision-makers, in all aspects related to the shaping of ICT policies and frameworks'. Government of India has taken conscious efforts to build the technical manpower through such initiatives as: (i) upgrading Industrial Training Institutes for providing training of skills for data entry, marketing, transcription, call centres, content creation and data processing; (ii) expanding Training Centre for the Unemployed Educated Youths; (iii) establishing IT Open University; (iv) setting up premier Indian Institute of Information Technology to impart high quality IT education and training to the people and (v) setting up Digital Media Library that would be a central storehouse of digitalised data containing government records, industry information and information on education, tourism and archaeology. In the year 2001, nearly 7929 colleges for general education and 2223 engineering and professional colleges were enrolling 36.9% of women in higher education.

NGOS INTIATIVES TOWARDS EDUCATING WOMEN IN ICT

The role of NGOs in proliferating the computer literacy among the rural women is noteworthy. Specific mention may be made about the initiatives taken by Datamation, MSSRF and SEWA. Datamation establishes that education and awareness through information is an indispensable input in the process of empowerment to facilitate women's decision- making capacities and capabilities to participate in governance. SEWA Bank in India uses the development communication wing of Indian Space Research Organisation (ISRO) to remote villages. Discussions on topics like women in development, nursery raising and forestry management, savings and credit are beamed to different villages through the use of satellite cable. The viewers can phone their enquiries which are answered promptly by a panel of experts. The M.S. Swaminathan Foundation (MSSRF) has established a high tech village information center in the state of Pondicherry in India. Villagers congregate around the center to get connected with the local news, Women get information about the markets and health from this center. Distance education is yet another significant areas where women stand to gain tremendously. Internet and television broadcasts open up avenues for women to continue with their education at their own pace and from the confines of their homes. The project 'Putting ICTs in the Hands of Poor Women' was initiated by Datamation (NGO) in 2002. It is one of the initiatives, which has been recognised as the 'Most Promising Social Entrepreneurs 2002' by Digital Partners. The Seelampur project entails 'Putting ICTs in the hands of the Muslim Women' in a slum area in Delhi has directly linked the use of ICTs to the alleviation of their poverty. This project seeks to modernise the vocational skills of Muslim women in the area in bead-making, dress-making, carpentry, and embroidery and lend marketing support to help them enhance their incomes. Datamation is in the process of developing 50 multimedia CDs focusing on skills enhancement, women's empowerment, and life skills. The CDs will be shown via the existing cable network. The project entitled IT Enabled Education for Rural Women (Tel-Nek) was initiated by an International NGO in 2001 The content of the course includes, Windows basics, MS -Office. Pagemaker, Graphic Designing etc., Local language softwares like Nudi, Baraha, i-Leap along with hardware basics, e-mail, Internet were also included. The course also focuses on IT security, computers and society. The training course is done in Kannada, the local language, and teaching manuals are also in the same language. Tel-Nek is keen on providing its current trainees, especially women, with teleworking opportunities. Future plans include, setting up of a Tele-centre, to provide facilities in training, data entry, and also double up as an Internet cafe. The project entitled 'Sumangali Seva Ashram IT Education Programme for Women and Children' was initiated by Sumangali Sewa Ashram (SSA) in 2002. It is implementing an IT Education program for children and women.

EFFORTS OF IT COMPANIES IN IMPROVING ICT EDUCATION OF GIRLS AND WOMEN

ICT organisations across the world are moving beyond their traditional roles of delighting the customer and meeting bottom lines. Indian IT companies too are moving in the same direction and giving precedence to their social commitments or what is called corporate social responsibility (CSR). A look at the scene in India reveals innumerable examples of corporate paying close attention to social issues and venturing into philanthropic endeavors. While a majority of the companies concentrate on children of the disadvantaged communities, only a very few concentrates on the girl-specific ICT training programs. For instance, Moksha is inspiring the industry with Project Prerna, under which it is educating young girls of "Navajeevana", with computers by providing the necessary hardware and training faculty. The girls are being made aware of the importance and relevance of computer education in their future career aspirations. The NUT is aiming to change the life of India's citizens through computer education. It has initiated projects such as Hole-in-the-Wall experiment, a brainchild of NIITian and R&D chief Dr Sugata Mitra, where slum children have successfully learnt to navigate the 'Net and "Web-enable" themselves. NUT has also developed special I-write and Learn packages for the physically challenged under a program called Computer Assisted Teaching and Rehabilitation (CATERED). Another program initiated by the company is NUT BOOT IT, a television-based distance learning project, to bring computer education free to the homes of millions of Indians. In an attempt to bridge the digital and gender divide, NUT has also launched initiatives such as World Computer Literacy Day and International Women's Month. NUT has also got underway an AIDS prevention and control program—a joint effort between NIS, USAID and the Government of Tamil Nadu. A unique project with the National Association of the Blind (NAB), Bangalore, has been initiated, where NUT made available its SWIFT India courseware for conversion into Braille and provided its faculty for training. The Cognisant Technology works closely with academia in providing advanced developmental programs for faculty and defines curricula and syllabi. The company also helps colleges and universities to set up solution labs and knowledge centers. TCS has developed computerised programs to address the adult literacy problem in India. The company has undertaken special adult education projects in states such as Andhra Pradesh and Tamil Nadu. With a strong belief, that India's educational system needs to be strengthened, Polaris has set up "Ullas" trust which gives monetary aid to students who cannot afford education on their own. Partly funded by employees of the company, Ullas has sponsored more than 2000 students scattered across 132 schools in Chennai City. It is also providing them free computer training at its office premises.

CONCLUSION

It is heartening to note that inspite of the best efforts taken by the government, NGOs and the IT companies, access to IT education and training is highly skewed towards urban centered, English speaking masses with a high socio-economic status. Government efforts to upgrade the institutions providing IT education strengthen only the caliber of IT training available to Indian elites, but had little impact on the deprived community especially the women community. There were no concrete efforts to uplift women's status in technology. The way things are moving would only widen the gender based digital divide and it is a serious concern which calls for the attention of the policy-makers. As rightly observed by Kofi Annan the Secretary-General of the UN, at the first World Summit on Information Society 'that the so- called digital divide is actually several divides: a technological divide in infrastructure, a language divide with much of the content in English, a gender divide for women in many nations, a commercial divide where e-commerce reaches only some'. Indeed the digital divide is the biggest non-tariff barrier to world trade today. It is difficult to captivate the digital divide precisely. From a policy angle, a specific absolute cut off line may be drawn up to denote the minimum level of IT knowledge required for any individual especially the women. Any shortfall denotes the distance to be covered by the individual suggesting that the State Government should initiate suitable steps to rectify the situation. This perhaps opens up a new area of further research.

About the contributor: Dr. Suriya is currently working as a Senior Professor and Head of the Department of Library and Information Science at Annamalai University and also heading the University library. She received her PhD degree (India) in

1990 and pursued her post-doctoral research at Warwick University (UK) in 1998. She was a Visiting Professor to the Institute of Informatics and Gesellschaft (Germany) in 2000 and worked as a visiting scholar in the Faculty of Media Studies at the University of Western Ontario (Canada) in 2001, and Department of Gender Studies at University of Essen (Germany) in 2002. Presently she is a Director (Interim Board Member) of IN WES (International Network of Women Engineers and Scientists), President of IA WES (Indian Association of Women Engineers and Scientists), and Indian Ambassador of the Association of Computing Machinery-Women's Chapter (ACM-W).

SECTION III

18

An Evolutionary Perspective of Research on 'Women in Informatics': A Cross-country Analysis

INTRODUCTION

The last two decades have witnessed a plethora of research publications on gender studies in informatics and they have brought to focus the global debate on women issues in computer education. These publications stand as a testimony not only to the progression that women have made in this field, but also indicate the emergence of a new discipline 'women in computing'. While research on this discipline is gaining momentum, evaluation of these research publications is seriously lacking. This situation has necessitated the development of some tools and techniques to explore the issues being discussed. The present study is an attempt to evaluate the gender research in informatics at two different levels. At one level, it is an attempt to characterise the discipline 'women in computer education' by identifying conceptual space of the discipline (central and the peripheral themes); and at another level, it is an attempt to consolidate the themes and the sub-themes around which the entire discipline is evolving through co-word analysis.

OBJECTIVES

The objective of this study is to review the research outputs (publications) depicting the gender issues in the field of women in computing and to map the factors attributing to the gender gap and decline in the participation of women in computer education. It would also portray the national and organisational initiatives to improve women's status in informatics. This study would also throw light on exogenous and indigenous factors that persuade or dissuade women from becoming active agents in such a leading-edge discipline as computing. It would offer a base for integrating the corpus of research outputs into the process of improvising the curriculum, recruitment and retention activities in computing in order to draw more women into computing. In short, this study takes stock of the research performance of the global countries on the key issues such as the shortage of women in computer education and the efforts being taken by various agencies to achieve gender equity in computer education.

METHODOLOGY

This study is based on a sample database of publications (1983-2003) in the field of 'women in computing'. The database consists of conference proceedings, journal articles, news items, projects and on-line discussions on this given subject. The co-word mapping technique is used to capture the dimensions of

Outline of the study

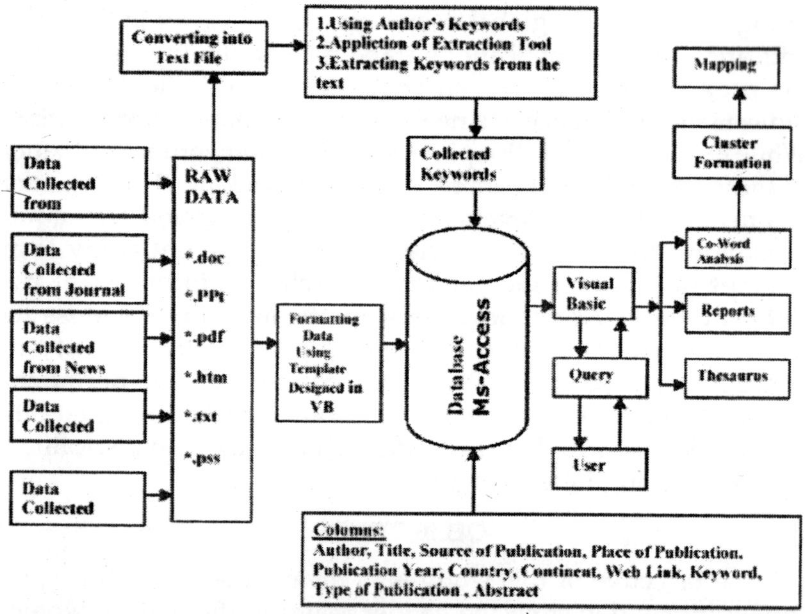

knowledge structure or cognitive themes in the field of women in informatics. This technique consists of (i) building keyword index from the bibliographic database, (ii) computing co-occurrences of keywords and measuring the similarity of keywords; (iii) cutting up the keyword associations network into clusters, (iv) classifying the documents into clusters and (v) building cognitive maps of the discipline. The plan of the study is given in Diagram-1.

ANALYSIS AND DISCUSSION

Source-wise Distribution of Publications in Gender in Informatics

The sources of publications/documents dealing with the gender issues in informatics is presented in Graph-2.

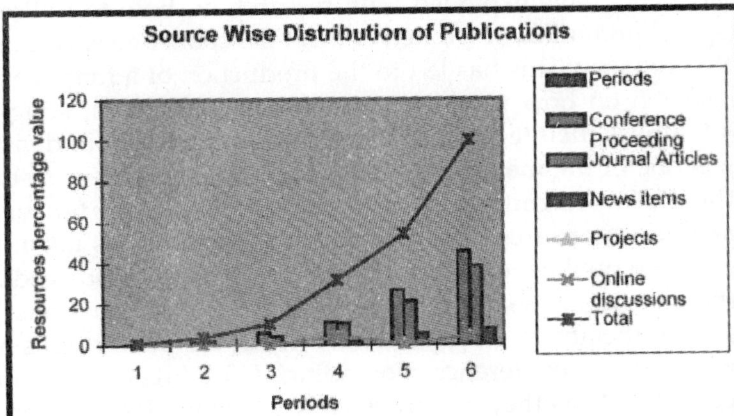

	I	II	III	IV	V	Total
Conference Proceeding	0.15	1.72	6.06	11	26.4	45.4
Journal Articles	0.47	1.87	4.35	10.4	21.3	38.4
News items	0	0	0	2.02	5.6	7.62
Projects	0	0	0	3.89	0.47	4.36
Online discussions	0	0	0	4.04	0.16	4.2

This study has taken into consideration the publication of documents for twenty years from 1984-2003. The total number of documents taken for the present study amounts to 643. For the purpose of analysis, the publication data has been grouped into five block periods (1984-87, 1988-91, 1992-95, 1996-99 & 2000-03). The data shows that the growth rate of publication is tremendous from 0.62% in the first period to 53.98% in the fifth period. However, the trend in the growth pattern is significant only in the last two periods. Roughly about 85% of the publications were brought out in the last ten years touching upon the issue of women's shortage in computer education. The above analysis shows the parallelism that exists between the actual field of work and the area of research. For instance, the later part of the 20th century has seen a dramatic growth in IT industry and its subsequent demand for IT workforce. This serious issue of shortage of IT skills have alerted research and academic institutions, professionals associations and government departments to accelerate research in the direction of exploring the means to produce adequate manpower to meet the demand. Consequently, the Computer Science and the Gender Studies departments have exploded with research on how to utilise the untapped potentials of women to meet the challenge encountered by the industry. This has led to the production of a huge volume of research on how to attract more women into computing and how to utilise their technical skills for meeting the labour demand. This is one of the major reasons for the accumulation of research in the field of women in informatics in the last ten years. Regarding the source of publications, this study has taken into account the publications appeared in the conference proceedings, journal articles, news items, projects and on line discussions. It is seen from the above graph that majority of the publications have appeared in the conference proceedings (45.41%) and the journal articles (38.41) as they are universally considered as the popular medium of communication. The contribution of the remaining sources are about 16.18%.

REGION-WISE DISTRIBUTION OF PUBLICATIONS IN GENDER IN INFORMATICS

A region-wise distribution of the publications (Total records= 643) indicates the research profiles of the individual nations in this discipline. The research contribution of the countries is calculated and presented in Graph-3.

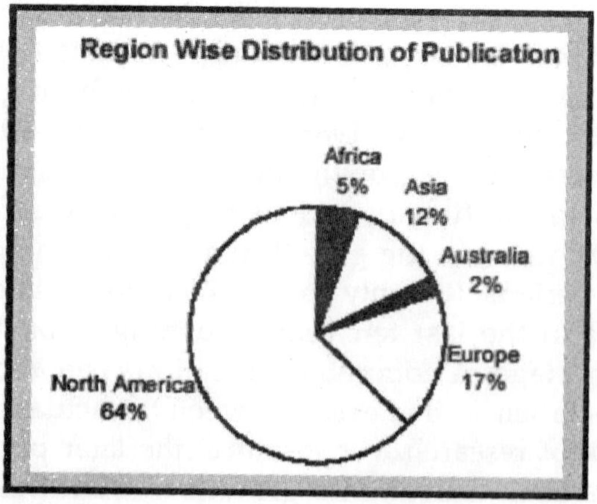

The above graph shows that the research profile of the discipline women in computing is much higher in the North-American regions (62.83%), followed by the European (17.43%), Asian (12.28%), African (5.13%) and Australian (2.33%) regions. An analysis of the publication profiles of the various countries shows that USA ranks high by producing more than 47 % of publications followed by Canada (16.3%), United Kingdom (12.6%), India (9.5%) and South Africa (2.6%). The rest of the countries are not very active in gender research in informatics and their overall contribution is inegligible.

THEMATIC DISTRIBUTION OF THE PUBLICATIONS IN GENDER IN INFORMATICS

The thematic distribution of the database of publications are analysed and presented in Graph-4.

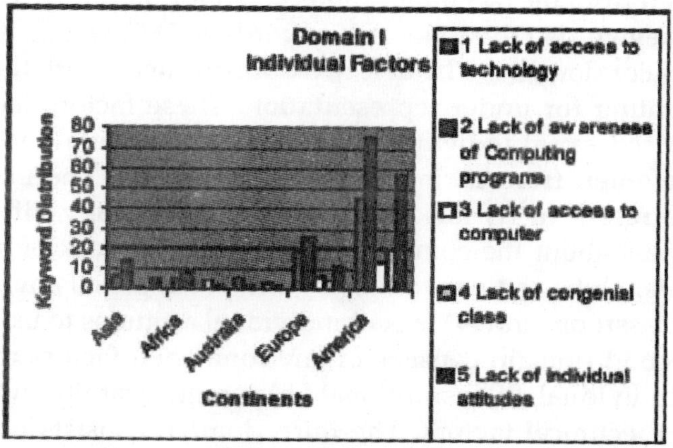

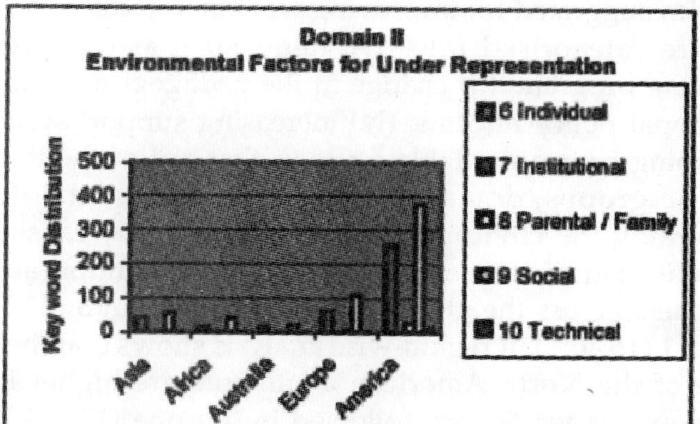

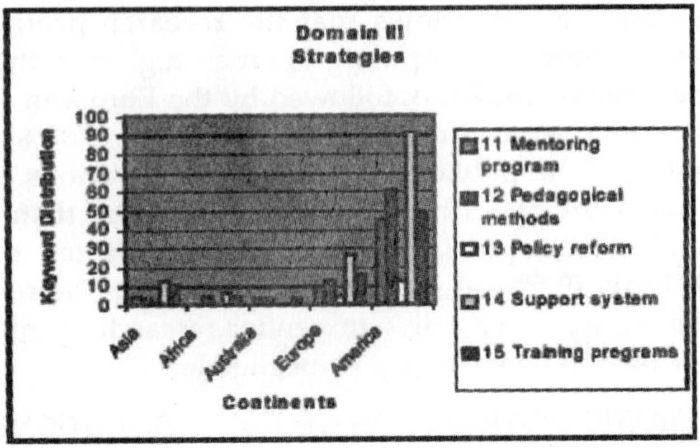

The publications has been categorised on the basis of their themes. A theme is a collection of keywords representing a homogeneous areas of research. About 1785 keywords have been extracted from the 643 publications taken for the study. The entire set of keywords (Total No of Keywords =1785) is classified into three major domains. The first two domains deals with the factors contributing for under-representation. These factors have been categorised as (a) individual and (b) environmental factors that deter women from taking active participation. The individual factors refers to (i) lack of access to technology, (ii) lack of awareness about the computing programs, (iii) lack of access to computer clubs and networks, (iv) lack of congenial environment in the classroom and (v) lack of individual attitudes to technology. The second domain consists of environmental factors related to the (i) individual, (ii) institutional (iii) parental/family, (iv) societal and (v) technical factors. The third domain consists of various strategies suggested for improving women's status in computing. They are categorised into five items such as (i) induction of mentoring program, (ii) change in the pedagogical methods, (iii) educational policy reforms, (iv) increasing support systems, and (v) training programs. Table 5 shows that out of the three major thematic groups/domains taken for analysis, the domain 2 representing the environmental factors (62.40%) causing under representation of women receives greater attention among the researchers across the globe followed by domain 3 (22.20%) and domain 1 (15.40%). A region-wise analysis shows that the research profile of the North American continents are higher in all the three domains viz 64.59% followed by Europe (17.55%) and the rest of the countries have a research profile of less than 10%. Out of the 15 thematic variables taken for analysis, lack of technical environment for women scores greater attention. More than 608 out of 1785 keywords taken from the 643 records are discussed about this issue. This trend seems to be common in all the regions. The next top priority is given to the theme related to lack of institutional environment for women to take up computing as a course of study (Table 5).

Table 5: Distribution of key terms among the Geographical region

No	*Key terms*	*Asia*	*Africa*	*Australia*	*Europe*	*America*	*Total*
	Domain I Individual factors						
1	Lack of access to technology	6	5	5	19	45	80 (4.48)
2	Lack of awareness of Computing programs	13	8	2	25	76	124 (6.94)
3	Lack of access to computer Groups & networks	1	0	0	6	14	21 (1.17)
4	Lack of congenial class Room environment	0	4	3	4	20	31 (1.73)
5	Lack of individual attitudes	5	2	2	11	57	19 (1.06)
	Domain I total	21	19	11	55	169	275 (15.4)
	Domain II Environmental factors						
6	Individual	40	16	15	59	255	77 (4.31)
7	Institutional	0	1	0	2	3	385 (21.56)
8	Parental/Family	2	2	1	5	28	6 (0.33)
9	Social	56	43	18	110	381	38 (2.12)
10	Technical	1	2	1	1	14	608 (34.06)
	Domain II total	103	64	36	187	724	1114 (62.4)

	Domain III Strategies						
11	Mentoring program	5	1	3	9	45	63 (3.52)
12	Pedagogical methods	4	5	4	13	61	87 (4.87)
13	Policy reform	2	0	1	5	13	21 (1.17)
14	Support system	13	7	1	27	92	140 (7.84)
15	Training programs	11	5	3	17	49	85 (4.76)
	Domain III total	35	18	12	71	260	396 (22.18)
	Over all Total	159 (8.90)	101 (5.65)	59 (3.30)	313 (17.53)	1153 (64.59)	1785 (100)

TRENDS IN THE PATTERN OF THEMATIC DISTRIBUTION OF THE PUBLICATIONS

The trend analysis is attempted to identify (i) which research themes in this discipline remain constant but with changing thrusts; (ii) which themes mature and diminish as major research topics and (iii) which themes remain transient or immature during the study period. The evolutionary pattern of the subject under consideration has been analysed and presented in Table 6. Trends in the pattern of thematic distribution of the publications:

Domain 1 : Factors Underrepresentation

Domains	*1984-1987*	*1988-1991*	*1996-1999*	*2000-2003*	*Total*
Access to technology	0 (0.00)	1(0.06)	38 (0.73)	28 (2.13)	80 (4.48)
Awareness2 (0.11)	2 (0.11)	36 (0.28)	79 (2.02)	124 (6.95)	
Computer clubs & networks	0 (0.00)	0 (0.00)	5 (0.06)	15(0.28)	21 (1.18)
Congenial class room environment	0 (0.00)	0 (0.00)	12 (0.22)	15 (0.67)	31(1.74)
Individual attitudes	0 (0.00)	0 (0.00)	4 (0.06)	14 (0.22)	19 (1.06)
Domain 2: Factors Declining Enrollment					
Environment: Individual	1(0.06)	1(0.06)	21 (0.50)	45 (1.18)	77 (4.31)
Environment: Institutional	2 (0.11)	19 (1.06)	101(2.13)	225 (5.66)	385 (21.57)
Environment: Parental/ Family	0 (0.00)	0 (0.00)	2 (0.06)	3 (0.11)	6 (0.34)

Environment: Social	0 (0.00)	0 (0.00)	12 (0.34)	20 (0.67)	38 (2.13)
Environment: Technical	3 (0.17)	13 (0.73)	215 (4.71)	293 (12.04)	608 (34.06)
Domain 3 : Strategies: Increasing Participation					
Mentoring program	0 (0.00)	0 (0.00)	16(0.28)	42 (0.90)	63 (3.53)
Pedagogical methods	0 (0.00)	2 (0.11)	38 (0.28)	42 (2.13)	87 (4.87)
Policy reform	1(0.06)	1(0.06)	7 (0.17)	9 (0.39)	21 (1.18)
Support system	0 (0.00)	2 (0.11)	48 (0.45)	82 (2.69)	140(7.84)
Training programs	0 (0.00)	1(0.06)	34 (0.39)	43(1.90)	85 (4.76)
Total 9 (0.50)	42 (2.35)	190 (10.64)	589 (33.00)	1785 (100)	

It is observed that out of the 15 major themes taken for analysis, only 4 themes have shown a constant growth in the last two decades. For instance, the themes on lack of technical environment and lack of institutional support in the domain-2 have witnessed a steady growth over the study period. These themes have shown manifold increase from the first period (984-87) to the last period (2000-03). Next to these, the theme related to lack of awareness as a factor for under representation of women received wider attention (domain-1). In domain-3 the theme representing the support system, as a measure to draw more women to the field of computing, has gained more importance. Out of the fifteen themes taken for the present study, 10 of them have started receiving attention only in late 90s. Almost all the themes taken for the present study are moving in the direction of development, although there exists a vast difference in their rate of growth. Themes such as, the need for 'educational policy reforms' to attract more women, and the need for 'parental or family support' to encourage women to take up computing as their course of study etc has not attracted many research publications.

MEASURING THE THEMATIC ASSOICATIONS

The relationship existing between the themes is analysed by means of the co-word occurrence. The co-word matrix is formed by identifying the pattern of associations among the key terms taken for the present study. The following matrix explains the strength of associations existing between the 15 thematic groups taken for the study (Table-7).

Table 7 : Coward Matrix

	G1	G2	G3	G4	G5	G6	G7	G8	G9	G10	G1	G12	G13	G14	G15
G1	80	24	5	7	1	10	47	7	78	3	11	14	4	26	18
G2	19	124	3	8	3	9	68	2	109	6	24	19	4	45	25
G3	4	8	21	1	1	4	9	1	26	1	5	8	1	13	11
G4	8	7	1	31	1	7	27	5	41	3	5	14	2	13	9
G5	1	7	1	1	6	1	5	1	13	1	6	2	0	8	3
G6	10	15	4	6	1	77	50	7	91	4	12	14	1	23	13
G7	27	55	9	14	4	38	385	18	265	11	31	45	7	61	25
G8	7	2	1	3	1	8	30	38	64	3	1	8	0	6	3
G9	46	71	13	19	4	49	206	26	608	13	35	58	14	69	47
G10	4	7	1	4	1	5	15	3	28	19	6	9	1	6	6
G11	6	27	2	4	3	11	38	1	53	6	63	18	3	20	9
G12	11	21	9	9	2	16	48	6	93	6	17	87	4	32	18
G13	9	4	1	3	0	1	12	0	23	1	4	5	21	3	4
G14	16	39	7	8	3	16	76	5	111	5	18	26	3	140	21
G15	15	26	7	7	1	10	33	4	91	5	9	15	4	24	85

G1 -» Access to technology
G2 -» Awareness
G3 -» Computer clubs & networks
G4 %* Congenial class room environment
G5 -» Environment: individual
G6 %* Environment: institutional
G7 -» Environment: parental/family
G8 %* Environment: social
G9 %* Environment: technical
G10-» Individual attitudes
Gil* Mentoring program
G12* Pedagogical methods
G13* Policy reform
G14* Support system
G15* Training programs

It is identified from the above matrix that the number of thematic groups have close relationship with other groups. The strength of relationship is categorised into three groups as high, medium and low. When the level of association of one group with the neighboring groups is greater than 10, it is considered as the core or central theme of the subject. When the level of association of one group with the neighboring groups falls between the range of 5 to 10, then it is considered as the neutral theme. If it falls below 5, then it is considered as the peripheral theme. From the above matrix it is noticed that the themes belong to G9, G7,G14,G2 & G12 are considered as the core themes of the discipline 'Gender in Informatics', since their level of association is greater than 10. At the next level the theme belongs to G15 is considered as the neutral theme since its level of association falls between the range of 5 to 10. The thematic groups belong to G11, G6 & G1 are considered as peripheral themes since their level of association falls below 5. The rest of the groups are not considered as very important since they have little role to play in the formation of the subject 'Gender in Informatics'.

CONCLUSION

This study is a maiden attempt to trace the historical development of the subject 'women in computing' by taking into consideration the publications. It is interesting to note that this subject has registered an enormous group. From a small branch of subject, it has reached the status of the full-fledged discipline in the last two decades. This study has reflected two important factors; one is : the globalisation of IT labour market, and the other is : the growing importance of women's role in international economy. The one another factor contributing for the dramatic change in the structural development of the discipline 'gender research in informatics' is due to the collaborative research across the global institutions dealing with the gender issues in computing.

19

Building A Knowledge Management System (Kms) for the Discipline 'Gender Studies in Informatics' (GSI)

ABSTRACT

The 21st century has witnessed an overwhelming research output on the subject 'Gender Studies in Informatics (GSI)' and it has created a need for building a better information management system on this discipline for quick transfer and retrieval of knowledge. The present study is an attempt to build a Knowledge Management System (KMS) in GSI by collecting the publication records from a wide variety of sources across the globe brought out in the last two decades (1985-2004). It involves such techniques as (i) creation of knowledge repositories; (ii) extracting data from heterogeneous databases; (iii) building a semantic index or thesaurus, and (iv) representing the data through knowledge maps. The knowledge repository of the subject GSI is built by collecting publication records from the conference proceedings, journal articles, news items, web publications, theses, reports, government documents, grey literature etc. Auto text extraction tools are adopted to cull out the text, tables, figures, images, graphs and bibliographical elements of the GSI publications. Each record in the database carries a subject tag for further manipulation of the concepts. As in most knowledge representation paradigms, the concepts are classified ontologically, i.e. on the basis of their knowledge content. The semantic index or taxonomy of concepts are built by using heuristic algorithms. This technique helps to categorise the text as well as other object-oriented information available in the database. The knowledge structure of the database is represented through semantic data model or knowledge maps. The primary objective of this study is to develop mechanisms to pool the publication data from several publication sources and to create a knowledge portal for the subject 'gender studies in informatics' which would act as a gateway for the specialists and researchers to access the database of world literature on the given discipline. The next objective is to build a thesaurus by listing the glossary of terms and establishing their hierarchical and associated relations through indexing tools. The yet another objective of this study is to develop practical strategies for (i) acquisition of knowledge from diverse formats like txt, xml, ppt, collaboration in order to build a collective repository; (ii) collaborate the data using knowledge engineering aids; (iii) represent the knowledge in the form of semantic data models, semantic nets, conceptual tress, graphs, lexi-maps, co-occurrence structures, scattered diagrams and clusters; and (iv) develop user interface for searching the relevant knowledge from the database of publications on GSI.

INTRODUCTION

The 21st century has witnessed an overwhelming research output on GSI but due to publication scattering and want of organised database, the outcome of these publications have not been visible to the policy-makers and gender scientists. Further, the traditional document management system put a heavy burden on the user in the process of information access, extraction and interpretation. Besides, the absence of domain-specific semantic index in the discipline GSI results in irrelevant retrieval of records resulting in high recall but low precision. In addition, the existing system makes the process of literature-search difficult and time consuming. The exponential growth of literature, the information overload, and the time wasted in searching and browsing in the field of GSI demanded a semantic information processing system. This situation calls for the development of Knowledge Management System (KMS) in GSI by building dynamic (i) knowledge repositories, (ii) semantic index and (iii) knowledge maps and thereby alleviates the problems encountered by the user in the traditional document management system.

NEED FOR KNOWLEDGE MANAGEMENT SYSTEM IN GSI

The gender problem received wider attention in the field of informatics across the globe in the recent years. While discussions about these gender issues are useful, there is no effort to consolidate these deliberations in an organised form. Similarly, research on GSI is gaining momentum in the last two decades but there is no knowledge management system (KMS) or subject portals in this area. Therefore, an attempt has been made in the direction of constructing a KMS on a sample database in the field of GSI. It further attempts to identify the modalities for organising knowledge in GSI, despite the fact that there is an absence of supporting tools like the semantic index or the subject thesaurus in this field. It further identifies the appropriate tools and techniques to standardise the unstructured and complex data in order to represent the knowledge in an accurate and precise manner without time consumption. Attempts have also been made to capture the intellectual structure of the domain through concept maps/topic maps.

FOCUS OF THE STUDY

The focus of the study is to trace the evolution of the research literature on GSI since the conceptual contours and their evolution in the discipline GSI is lacking. A large number of publications from 1983-2003 are analysed to determine themes and trends in GSI.

- The study also aims at creating different knowledge maps consisting of different types of objects like keywords, institutions and authors.
- It further aims at designing efficient information retrieval tools in GSI using co-occurrence analysis.

BACKGROUNDS AND PREVIOUS WORK

Creation of knowledge database like CiteSeer Citation index that provides access to over 300,000 articles is a pre-requisite to promote research in GSI. Automatic indexing and categorisation of publication have become an integral part of establishing knowledge repositories in the recent years. The propagation of digital libraries has fuelled much work in the area of automatic categorisation and meta-data extraction.. Topic maps for repositories and for knowledge organisation have been the trend in the last decade, which is a step forward in the area of KMS. It is interesting to note that the application of co-occurrences of the word have become a common phenomena in the area of concepts categorisation and formation of semantic maps. The technique of co-word analysis also has been used for building thematic maps in the last years: Callon 86, Callon 91, Courtial 89, Law 92, and Whitaker 89. Based on these review of literature, the following research questions were generated pertaining to the present study: (i) How to define, organize knowledge structures in GSI in a principled way? (ii) How to deal with the heterogeneous subject data in GSI? (iii) Which semantic relation types should we use and standardise in organising the dataset in GSI? (iv) How to construct the knowledge maps and what could be inferred from the maps?

METHODOLOGY

Topic map creation is a multi-stage modularised process and the following steps are followed in designing the topic maps for GSI. They are (i) extraction of concepts from the keywords; (ii) fixing their semantic relations; and (iii) creation of topic maps.

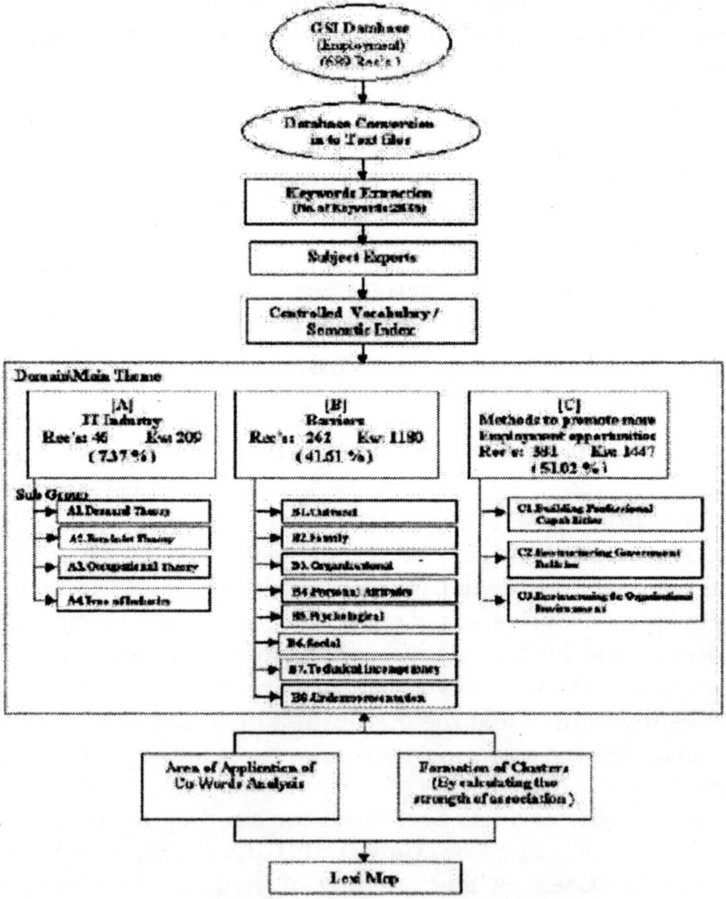

Fig. 1. Activities involved in building Topic Maps using Lexi maps & JCP techniques

A concept, in its most generic sense, can be any "thing" whatsoever—a person, an entity, really anything—regardless of whether it exists or has an other specific characteristics, about which anything whatsoever may be asserted by any means whatsoever. (H.H. Rath). Concept extractions are carried out by means of text mining. The process involved in the text mining are (a) segmentation; (b) phrase detection; (c) calculation of collocations; and (d) integration of external knowledge. This process is carried out for all word types in the corpus. Semantic relation refers to the ' collocation of words' or the 'concept association between two words' and it is computed by joint occurrence of two given words A and B within a context. Creation of topic maps involves (i) formation of co-occurrence matrix (ii) cluster formation and (iii) creation of maps. The following diagram represents the flow of activities in the formation of the topic maps.

Concept Extraction by Means of Keyword Analysis:

For the purpose of the present study, about 689 documents dealing with the subject GSI were selected. The main concepts of these documents are identified by means of text mining. Text mining, also known as document information mining, text data mining, or knowledge discovery in textual database is an apt technology for analysing large domains of unstructured data in order to extract relevant patterns or knowledge. Here, the text mining tools like TexNet32 and Site Content Analyser were applied on the GSI database to get the relevant words. These tools extract the words, word-phrases and context-relevant passages representing the contents of the publications by adopting the stemming procedure based on the context sensitive longest-match principle and a phrase recognition algorithm. The extracted word lists were standardised by involving the domain-experts. Due to non-availability of subject thesaurus in the discipline GSI, the experts attempted to build a macro-thesaurus by collating the unique, unambiguous and concept-related words out of the pool of words. The homonyms were disambiguated and the synonyms were hooked to one hub term as the preferred term. The filtered keywords were organised into a database with their appropriate broader terms, narrower terms and associative terms. Once extracted, the words are standardised and stored in a database (thesaurus) in order to be queried, data mined, summarised in natural language.

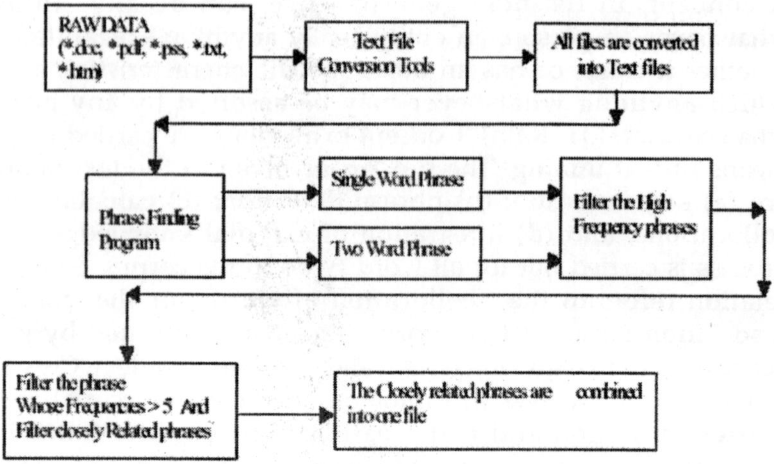

Fig. 2. Methods Used for Extraction of Keywords from the Textual Corpus on GSI

Co-occurrence of Semantically Related Concepts

Since single concept does not convey meaningful connotations of a topic, associations of semantically related concepts are identified to form the domains and sub-domains of the subject GSI. The Salton's co-occurrence procedure is adopted to compute the cohesion between the pairs of concepts in the given database and the results are presented in the co-occurrence matrix. Here, co-words are constructed by identifying the linkages or strength among the important concepts (keywords). The frequencies of co-occurrences of the concepts are ranked to form a matrix of co-word pairs. In this context, the occurrences of single concept in the whole sample were not taken into consideration for the formation of co-word matrix in order to avoid the spurious linkages. In the co-occurrence matrix, each cell in this symmetric matrix represents the number of times two concepts co-occur together (Cij). This method is followed by the 'co word clustering method' and its purpose is to create groups or clusters of associated keywords (co-words) as a means to trace the numbers of research topics in the GSI database.

Building Lexi-Maps based on Co-occurrence Matrix

To understand the nature of relationship among the co-occurrence of concepts, lexi-map technique is adopted. In this method, each concept is considered as a node connected by the relation of co-occurrence to another node. Co-occurrences are the ties or the links. The lexi-map is formed out of the co-occurrence matrix. The strength of the linkage 'S' of the co-occurrences are measured by using the formula: S(Ci,Cj, Cij)= Cij*Cij / CiCj 0 S 1 where 'Cij' is the number of co-occurrence of concepts i and j. Here, the occurrence of a single concept i within a set of publications is denoted as Ci.[2]. The higher (1) or the lower (0) strength of the co-occurrence is determined by the number of times a co-word pair occurs together in a given document or in a database of a specific subject. As the strength of the co-occurrence ranges between 0 and 1, it is necessary to fix certain thresholds in order to filter the 'uninteresting co-occurrences'. This implies that the ' co-word pairs' with a co-occurrence frequency under a certain threshold value, are filtered out. The height of such a 'noise' reduction threshold is determined in an ad hoc fashion and is usually set somewhere between 0.05 and 0.25 in this context in order to obtain a map representing the main linkages. The higher the occurrence of the co-word pair, the greater will be the strength of their association and vice-versa. From the strength of association, one could identify the semantic relationship existing between the concepts. This also reflects the semantic structure of the existing subject.

Building Topic Maps of the Discipline GSI using JCP and Inclusion Index

Though 'Leximap' is a commonly used technique for the creation of topic maps, it has not given a methodology for positioning the neighboring concepts. Therefore, attempts have been made to adopt the 'Inclusion Index' and the 'Joint Conditional Probability Index' (JCP) to convert the co-occurrence data into a spatial configuration (or a map). While the Inclusion index determines the spatial occurrences of the concepts (distance) on the Topic maps, the JCP determines their strength of relations. Inclusion Index (I) is computed by using formula: (Cij/min(Ci, Cj)) where Cij is the count of all records in which the two concepts co-occur, and Ci and (Cj) are respectively counts of all records indexed. The degree of relatedness may vary between 0 to 1 where '0' indicates the state of no-co-occurrence; and 'V' complete co-occurrence. The identification of relevant or master keywords can be fixed by setting a threshold value (5 occurrences). Only those nodes that have "I" values between 0.25 and above are taken for analysis. The distances on the map, in this study are not an indication of the intensity of relationships. The strength of inclusion between concepts is determined by their co-occurrences. In this context, Joint Conditional Probability is used to measure the strength of relationship between a given pair of entities. The JCP of the co-occurrences of the concepts in a GSI database is calculated using the formula: ((Cij / Ci) + Cij /Cj)) /2 where Cij is the count of all records in which two concepts co-occur, and Ci (Cj) are the count of all records indexed. The JCP is 0 when the two concepts are never assigned to the same record, and approaches 1 as a joint assignment of that two concepts increase proportionately in comparison of that frequency of assignment in the database as a whole. The higher the JCP values, the stronger the links between the concepts. While the spatial distribution of the nodes are determined by the inclusion index, their strength of relations are fixed by the JCP index. It is the link between the concepts that are of interest, rather than the spatial arrangement; thus the structure of GSI has been arranged keeping in mind the better graphic display of the links.

ANALYSIS AND INTERPRETATION

Details of the Database Selected for the Present Study

The publication trend of the discipline 'Gender Studies in Informatics' has gained a momentum in the recent years. These publications have deliberated on a wide variety of topics viz. (i) gender situation in the IT labour market i.e. in the software, hardware, telecom, IT-enabled and business processing sectors; (ii) gender related barriers prevailing in the IT related industries; (iii) and the strategies to maintain gender equity in the field of informatics etc. Parallel to the growth of publications on this discipline, there is a corresponding demand for literature on this area of research. This situation has demanded data consolidation and topic map generation to meet the user requirements. For the purpose of this study a sample database of 689 records covering 2836 keywords have been selected. Topic map techniques were applied on this basic data.

Outline of the Semantic Structure of the Discipline GSI

The 'knowledge management system (KMS)' of the discipline 'Gender Studies in Informatics' is built on three major inter-related activities viz: (i) building a dynamic knowledge repository; (ii) developing a comprehensive and interactive semantic index or thesaurus and (iii) creating a knowledge or topic maps. The 'knowledge repository' component of the KMS involves in acquiring domain-specific knowledge in diverse forms (xml, html, doc, ps., etc) from heterogeneous sources like WWW, Journals, Conference Proceedings, Reports and Projects. The 'semantic index' component of the KMS involves in organising the heterogeneous knowledge on the basis of their epistemological and ontological structures. Such kind of organisation results in dichotomous division of knowledge as 'conceptual model' and the 'representation paradigms' of the domain GSI. The following diagram explains the KMS of the discipline GSI.

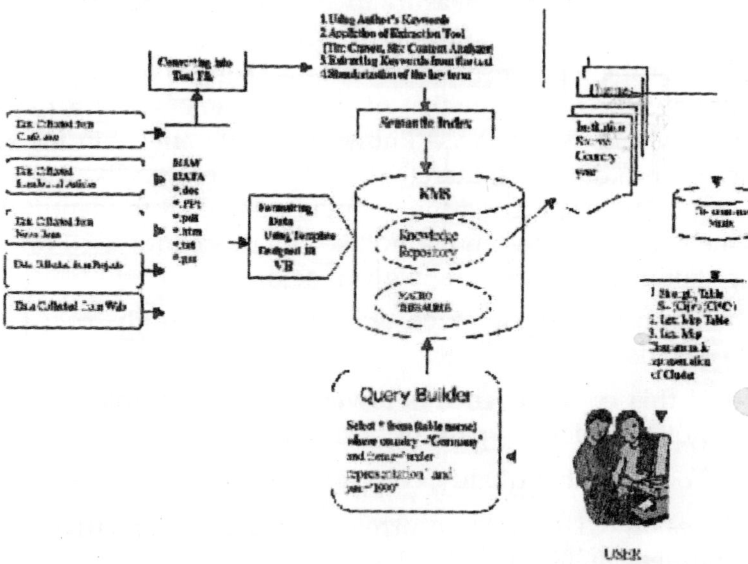

Fig. 3 : An Outline of Knowledge Management System in GSI

Co-Occurrence Matrix

It is noticed that themes or topics are formed not by a single concept represented through a keyword but through a collection or combination of concepts (keywords) . S. R. Ranganathan in his theory of 'Knowledge organisation' has discussed the various modes through which words would combine together and generate a new themes or topics. In this study, the co-word method is adopted to trace the formation of new themes.

Co-occurrence matrix depicts the number of times each concept (i) co-occurs with another concept (j) in the database taken for analysis. The cell value in the co-occurrence matrix represents the co-word pairs (Cij) selected for the current study. For instance, the theme 'C3' in Co-occurrence matrix associates with theme 'B3' 143 times & with 'C1' 172 times within a database of 689 documents having 2836 descriptors or keywords. In the same manner the concept 'B3' co-occurs with concepts 'A1 & C1' 18 times and 110 times respectively. Similar is the case with concept 'A'. There is a closer correlation between the co-occurrence of the keywords and the formation of new themes. The more the co-occurrences of the keywords, the higher will be the emergence of new themes in any given subject. Though co-occurrence of themes is a meaningful measure to identify the cohesion existing between two thematic groups, it will not show the type and intensity of the relationship between the thematic pairs. In other words, absolute frequencies of co-occurrences are a biased measure, which is otherwise known as "scale effect" in the raw co-occurrence data and, therefore, a further analysis like leximap techniques are applied on the co-occurrence data to identify the specific relations between the nodes. The procedure used for the computation of the leximap is given below:

- Compute pairwise co-occurrence for high-frequency words.
- If this co-occurrence is lower than a threshold, then do not consider the pair any further.
- For pairs that qualify, compute the cohesion value.

Cohesion (Ci, Cj)= co-occurrence-frequency/(sqrt (frequency (Ci)*frequency(Cj))) (1)

Leximap-Table Indicating the Strength of Relationship Between the Thematic Groups in GSI

Leximap table is based on the co-word pairs given in the co-occurrence matrix. The 15 thematic groups or sub-domains derived out of the 2836 keywords representing the concepts in the GSI database have formed a 15 X 15 matrix. Out of the 105 possible co-occurrences of themes formed from the above matrix, only 27 thematic pairs were chosen based on the threshold value prescribed (maximum>=5 co-occurrences). Here, the words representing each theme is considered as a node and the combination of these nodes with other nodes is measured by their strength value. Based on the calculated strength value (S), the type of relation existing between the thematic pairs viz: high, medium and low is determined. The following table illustrates the type of relationship that exists between the co-word pairs, whose strength(s) values are high.

Table 1. Co-Word Pairs Showing the Strength of Relationship Between the Thematic Groups in GSI

Ord.	*IVoifc i(cl)*			*Strengths*	*Range*
1.	Building Professional Capabilities <;C 1) [291]	Restructuring the Organisational Eti-<nronment <C3;i [105]	172	0.271S	High
2.	Organisational Barriers(B3) [232]	Restructuring the Organisational Eti-^nronment <C3r) [105]	143	0.2357	High
3.	Organisational Barriers(B3) [232]	Building Professional C apatiilities CC 1) [291]	110	0.1792	High
4.	Reconstructing Government policies<C2) [172]	Restructuring the Organisational Environments <C3r) [105]	105	0.1714	High
5.	Organisational Barriers(B3) [232]	Underrepres entation:tXBg) [170]	SI	0.1664	High
6.	Underrepre sentation (Bg^i[170]	Restructuring the Organisational Environment <C35 p. 05]	99	0.1542	High
7.	Technical Incompetency (B71 [142]	Restructuring the Organisational Environment <C35 p. 05]	36	0.1393	High
8.	Underrepres entatioruT38^i [170]	Building Professional C apabilities CC 1) [291]	SO	0.1294	High
9.	Building Professional Capabilities <C 1) [291]	Reconstructing Government policies; C3)[172]	79	0.1247	High

10.	Organisational Barriers (T33) [232]	Technical Incompetence vfT=-7) fl 42]	63	0.1205	High
11.	Social Barriers (136) [133]	Restructuring the Organisational Environment; C3;i p. 05]	76	0.1161	High
12.	Cultural Barriers (Br>[120]	Organisational Barriers CB33 P32]	56	0.1126	High

The above table shows the linkages between the thematic pairs. For instance, the association of the node C3 is strong with a set of nodes as C1, B3, C2, B7 and B6; it is medium with another set of nodes such as A3 & A4 and it is weak with respect to B2 & B5. Similarly, the association of B3 is strong with respect to C1, B8, B7 & B1; and it is weak with respect to A1, A3 and B4. Same is the case with the other nodes. The association existing between the nodes given in table may be represented in a more vivid manner through a diagram.

Leximap

The leximap shows the degrees of nodes on the map. The degree of a node 'X' is defined as a number of links incident with X and is denoted by d (X). The strong degree, medium degree and weak degree of a node ' X' is defined as number of strong, weak and medium links incident with it and it is denoted by $d_s(X)$, $d_m(X)$, $d_w(X)$ respectively. It is easy to verify that $d(X)=d_s(X)+d_m(X)+ d_w(X)$. The above lexi-map indicates that d (C3) = 10 , $d_s(C3)$ =6, $d_m(C3)$=2, $d_w(C3)$=2; d (B3) = 8 , $d_s(B3)$ =4, $d_m(B3)$=1, $d_w(B3)$=3; d(C1) = 8, ds(C1) =4, $d_m(C1)$=3, $d_w(C1)$=1; d(B8) = 4, $d_s(B8)$ =3, $d_m(B8)$=1, $d_w(B8)$=0; d(B1) = 3, ds(B1) =0, $d_m(B1)$=2, $d_w(B1)$=1; d(C2) = 3, $d_s(C2)$ =2, $d_m(C2)$=1, $d_w(C2)$=0; d(A4) = 3, $d_s(A4)$ =0, $d_m(A4)$=2, $d_w(A4)$=1; d(A3) = 3, $d_s(A3)$ =0, $d_m(A3)$=1, $d_w(A3)$=2; We declare a node X as a 'cluster' if d_s (X) >= n, for a given n. We take n =4 in the present context. Based on this criteria, it is observed that C1, C3 & B3 are clusters. Out of the 105 co-word combination for the 15 subject categories [n (n-1)/2], only 27 pairs have been taken for analysis filtering out the word-pairs fall below the threshold value (<5). It is observed from the Lexi-map that these 27 word pairs have lent themselves into three meaningful clusters. It is interesting to note that the subject C3 has linked with 9 other subject headings viz: A3, A4, B2, B3, B5,B6,B7,C1, C2 and formed the primary cluster. Similarly, the subject B3 has linked with 7 other subject headings viz; A1,A3,B1, B4, B7,B8, C1 and formed a secondary cluster. The tertiary cluster is formed by C1 in association with other subject headings like A1, B1, B6, B8, C2. The following diagram illustrates the formation of the above mentioned clusters.

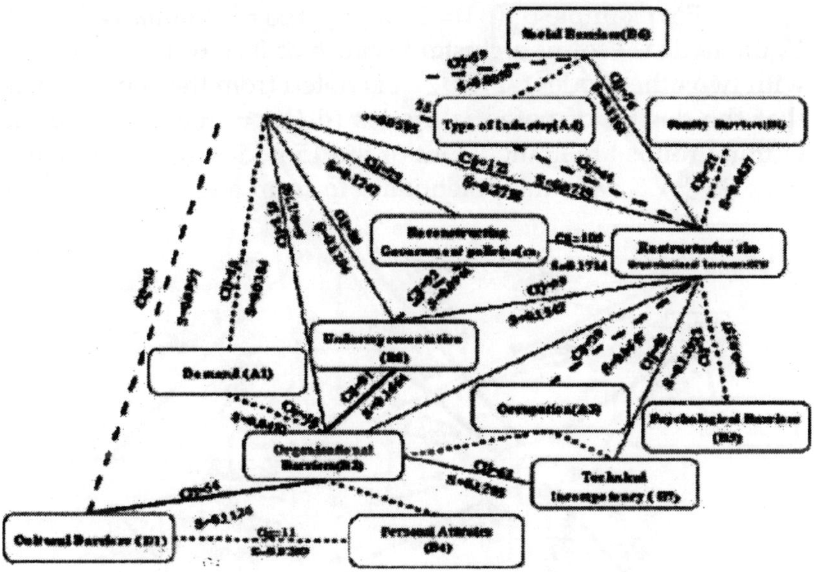

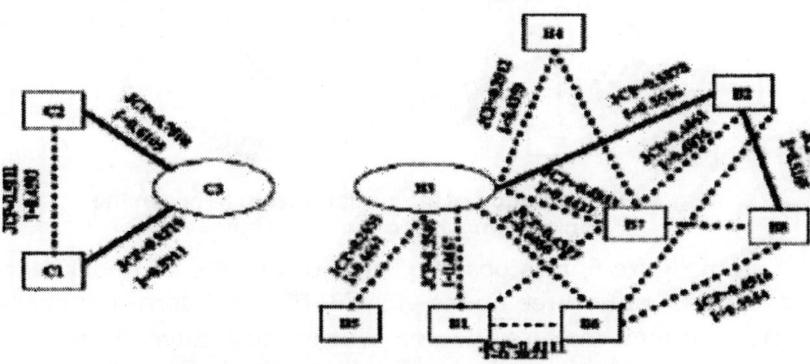

Fig. 5 : Computation of Inter-relationship between the topics using JCP and Inclusion index

The inter and intra-relationship between the nodes have been calculated by using the Inclusion Index (I) and the Joint Conditional

Probability Index (JCP). The inter-cluster relationships of the nodes A1-A4; B1-B8 and C1-C3 have been analysed. Based on the calculated values, the co-occurrence structure for the individual nodes are formed (Fig. 4). While considering the individual nodes in the group A, it is identified that none of the nodes in this group has any meaningful co-occurrence. On the other hand, in group B, the node B3, form a cluster because of its strong and medium co-occurrence relationship with other nodes within their groups. For example d_s (B3)= 1 and d_m(B3) =5. Similarly, in group C, the node C3 forms a cluster because of its stronger association with two other nodes C1 & C2. It is noted from the above analysis that the degree of potential nodes (d (X) = that form a cluster within groups are limited. Out of the 15 nodes taken for analysis only B3 & C3 have the potentiality to form a cluster.

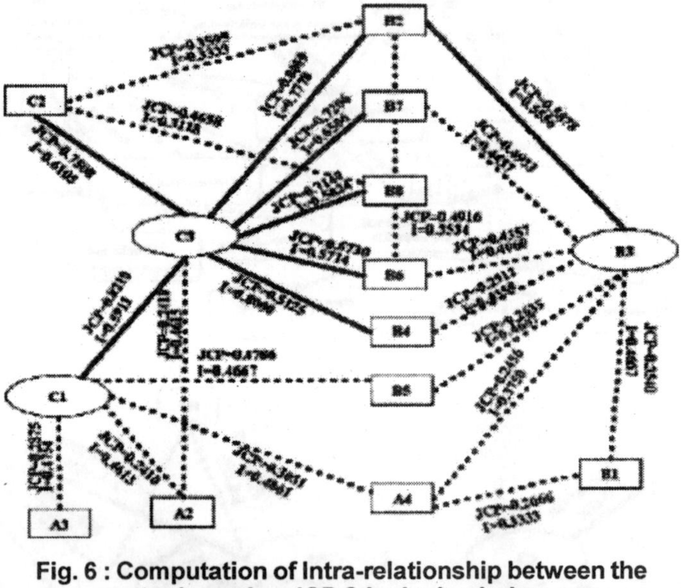

Fig. 6 : Computation of Intra-relationship between the topics using JCP & Inclusion index

From figure 6, it is observed that out of the 15 nodes taken for analysis, only three nodes viz: C3, B3 & C1 form the cluster because of their maximal degree. Out of these three clusters, the C3 has formed a larger cluster. For instance, d (C3) = 8 where d_s (C3) =7, and d_m (C3) =1. In the same manner, d (B3) = 7; where d_s (B3) =1, and d_m (B3) =6. Similarly, d (C1) = 6 where d_s (C3) =1, and d_m (C3) =5. It is interesting to note that the intra relationship of the cluster C3 is stronger than the other clusters because of its stronger association both within (C1 & C2) and outside the clusters viz: B2, B4, B6, B7, B8 & A2.

CONCLUSION

In this paper an attempt has been made to map the structure of 'Gender Studies in Informatics' over a period of twenty years. This study has experimented with several techniques like the leximap, inclusion index, joint probability index etc in order to create topic maps of the given discipline. The inter and intra cluster maps applied here help to trace out the interactions among the sub-domains in the discipline GSI.

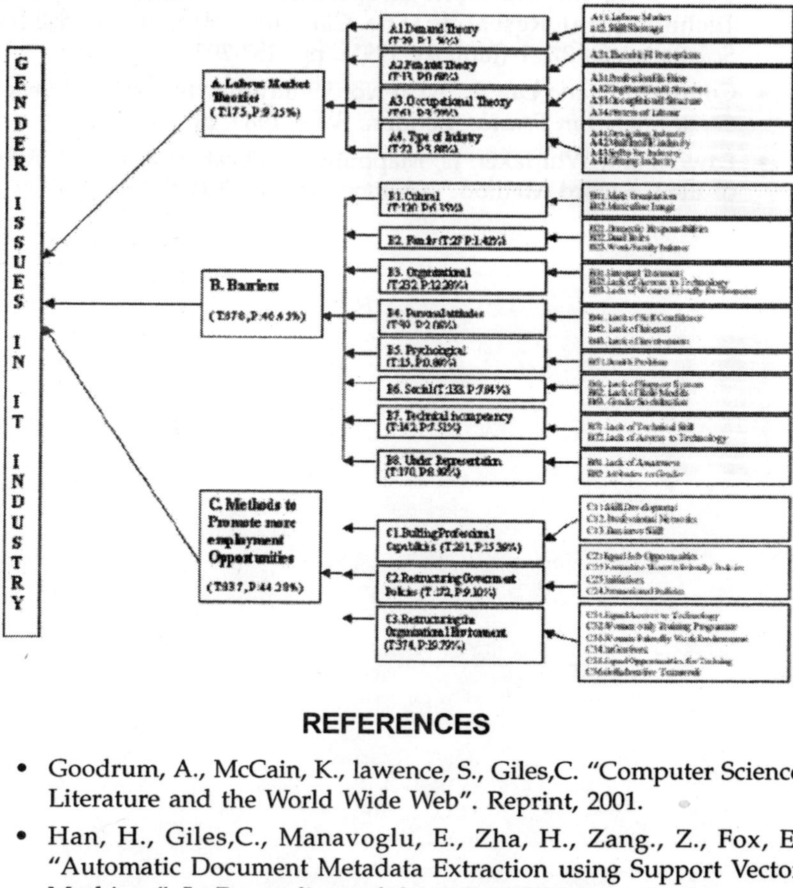

REFERENCES

- Goodrum, A., McCain, K., lawence, S., Giles,C. "Computer Science Literature and the World Wide Web". Reprint, 2001.
- Han, H., Giles,C., Manavoglu, E., Zha, H., Zang., Z., Fox, E. "Automatic Document Metadata Extraction using Support Vector Machines". In Proceedings of the ACM/IEEE Joint Conference on Digital Libraries. 2003.

- Giuffridu, G., Shek, E.,Yang, J. "Knowledge Based Metadata Extraction from Postscript Files". In Proceedings of the Fifth ACM International Conference on Digital Libraries. 2000.
- Kal Ahmed. "Topic Maps for Repositors" www.Topic Maps for repositories.htm
- Alexander Siegel M.A. "Towards Knowledge Organisation with Topic Maps" www.To wards Knowledge organization with Topic Maps.htm
- Callon, M., Law, J., and Rip, A." Quantitative scientometrics." *Mapping of the Dynamics of Science and Technology*. London. Mcmillian. 1986.
- Callon, M., Courtial, J.P., Laville, F."Co-word analysis as a tool for describing the Network of Interactions between Basic and Technological Research: The Case of Polymer Chemistry." *Scientometrics* 22, 1 (January 1991). pp. 153-203.
- Courtial, J.P., and Law, J. "A Co-word Study of Artificial Intelligence". *Social Studies in Science*. London. Sage. 1989. pp. 301-311.
- Law, J., and Whittaker, J. "Mapping Acidification Research: A Test of the Co-word Method." *Scientometrics* 23, 3 (1992). pp. 417-461.

20

Mapping of Gender Studies in Informatics

ABSTRACT

Information technology intervenes and shapes people's everyday lives. In democratic information society, one basic principle must be a guarantee of equal access. The Present study focuses on mapping the research dynamics of the field gender issues in informatics. It aims at evaluating the research activity of the countries on gender development in informatics by means of their bibliographic output. In recent years, there have been a rapid growing interest in the use of quantitative parameters for assessing the quality of research carried out in research institutions, Universities and so on. The need for the study is realised to identify the existing research trends, thrust areas, priorities, gaps and future requirements.

This study is designed to analyse the research output pertaining to the gender issues in the field of informatics and to map the factors attributing to the alarming gender gap and a paucity of women's participation in this field. The analysis is based on the emergence of research areas, research groups and countries with a view to map the cognitive or intellectual structure of research. Further, this study spells out the relationship between authors and institutions, as a means of assisting the peer review procedure.

The mapping process consists of conversion of these publication records into a bibliographic database in English language. This technique consist of building keyword index from the bibliographic database, computing co-occurrence of keywords and measuring the similarity of keywords, cutting up the keyword associations network into clusters, classifying the documents into clusters and building scatter diagrams or maps.

Hence, the major focus of this study is to collect the research outputs of the countries in the world on the areas of women in informatics for the International Conference on Women in Digital Era : Opportunities and Challenges to produce cognitive maps. This study evaluates the research scenario of these countries with respect to women in information technology education, women in IT industry and gender gap in IT labour market and IT education. The map highlights the strength and weakness of the research efforts. These maps illustrate the research status of the individual countries, the most focused area of specialty (themes/issues), the most active countries in conducting research, and its impact of this research on gender development.

INTRODUCTION

The period since the Second World War has seen major changes in the patterns of industrial employment around the world. Industrial development in the Third World' has been variable, the rapid transformation of the socalled newly industrialising countries contrasting with the far more modest industrialisation. National boundaries have become increasingly permeable to transnational capital and a new international division of labour has been established. These changes have had important implications for the gender composition of employment and of the work force, and have led to considerable debate about the implications for the structure of gender relations and the degree of gender inequality. A large body of work has been generated on the topic of gender and industrialisation. We lack an up-to-date overview of the field, which is global in coverage and incudes information about the scope of research and research methodologies as well as research findings. As a preliminary step, now we have summarised the research papers submitted to the International Conference on Women in the Digital Era: Opportunities and Challenges Organised by Annamalai University and Software Technology Parks of India. Our paper fills the gap, and contributes to the synthesis and interpretation of a field of research on progress. This paper is based on constructing a database as a research tool. Items have been selected for inclusion in the database on the grounds of both relevance and accessibility. The characteristics of the database, in particular the keywords developed during the research is based on (a) geographical coverage; (b) institutonal coverage; (c) authorship pattern; (d) Collaboration pattern; (e) themes covered.

Geographical coverage

(a) Country-wise Coverage

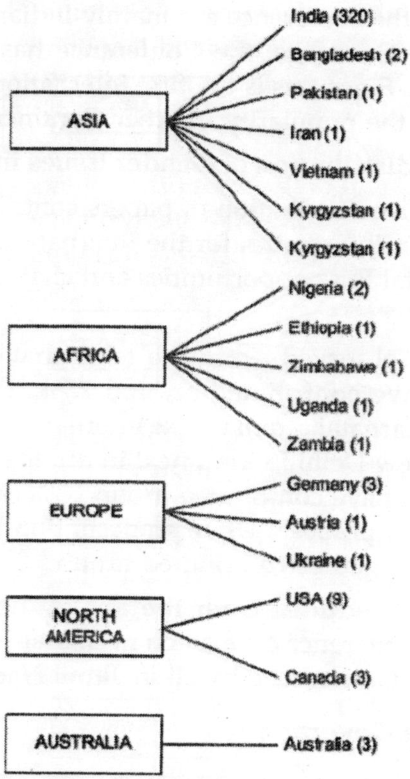

Fig. 1.

Country-wise distribution of Gender issues in Informatics

The country-wise distribution of papers contributed on gender issues in informatics for the International conference on women in Digital Era: opportunities and challenges is presented in Graph 1. It could be observed from the graph that Indian researchers have contributed their research papers more in number to the conference.

India rank first in order with 320 (90.91%) papers, U.S.A. ranks second in order with 9 (2.55%). Germany, Canada, Australia, follows next in order with 0.85% each in this regard. Nigeria, Bangladesh ranks next in order with 0.57% each. Iran, Kyrgyzstan, Pakistan, Uganda, Ukraine, Vietnam, Zambia,

Zimbabwe, US, Austria, Ethiopia have contributed one research paper each.

It could be deduced from the above discussion that the contributors to the conference are mainly Indians. Regarding the Continent-wise Coverage, the Conference has reached well in Asia and Africa. Since this is the first International Conference, it has not gained the popularity in other Continents.

State-wise distribution of Gender issues in Informatics.

The state-wise distribution of papers contributed in India on Gender issues in Informatics for the International Conference on women in Digital Era : opportunities and challenges is presented in Graph-2.

It could be observed, from the table that researchers from Tamil Nadu have contributed around 75%. Tamil Nadu ranks first in order. Karnataka ranks next in order with 6.25%. Andhra Pradesh and New Delhi follows next in order with 4.06%. Kerala and Maharastra have contributed around 3% each in this regard. Gujarat, Madhya pradesh, Uttar pradesh, Pondicherry, Haryana, Orissa, Punjab together contributed around 5%.

It could be deduced from the above discussion that the International Conference on women in Digital Era : Opportunities and challenges have reached well in Tamil Nadu.

(b) State-wise Coverage

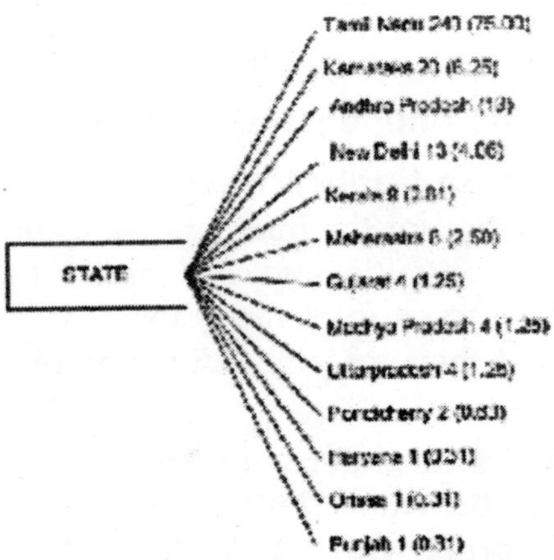

Fig. 2.

(c) District-wise Coverage

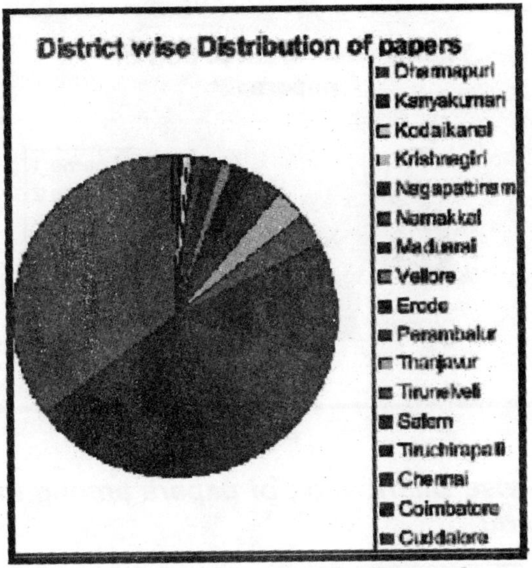

Fig. 3.

Graph-3 shows the District-wise distribution of papers contributed on gender issues in Informatics for the International Conference on Women in Digital Era: Opportunities and Challenges. It could be observed from the graph that maximum numbers of the papers have been contributed in Cuddalore District. It is followed by Coimbatore, Chennai, Tiruchirapalli. The papers from the remaining Districts contributed less number of papers.

(d) Theme-wise Distribution of Papers

Graph-4 shows the Theme-wise distribution of papers contributed on gender issues in Informatics for the International Conference on Women in Digital Era: Opportunities and Challenges. It could be observed from the graph that around 37% of papers have been contributed on Sub themes of Theme 1. Theme-1 ranks first in order with 37%. The next place is occupied by Theme-3 with 24%. The next place is occupied by Theme-5 with 15% of papers. The Fourth place is occupied by Theme-2 with 11% of papers. The remaining Themes namely Theme 4, 6, 7 and 8 together contributes around 15%. It could be deduced from the above discussion that the Concentration of Themes-4, 6, 7 & 8 received less attention.

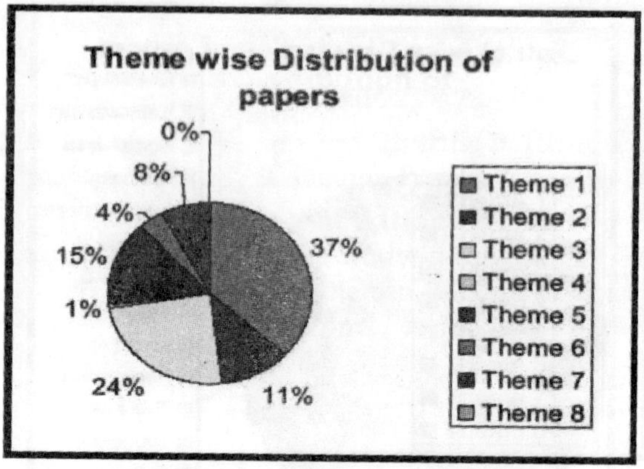

Fig. 4.

(e) Theme-wise Distribution of papers among the Districts of Tamil Nadu

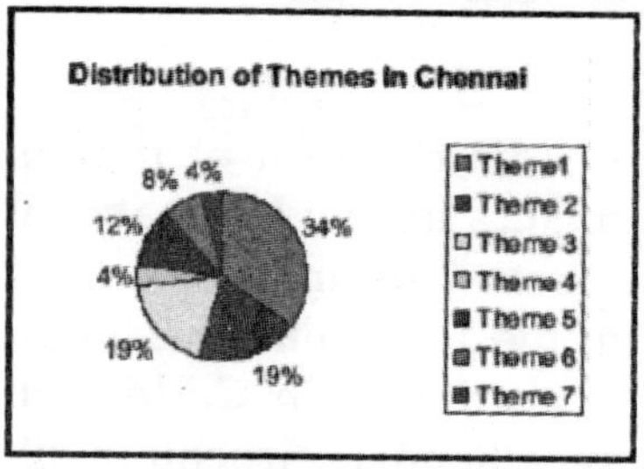

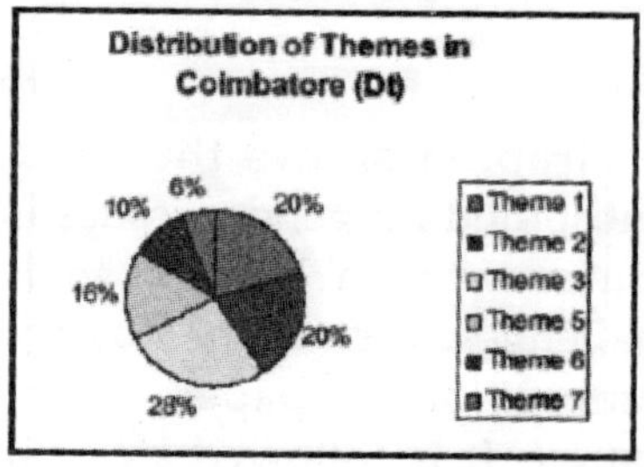

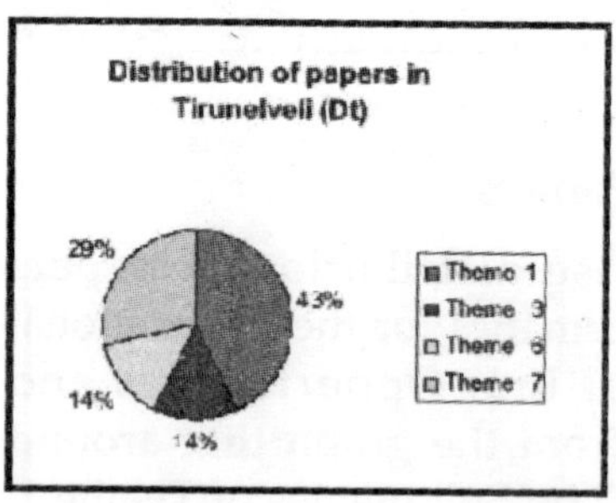

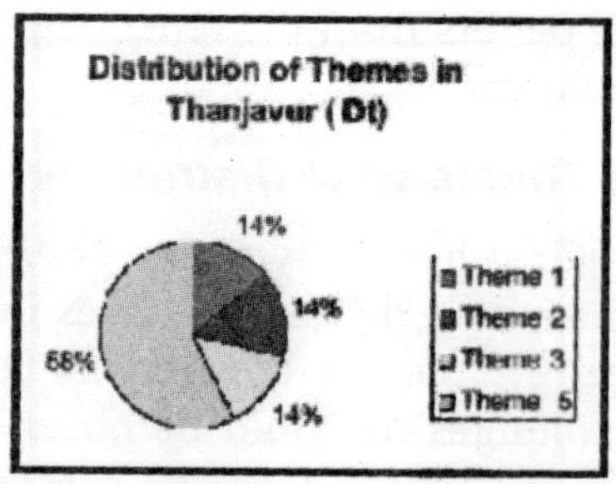

AUTHORSHIP PATTERN

The objective of the study of Authorship pattern is to bring out research pattern in a discipline. The extent of research

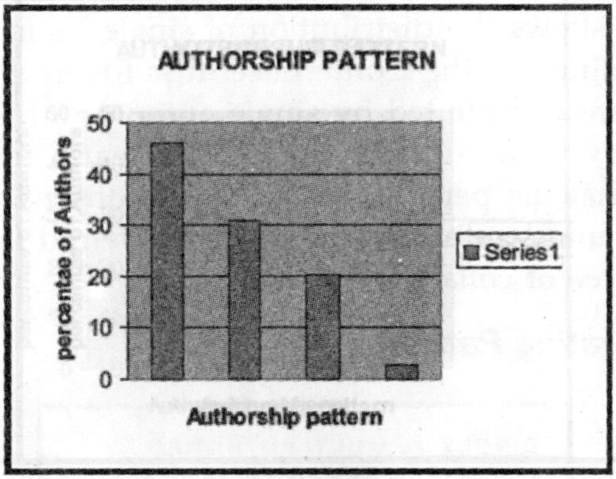

Fig. 5.

contribution by the researchers is explained in the analysis of Authorship pattern. It is well known that now a day's research is carried out by a group of researchers rather than by a single author. In the light of the above fact, an attempt is made to identify the nature of authorship pattern in the field Gender issues in Informatics.

Graph-11 indicates the authorship pattern and their percentage of research output. The total contribution submitted to International conference on women in Digital Era : opportunities and challenges is calculated as 352. It could be noted that single authored papers rank first in order sharing 46.02%. Double authored papers ranks second in order sharing 109 Contributions (30.97%). Three authored papers ranks next in order sharing 71 Contributions (20.17%). Papers with four and more authors rank next in order sharing 9 Contributions (2.56%).

(g) Single Vs Multi Authored Papers

Fig. 6.

Graph-6 shows the distribution of single Vs multi authored papers submitted to the Conference. It is found that 50.62% of the papers are contributed by single authors and 59.38% of the papers are by multi authors. It could be learnt fom the above discussion that the percentage of single authored paper is less than that of multi-authored papers. It is inferred from the table that the degree of collaboration is 0.54.

(h) Collaborating Pattern

Fig. 7.

Graph-7 shows the distribution of collaboration between institutions. Out of 190 Collaborated papers, 113 (68.95%) of the papers are Collaborated with the researches of the same institution; 59 (31.05%) of the papers are collaborated with neighboring institutions.

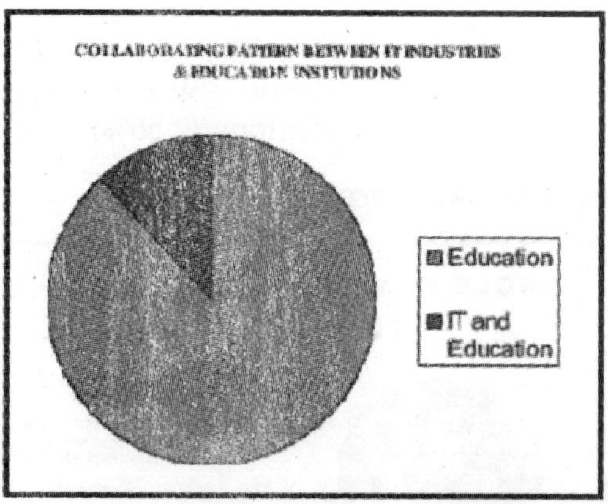

Fig. 8.

Graph-8 shows the Collaborating institutions. Out of 59 Collaborated papers with different institution, 52 papers are collaborated with Education Institution. Only 7 papers are found collaborated with IT industries. Thus it can be found that the Collaboration between IT industries with Education Institutions are very limited.

Institution-wise Distribution

Table Showing Institution-wise output

Institutions	*Number*
Annamlai University	73
DIET	26
Avinashilingam University	17
PSG College of Technology and Polytechnic College	13
Bishop Heber College	11
Sri Paramakalyani College	10
Kristu Jayanti College of Management and Technology	8
Tapiaco and Castor Research Station	8
P.S.G. College of Arts and Science	5
Mangalore University	4
Periyar Manimammai College of Technology For Women	4
Vikram Sarabhai Space Centre	4
Bharathiar University	3
Ethiraj College for Women	3
Kerala Agricultural University	3
Kongu Engineering College	3
NIEPA	3
Periyar Centenary Polytechnic College	3
St. Joseph's College	3
University of Madras	3
Aligarh Muslim University	2
Amravati University	2
Anna University	2
Bangalore University	2
Dr. G.R.D. College of Science	2
Indian Institute of Technology	2
Knowledge Point Online Services Pvt. Ltd.	2

Manonmaniam Sundaranar University	2
Mother Teresa Women's University	2
NIRMALA COLLEGE FOR WOMEN	2
P. M.T. College	2
P.S.G.R Krishnammal College	2
Pachaiyappa's College for Women	2
Presidency College	2
PSG Institute of Management	2
S.T.Hindu College	2
Shri Vaishnav Institute of Management	2
Tamil Nadu Agricultural University	2
University of Poona	2
Vellalar College for Women	2
Other Institution	108

Table -1 indicates the institution-wise research output to the Conference. It could be observed that Annamalai University ranks first in order among other institutions Contributing about 73 papers.

DIET ranks second in order contributing 26 papa's. Avinashillingam University ranks third in order contributing 17 papers. PSG college of technology is placed next in order sharing 13 papers. PSG College of technology is placed next in order sharing 13 papers.

Bishop Heber College is placed next in order sharing 11 papers.

The other various numbers of minor institutions have individually contributed less than 10 papers each.

It could be deduced from the above disscussion that Annamalai university, DIET, Avinashiligam university, PSG college of tech, Bishop Heber college are predominant Institutions in contributing more number of research papers.

CONCLUSION

The findings of the present study as derived from the analysis are summarised as follows:

(1) The country-wise distribution of papers contributed to the International conference revealed that the major

contributors are Indians. Regarding continent-wise coverage, the conference has reached well in Asia and Africa and Europe.

(2) The State-wise distribution of papers revealed that the major contributions are from Tamil Nadu.

(3) The District-wise distribution of papers revealed that the major contributions are from Cuddalore, Coimbatore and Chennai District.

(4) The analysis of Authorship pattern revealed that single authored papers ranks first in order, followed by Double Authored, Triple authored papers.

(5) The analysis of collaboration between institutions revealed that the authors mainly collaborate with the same institution.

(6) The analysis of Institution-wise research output revealed that Annamalai University ranks first in order. It is followed by DIET, Avinashiligam University, PSG College of Technology, Bishop Heber College.

21

Mapping the Structure of the Discipline 'Women in* Informatics' Using Co-word Analysis

ABSTRACT

The present study attempts to identify the microstructure of the discipline 'women in informatics' by using the co-word analysis. It takes into consideration three-time periods viz: 1984-1989, 1990-1994, 1995-2003. Based on the publications of this discipline collected for these periods, a databases is created using 'Procite' (bibliographic management software). By adopting various word extraction techniques, keywords and word phrases representing the thematic structures of this discipline are constructed. The strength of linkage between co-word pairs are explored further to understand the core, neutral and peripheral themes. Such thematic structures represent the trend and pattern of research activities within the discipline taken for analysis. The results are projected through lexi-maps.

INTRODUCTION

Mapping the structure of a discipline indicates the dimension in which the intellectual discourse in a discipline is developing. On the basis of these thematic maps, two types of information analysis can be considered: (i) one is the analysis of the thematic structure of the database itself (What is in the database?); and (ii) the other is the observation of the research field (Who does what, where and when?). This study attempts to map the structure of the subject 'women in informatics' in order to identify the components or themes that build the structure of this subject. Though it is an emerging discipline, the volume of publication on this subject is quite enormous which warrants an evaluation of the direction and the pattern of the growth and development of this subject. This study is a maiden attempt to evaluate the status of this discipline through published literature across the globe. Besides, it is an effort towards organising the scattered resources of information on this discipline for the purpose of undertaking further research. Enough attention is given to create, organise and map the gender specific information in computing in order to provide wider visibility to the existing knowledge, which could be used as an input to promote women's status in informatics. For the purpose of the present study, a sample database on the given subject is developed by collecting and organising the related literature available in the journal articles, books, conference proceedings, project reports etc. Besides, the keywords representing the themes and the sub-themes of the subject are extracted in order to map the semantic structure of the discipline. This cognitive structure of the discipline explains the importance that this subject gains in the last two decades and serves as a base for planning the future research.

CONCEPTUAL DISCUSSION

This study is based on the fact that a network of co-occurrences between different words, collected on a specific set of publications, allows a quantitative study of the structure of publications. The contents or the concepts (keywords) of the publications are analysed in order to understand the nature and strength of linkages between the pairs of words. This method labeled as co-word analysis, provides a direct quantitative way of linking the conceptual contents of publications, by comparing and classifying publications with respect to the occurrences of similar word-pairs. Hence, such a co-word structure can represent activities within a scientific area. It does so through the depiction of the state-of-art research in that scientific area by delineating and underscoring the relations between various themes. The value of this analysis lies chiefly in identifying the emerging research areas—both within the specialty and across specialties i.e interdisciplinary areas[1].

In this study, co-word approach is used to understand the dynamics and the internal structure of the field 'women in informatics'. The aim is to identify the core, neutral and the peripheral areas of research apart from tracing the emerging field in this discipline during the period 1984 and 2003. It also aims to project the constant and the extinct nature of the themes of this discipline. The lexi-maps used in this study provide a pictorial representation of the research areas of the subject 'women in informatics'.

METHODOLOGY

Methods used for standardising the Keywords

Keywords are extracted from the sample publications on the discipline 'women in informatics' by adopting Tim Caravan's tools. The extracted words were ranked on the basis of their higher order of frequency i.e words having maximum frequency in a given document (>5). It is presumed that words that have maximum occurrence represent the relevant concepts in the areas of research taken for analysis. In this manner, keywords for the entire set of sample documents (639 records) were collected. The collated keyword were converted into a standard thesaurus. The following diagram explains the manner in which the keywords are built in to an organised database of keywords.

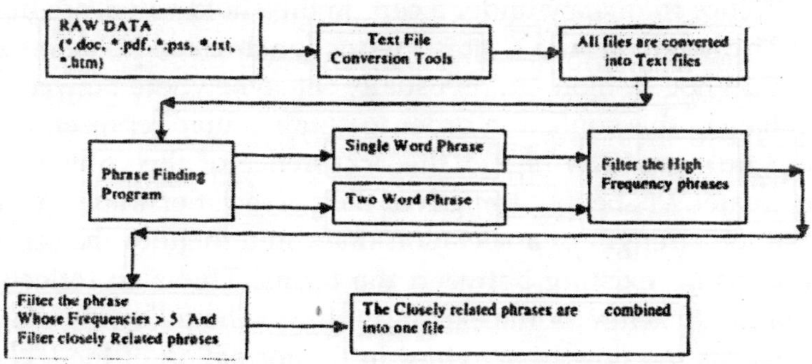

Methods Used to Form the Co-words (Co-occurrence of words)

Co-words are constructed by identifying the linkages or strength among the important concepts (keywords). The frequencies of the co-occurrences of words are ranked to form a matrix of co-word pairs. In this context, the occurrence of single words in the whole sample were not taken into consideration for the formation of co-word matrix in order to avoid the spurious linkages. In the co-occurrence matrix, each cell in this symmetric matrix represents the number of times two words co-occur together (C_{ij}).

Methods Used to Form the Lexi-Map

To understand the nature of relationship among the co-occurrence of words, lexi-map technique is adopted. In this method, each word is considered as a node connected by the relation of co-occurrence to another node. Co-occurrences are the ties or the links. The lexi-map is formed out of the co-occurrence matrix. The strength of the linkage 'S' of the co-ocrrences are measured by the number by using the formula: $S(Ci.Cij)=Cij*Cij / CiCj$ $0<S<1$ where'Cij' is the number of co-occurrence of terms I and j. Here, the occurrence of a single word I within a set of publications is denoted as C_1.[2] The higher (1) or the lower (0) strength of the co-occurrence is determined by the number of times a co-word pair occurs together in a given document or in a database of a specific subject. As the strength of the co-occurrence ranges between 0 and 1, it is necessary to fix certain thresholds in order to filter the 'uninteresting co-occurrences'. This implies that the 'co-word pairs' with a co-occurrence frequency under a certain threshold value, are filtered out. The height of such a 'noise' reduction threshold is determined in an ad hoc fashion and is usually set somewhere between 0.05 and 0.25 in this context in order to obtain a map representing the main linkages. The higher the occurrence of the co-word pair, the greater will be the strength of their association and vice-versa. From the strength of association one could identify the semantic relationship existing between the terms. This also reflects the semantic structure of the existing subject. The following diagram represents the flow of activities in the formation of the lexi-map which is ~ reflective of the structure of the discipline 'women in informatics'.

ANALYSIS AND INTERPRETAITON

Growth in the Publication Pattern of the Discipline 'Women in Informatics'

It is interesting to note (vide Table-I) that the publication trend of the subject 'women in informatics' is gaining momentum in the recent years. The number of documents in the sample database has shown a manifold increase from 8 publications in the early 80s to 347 publications in the early 2000s indicating that

Data Flow Diagram:

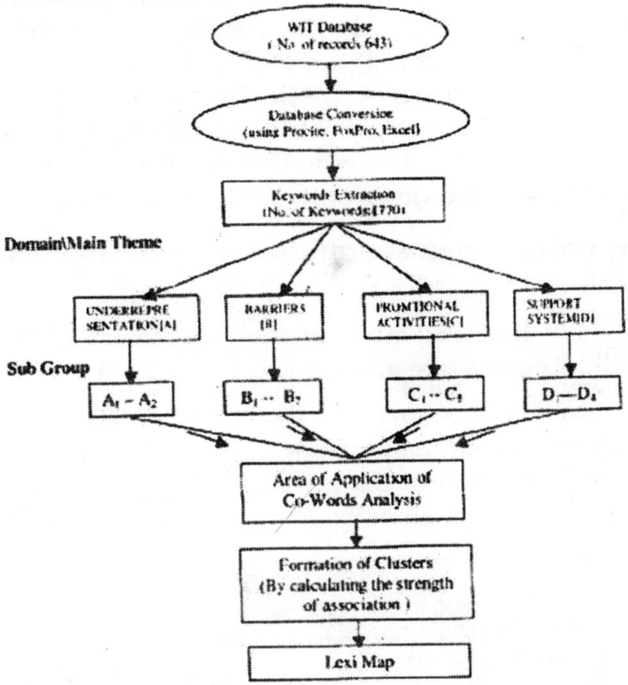

the concept 'women in informatics' has gradually progressed into a full-fledged discipline in the last two decades. The phenomenal growth in the publication is an indication of the importance that this discipline has gained among the scholars in gender research. It further reflects the concern of the academicians in the lower

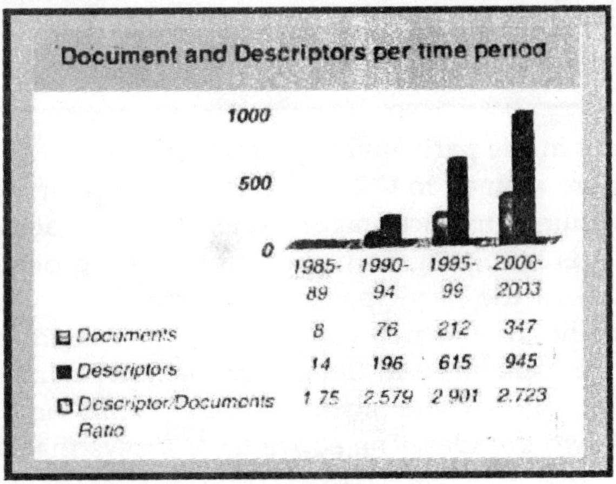

participation of women in the newly emerging technology. Parallel to the development in the number of publications, the descriptors or keywords explaining the problems in the field are also increasing at a faster rate. It is noticed from that the number of descriptors are increasing from 14 to 945 in the sample database, which again is the indication of the growing popularity of the above field. One could observe a direct proportion to the number of documents and the descriptors in the given discipline.

Chronological Representation of the Themes of the Discipline

The major thematic facets or the constituents of the subject 'women informatics' are analysed and presented in Table 2.

The above table shows that the subject under consideration has been built on four major themes. The specific issues that have attracted the attention of the gender specialists include 'Under-representation of women in Computer Science 'Education (CSE)'

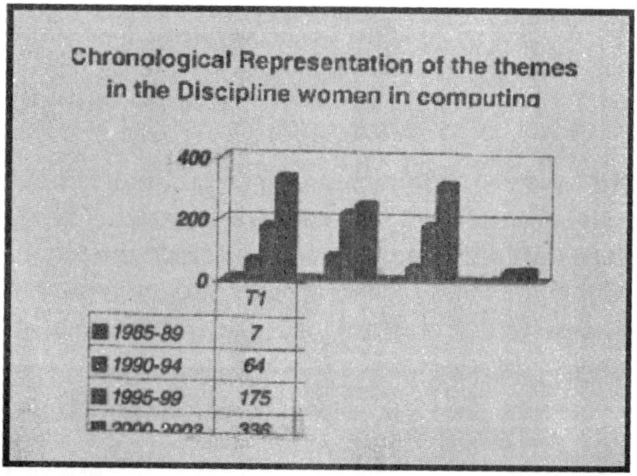

(Tl); 'Barrier in the participation, women in CSE' (T2); 'Strategies to draw more women to CSE' (T3) and the 'Support system' (T4) that are required to encourage women to be an active agent in the CSE. It is seen that contrary to the existing demand in the labour market, the participation of women and minorities are limited in the area which caused a great concern among the industrialists, scholars and the government departments dealing with labour issues. These factors are reflected in the publications of the last two decades. The above table shows that the number of publications on T1 (under representation of women in CSE) has increased from 7 to 175 registering a 25-fold increase over the period of time. Similarly, the discussions on T2 (barriers to participate in CSE) has increased from 2 to 221 in the last three periods indicating the importance of this issue. In the same manner, the number of publications delineating the strategies for involving more women in CSE and training has increased from 5 to 183. The need for developing a support system both in the family and the work place has been the target of discussion in the last two periods. In short, theme 2 received higher priority with 303 publications followed by theme 1 (246 publications), theme 3 (233 publications) and theme 4 (43 publications).

Co-occurence Matrix for the Main Themes

It is noticed that themes are formed not by a single keyword but through a collection or combination of keywords. S. R. Ranganathan in his theory of 'Knowledge organisation' has discussed the various modes through which words would combine together and generate a new themes or knowledge. In this study, the co-word method is adopted to trace the formation of new themes. Table 3 depicts the number of times each keyword (i) co-occurs with another keyword (j) in the database taken for analysis. The cell value in the co-occurrence matrix represents the co-word pairs (C_{ij}) selected for the current study. For instance, the theme 'A' in Table-3 co-occurs with theme 'B' 148 times & with 'C' 167 times within a database of 639 documents having 1770 descriptors or keywords. In the same manner the concept

Table 3 : Matrix Representing the Co-occurrence of the Major Themes

Thematic Groups	*A*	*B*	*C*	*D*	*Total*
A	373	148	167	43	731
B	148	319	142	29	638
C	167	142	318	47	674
D	43	29	47	73	192

Group 'A' indicates Under-representation of women in CSE
Group 'B' indicates Barriers in participation in CSE course
Group 'C' indicates Promotional activities to draw more women
Group 'D' indicates Support System

'B' co-occurs with concepts 'A & C' more than 100 times. Similar is the case with concept 'C'. There is a closer correlation between the co-occurrence of the keywords and the formation of new themes. The more the co-occurrences of the keywords, the higher will be the emergence of new themes in any given subject.

Determination of Word-Linkage Strength

Table 4 shows that the linkages or the associations are stronger between the co-word pairs: A & C; B & C. The linkages are weaker between the co-word pairs: A&D; and B&D. The medium linkages are observed between the pairs: A&B; D&C. The above analysis brings to the lime light the fact that out of the 639 publications (1770 keywords), most of them have discussed about the issues concerning women's under representation (A) in the field of computing and the need to formulate strategies for promoting more women (C) to this field which is notified in the strong association between the co-word pair A &C where the 'S' value is greater than 0.25. Similarly, publications have deliberated on the barriers (B) that deter women from taking active participation in computing education and suggested the context-specific methodologies for promoting women (C) in computing which is seen from the strong linkages between the co-word pair B & C. The word-linkage strength value also confirms this. The number of publications covering the themes under representation of women (A) and the barriers (B) are found at a moderate level (Strength of A&B = 0.184). Similar is the case with the co-word pairs C&B, C&D whose strength of associations are 0.199 & 0.148. The word-linkage strength of the rest of the pairs *viz*: A&D, B&D are low i.e. 0.106 & 0.056 respectively.

Table 4 : Matrix Depicting the Strength of Relationship between the Major Themes

Groups	*A*	*B*	*C*	*D*
A	1	0.184	0.235	0.016
B	0.184	1	0.199	0.056
C	0.235	0.199	1	0.148
D	0.106	0.056	0.148	1

The lexi-map gives a pictorial representation of not only the association existing between the co-word pairs but also the level of relation existing between them. The thick lines in the lexi-map indicate the stronger association of co-word pairs A&C and B&C.

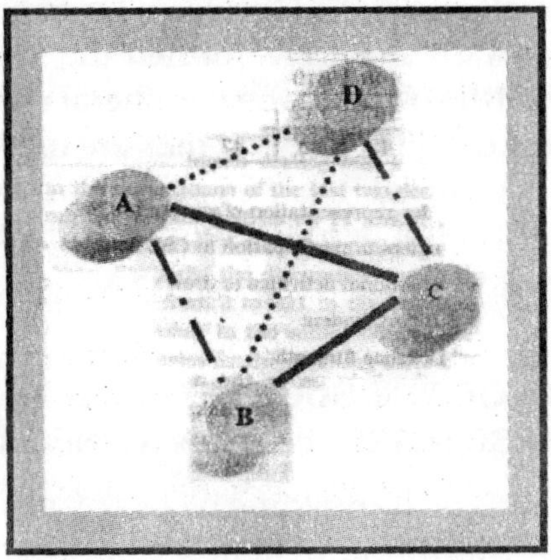

Table 5: Lexi Map Table Depicting the Strength of Relationship between the Major Thematic Groups

Order	*Ci*	*Cj*	*Cij*	*S*	*Intensity of Strength*
1.	Under representation [A) [373]	Promotional activities [C) [318]	167	0.235	High
2.	Barriers (B) [319]	Promotional activities [C) [318]	142	0.199	High
3.	Under representation [A) [373]	Barriers (B) [319]	148	0.184	Medium
4.	Promotional activities [C)[318]	Support system (D) [73]	47	0.148	Medium
5.	Under representation [A) [373]	Support system (D)[73]	43	0.106	Low
6.	Barriers (B)[319]	Support system(D) [73]	29	0.056	Low

Note: High level of association is identified between the groups A-C & B-C. Medium level of association is identified between the groups A-B & C-D. Lower level of association is identified between the groups A-D & B-D

As against this, a moderate level of linkages are indicated through the intermittent lines A&B and D&C. Out of the 6 co-word pairs taken for analysis, the pairs A&C and B&C formed the core theme; the co-word pairs A&B and D&C formed the neutral theme; and the pairs A&D and B&D formed the peripheral theme of the subject 'women in informatics'. The core themes are represented through thick lines; the neutral themes are represented through intermittent lines and the peripherals are notified through dotted lines. The lexi-map table given in Table-5 also reinstate the above findings.

CONTRIBUTION OF THE SUB-THEMES IN THE FORMATION OF THE DISCIPLINE 'WOMEN IN INFORMATICS'

The sub-themes are the building blocks of any given discipline. The growth of a discipline depends to a larger extent on the proliferation of the sub-fields emerged within the discipline and also on the tendency of the discipline to interact with other discipline.

The following table indicates the number of sub-themes that have contributed for the growth and development of the discipline under consideration. It is observed that the contribution of the sub-themes 'Branch of Study (A1) and Level of Course (A2) in CSE to 'Theme A' is 32%. Similarly, 'Theme B' is constituted by barriers of various kinds such as Social Barriers (B); Cultural Barriers (B2); Family Barriers (B3); Institutional Barriers (B4); Technological Barriers (B5); Attitudinal Barriers (B6); Lack of Technical Competency (B7) and the proportion contribution of these sub-themes to the growth of the subject is 31%. Similarly 'Theme C' is made up of eight sub-themes viz: Formulation of women-friendly policies (C1); Career Counseling (C2); Changes in the academic environment (C3); Propagating computer education (C4); Special programmes to encourage girls and women (C5); Outreach programmes (C6); Skill Development (C7); and Awareness (C8) and their collective contribution to the growth of the discipline is 32%. 'Theme 4' is composed of the following four sub-themes i.e Family support (D1); Financial support (D2); Support from the Government (D3); and Institutional Programmes (D4) to encourage women. The overall contribution of these themes for the development of the discipline is just 6%. Out of the 21 sub-themes, only a very few themes such as the under representation of women in the various branches of CSE courses (Al=25%), the technical in-competencies of women to participate in the CSE course (B7=10%) or and the need for skill development (C7=9%} to involve more women into computing have received wider attention among the gender specialists and, therefore, their contribution to the growth of the discipline is found to be significant. Table 6 explains the proportion of contribution of the individual themes to the structural growth of the discipline under consideration till the last two decades.

Table 6: Sub-themes Contribution to the Growth of the Discipline

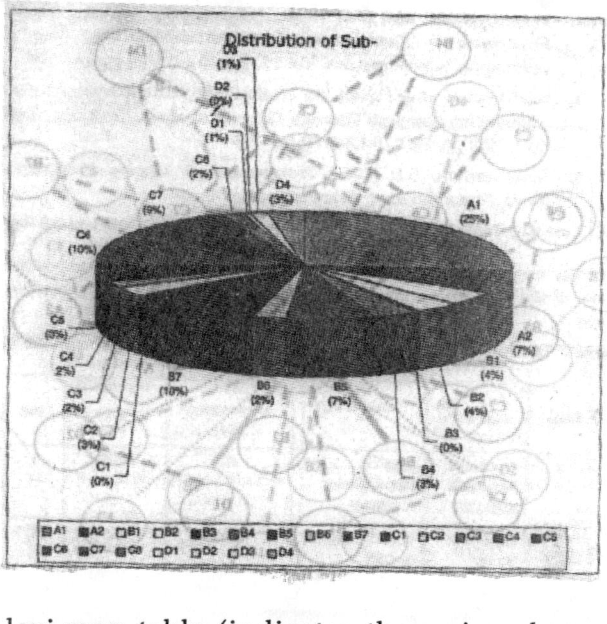

The lexi-map table (indicates the major players or the contributors to the structural development of the discipline. It is observed that the primary network or the core themes are formed by the nodes or the sub-themes A1, A2,B5.B6,C6, &C7 which have contributed significantly in the building of the core theme of the subject 'women in informatics'. The first network is formed by the nodes C6&C7 whose 'S' value is 0.1022. The second network is formed by the association of the node A1 with several other nodes A2, C7, B6, & C6 and their 'S' values are ranging between 0.0771 to 0.0655. The third network is formed by the association of the nodes B5 & C6 whose 'S' value is 0.0605.

The secondary networks are formed by the nodes A1, A2, B5, B7, C6, C7 & C3. Here A1 has formed a larger network with

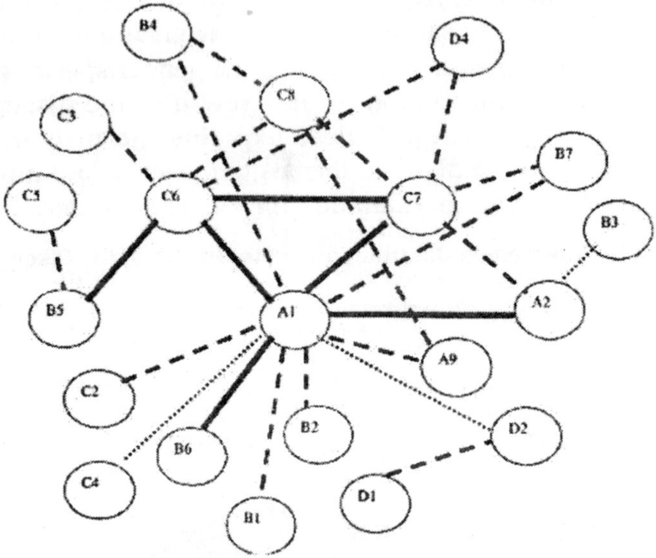

other nodes such as B2 (S = 0.0489), B7 (S = 0.0469), B1(S = 0.0456), C2(S = 0.046) B4(S = 0.0416). Next in the order of priority comes A2 that has formed network with C7 (S = 0.0443) & C6 (S=0.0441).

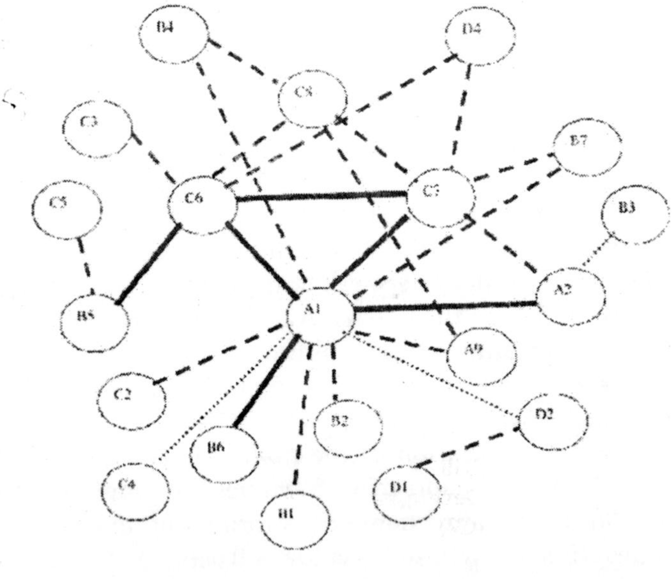

The other network in the second category is formed by the node B7 with C7 (S = 0.578) and C8 (S = 0.042). The other nodes that are involved in the formation of the secondary networks include B5 & B7, C6 & C8, C7 & D4, C6 & D4, C7 & C8, C3 & C8. The co-word pairs in the secondary networks indicate the themes that are in the process of development. The third category of network is formed between the nodes B5 & C5(S = 0.04) and Al&C4 (0.045) which explains the emerging trend of publication on these themes. The following lexi-map also supports the results given above.

CONCLUSION

This study demonstrates the feasibility of co-word analysis as a viable approach for extracting patterns of development of subject from the publications. It also shows the status report of the growth of the subject in the last two years which is a base for predicting the future of the subject. It also shows the multi-disciplinary trend that contributes for the fast growth of the subject. On the whole, the fast expansion in the development of the subject 'women in informatics' is gauged through an appropriate methodology.

Lexi Map Table Depicting the Strength of Relationship between the Sub-Themes

The co-word pairs that constitute the core, neutral and the peripheral areas of the discipline under study have been analysed and presented in Table 7.

Table 7: Co-word Pairs showing the Strength of Relationship between the Sub-Themes

Order	Node-I [Ci)	Node-II [Cj)	Co-occurrence	Strength (S)	Link
1	Outreach Programs (C6)(137)	Skill Development (C7) (126)	42	0.1022	1
2	Branch of Study (A1)(313)	Level of Course in CSE (A2)(112)	52	0.0771	1
3	Branch of Study (A1)(313)	Skill Development (C7) (126)	55	0.0767	1

4	Branch of Study (A1)(313)	Personal Attitudes (B6)(38)	28	0.0659	1
5	Branch of Study (A1)(313)	Outreach Programe (C6)(137)	53	0.0655	1
6	Lack of Access To Computer Infrastructure (B5)(88)	Outreach Programe (C6)(137)	27	0.0605	1
7.	Technical Incompetency (B7)(132)	Skill Development (C7) (126)	31	0.0578	2
8.	Outreach Programs (C6)(137)	Treatment (C8((26)	14	0.055	2
9.	Skill Development (C7) (126)	Institutional Programmes (D4)(40)	6	0.0508	2
10.	Branch of Study (A1)(313)	Cultural Barriers (B2)(55)	29	0.0489	2
11.	Branch of Study (A1)(313)	Technical Incompetency (B7)(132)	44	0.0469	2
12.	Outreach Programmes (C6)(137)	Institutional Programmes (D4)(40)	16	0.0467	2
13.	Branch of Study (A1)(313)	Career Counseling (C2)(47)	26	0.046	2
14.	Branch of Study (A1)(313)	Social Barriers (B1)(63)	30	0.0456	2
15.	Level of Course in CSE (A2)(112)	Skill Development (C7) (126)	25	0.0443	2
16.	Level of Course in CSE (A2)(112)	Outreach Programmes (C6)(137)	26	0.0441	2

17.	Skill Development (C7) (126)	Treatment (C8)(26)	12	0.044	2
18.	Technical Incompetency (B7)(132)	Treatment (C8((26)	12	0.042	2
19.	Lack of Access to Computer Infrastructure (B5)(88)	Technical Incompetency (B7)(132)	22	0.0417	2
20.	Branch of Study (A1)(313)	Institutional Barriers (B4)(56)	27	0.0416	2
21.	Change in Academic Environment (C3)(33)	Outreach Programs (C6)(137)	15	0.0409	2
22.	Lack of Access To Computer Infrastructure (B5)(88)	Programmes To Encourage Girls and Women (C5)(48)	13	0.04	3
23.	Branch of Study (A1)(313)	Popularise Computer Education (C4)(37)	20	0.0345	3

1 – Core Theme 2 – Neutral Theme 3 – Peripheral Theme

REFERENCES

- Tijssen, R.J.W and Van Raan, A.F.J (1989). "Mapping Co-Word Structures: A Comparison of Multidimensional Scaling and Leximappe". *Scientometrics,* Vol. 15. Nos 3-4 (1989). pp. 283-295.
- Neal Coulter et.al (1996). "An Evolutionary Perspective of Software Engineering Research Through Co-word analysis". *Technical Report,* CMU/SEI-95-TR-019 ESC-TR-95-019
- Ranganathan, S.R (1967). *Prolegomena to Library Classification.* Third Edition. London. Asia Publishing House.

22

Building an Ontology-based Open Access Digital Archives for ICWES Proceedings (1964-2005)

ABSTRACT

The aims of this paper are (i) to establish an open access repository for the entire ICWES publications to facilitate wider access to the scholarly information among the gender scientists (ii) to develop an appropriate mechanism for concept representation and storage for easy retrieval of the conference papers (iii) to develop an ontology-based knowledge management system for the ICWES by combining metadata approach as well as ontology-based information systems approach and (iv) to examine the possibilities of utilising the existing 'subject classification systems' like the Dewey Decimal Classification systems (DDC) for tagging and mapping the information.

INTRODUCTION

The beginning of the third millennium has witnessed unprecedented changes in the domain of science, technology and the world of work. The socio-economic and political forces across the globe have brought out challenging pressures on the growing issues of gender within the developed and developing world. New paradigm orders are rapidly shifting their importance with respect to the overall welfare of humankind and thus International Conference of Women Engineers and Scientists (ICWES) has become a well-organised association, which aims at contributing through Science and Technology, towards the promotion of gender equity and distributive justice. The ICWES international conferences are held every three years and have been central in establishing strong and influential networks of individuals and organisations that are engaged in research and grassroots activities with a view to promoting gender equity in science and technology. The research contributions and proceedings of ICWES conferences provide an important source of information on research and interventions in the field of gender, science and technology. Ironically, the availability and the accessibility to the resources of the ICWES have been constrained by various factors. None of the engineering databases like the INSPEC, COMPENDX, IEEE have captured the papers published in the proceedings of the ICWES. This means that the visibility of these research papers remain like a block box not to be reached to the research community in gender studies. To alleviate this problem, the International Network of Women Engineers and Scientists (INWES) have come out with a proposal of digitising the proceedings and establishing an open access digital repository. This project was commenced in October 2004 and completed in March 2005.

HISTORICAL OVERVIEW OF ICWES

ICWES provides an international forum for sharing research findings and strengthening global networks. ICWES held its first International Conference in 1964 in New York, (USA). The subsequent conferences were held in: 1967 Cambridge (UK), 1971 Torino (Italy), 1975 Cracow (Poland), 1978 Rouen (France), 1981 Bombay (India), 1984 Washington, DC (USA), 1987 (Ivory Coast), 1991 Coventry (England), 1996 Budapest (Hungary), 1999 Tokyo (Japan) , 2002 Ottawa (Canada) and 2005 Seuol (Korea). The theme of the First ICWES Conference was: Focus on the Future and this conference was structured around the theme of building engineering and scientific talents to solve basic human needs such as water, clothing, shelter, transport and energy. The rest of the conferences have focused their themes on (i) Application of Technology to World Food Problems; (ii) Planning for Progress; (iii) Sociological Problems of Women Engineers and Scientists; (iv) Technology and Freedom; (v) Science, Technology and Society; (vi) Technology-An International Bridge; (vii) Science, Technology and Development; (viii) Communication; (ix) Towards the Third Millennium: The Role of the Intellectual Potential in a New World; (x) Science and Technology for Global; (xi) Women in a Knowledge Based Society; (xii) Women Engineers and Scientists: Main Force to Reshape the Future World.

PROBLEM STATEMENT

Over the last decade, there has been increasing debate over the reasons underlying the dearth of women at all levels in SET. Many initiatives have been taken up like the one organised by UNESCO at Budapest in 1999 (World Women Science Conference) for promoting women in the field of science and technology. A quick review of the conferences being organised in the domain of 'women in science and engineering' down the line has shown that ICWES was one of the pioneering efforts. The compendium of papers published in the conference proceedings from 1964-2005 provides a rich source of information specific to gender inclusive science and technology. However, an analysis of the secondary engineering databases like the INSPEC and the science citation index reveals that they have not captured the publications of these ICWES conference proceedings, reflecting the limited usability of these resources by a wider gender research community. The major problem is that these proceedings are not only scattered but also poorly organised leading to limited utility by the special interest groups. This situation has prompted the organisers of the ICWES to go in for a digital archive of their conference proceedings in order to make it accessible worldwide. One of the challenges in transforming this concept into reality is to identify the institutional and individual sources to pool the printed version of the proceedings. The next challenge is to identify an appropriate and cost-effective technology to create an open access repository that could be accessible world-wide. The other major concerns are (i) identification and organisation of the content metadata of the conference papers; (ii) grouping or categorising the contents into hierarchical directories in the repository; (iii) creating bibliographic metadata of the conference papers and (iv) building an association between the concept metadata, bibliographic metadata, and the documents in the knowledge repository.

SCOPE AND OBJECTIVES

The aims of this paper are (i) to establish an open access repository for the entire ICWES publications to facilitate wider access to the scholarly information among the gender scientists (ii) to develop an appropriate mechanism for concept representation and storage for easy retrieval of the conference papers (iii) to develop an ontology-based knowledge management system for the ICWES by combining metadata approach as well as ontology-based information systems approach and (iv) to examine the possibilities of utilising the existing 'subject classification systems' like the Dewey Decimal Classification systems (DDC) for tagging and mapping the information.

REVIEW OF LITERATURE

Open Archives Initiatives

The open archives initiatives take a momentum in the recent years and they take one of the following forms: (i) institutional repositories; (ii) discipline-specific open archives; and (iii) material-type-specific digital repositories. There seems to be a big move in the direction of creating institutional repositories in academic and research institutions to cope with the globalisation of education. On the other hand, the growth of subject-specific open archives are very slow due to want of subject-related thesaurus or taxonomies for the emerging subjects. However, efforts are being taken in the direction of either building domain-specific taxonomies for organising knowledge or to adopt the existing subject classification systems with modifications.

Use of DDC for Knowledge Organisations (KO)

Several new techniques have been introduced for organising discipline-specific open archives. The relevance of DDC as an effective tool for knowledge organisation in the web environment is well established. Koch et al. (1997) reviewed major classification schemes that are being used on the Internet and concluded that DDC was used more frequently than any other knowledge organisation scheme. Williamson (1997) and Saeed and Chaudhry (2001) pointed out that the features available in the latest version of DDC could have been exploited in more innovative ways to provide better support for organisation of digital information resources. One possibility in this regard is to exploit the potential of knowledge structure of DDC to develop a taxonomy system that can be used for categorisation of information resources. Drawing inspiration from the above literature, the present study makes an attempt to build a taxonomy for organising the subject 'women in science and engineering'.

METHODOLOGY

The key issues raised at the commencement of the ICWES open access digital archives project were mainly centering around (i) how to organise the content and how to group the digital objects; and (ii) how to create a semantic-based knowledge management system. The complexity of these issues were resolved by fragmenting the process into different activities as (i) creating a digital repository of the printed texts (lowest level); (ii) designing a metadata repository for the content and the context of the documents (intermediate level) ; and (iii) building a web-based access mechanisms (highest level).

Process of Creating Digital Repository for ICWES

In step 1, the printed copies of the ICWES conference proceedings (ICWES 1- ICWES 13) were scanned in different resolutions. Nearly about 1900 papers covering 6184 pages were scanned in 300 dpi with 256 gray levels and saved in a file. In step 2, the scanned images of the document were transformed into a digitised representation of the page content i.e. a character-by-character representation rather than a pixel-by-pixel one. In step 3, the anomalies caused by special terminologies, small type printing, unusual page layouts, over-dark characters, were resolved using interactive OCR software. In step 4, the digital contents were segmented into blocks such as text blocks, table blocks, picture blocks etc and they were tagged and stored in separate file formats viz: html, doc, plain text and pdf etc. Fig. 1 presents the process of building the digital repository of the ICWES papers.

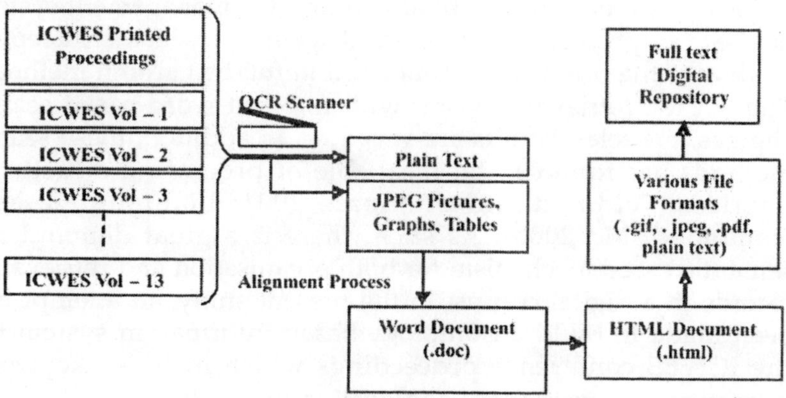

Process of Creating Metadata Repository for the Digital Objects in ICWES

In general all information objects, regardless of the physical or intellectual form will have three features - content, context and structure - all of which can be reflected through Metadata. Content relates to what the object contains or is about, and is intrinsic to an information object. Context indicates who, what, why, where, how aspects associated with the object's creation and is extrinsic to an information object and structure relates to the formal set of associations within or among individual information objects. In a digital repository environment, metadata is created for almost every conceivable object or group of objects stored in electronic form. Multiple standards are available for metadata creation. In the present study, simple but effective tools and techniques have been exploited for generating the content metadata, context or document metadata and the structural metadata.

Creating Context Metadata or Document Description Model

The schema of the context or document description metadata contains data relating to the (i) contributors (ii) organisers; and the (iii) publishers of the ICWES conference and it acts as a document identifier. Based on predefined templates for documents, the context metadata were extracted. Microsoft MS-Access is used for capturing the bibliographic elements of the conference papers.

Creating Content Metadata

The need for ontology based knowledge management system has been emphasized from time and again by researchers keeping in view of the problems encountered in full-text search methods. Though the retrieval is faster with free-text word-based search engines, the relevant hits are very low. In addition, these search methods are found to be incapable of processing structured queries. (Feldman and Sherman, 2001; Liautaud, B. and Hammond, M., 2000). As such, there is a great demand for semantic based mechanism for both organisation and retrieval of records in a digital corpus. In the present study, an attempt has been made to build an ontology-based information system for the ICWES conference proceedings which includes keyword extraction, categorisation, aggregation and validation.

Keyword Extraction

A keyword is a single word or multiple-words present in the documents that can characterise and summarise the topics covered by documents. In the present study, the freely available text mining and extraction techniques are applied to extract keywords from the textual digital data. It is clear that all the words do not have the same prior chance to be a keyword in a document. Firstly, using delimiters such as spaces, tabs, new lines, dots, etc all token words in the documents are identified. The choice of keywords are decided by making use of the parameters (i) frequency (ii) specialty of the word in the document. By using the following metric, keywords are extracted for the test data in our project. Standard key word extraction metric is *TFxIDF* (standing for Term Frequency x Inverse Document Frequency) score. A word W in document D, is defined as *TFxIDF (P, D)* = P(word in D is W) x [- log P(W in a document)]. The first term in this formula is calculated by counting the number of times the word occurs in the document and dividing it to the total number of words in it. The second term is calculated by counting the number of documents in the training set that the word occurs in except D and dividing it by the total number of documents in the training set. By adopting this algorithm, the keywords are extracted from the ICWES documents. The total number of keywords generated for the entire set of ICWES proceedings (1900 papers) amounts to more than 10,00,000 words. Since there is a problem in managing these unorganised data both for storing and retrieval purpose, we have decided to adopt a controlled vocabulary system for grouping these keywords into semantically-structured format.

Text Categorisation

DDC was used to structure the keywords generated from the ICWES proceedings. This system facilitated the process of mapping the voluminous terms into semantic categories. DDC taxonomy building process involves: (i) identification of relevant hierarchies from DDC schedules, (ii) combining terms from DDC indexes, (iii) adding controlled vocabulary to the hierarchy. The Figure-2 explains how the concepts were organised into a hierarchical structure. It is interesting to note that the entire set of keywords have been classified into 250 broad categories.

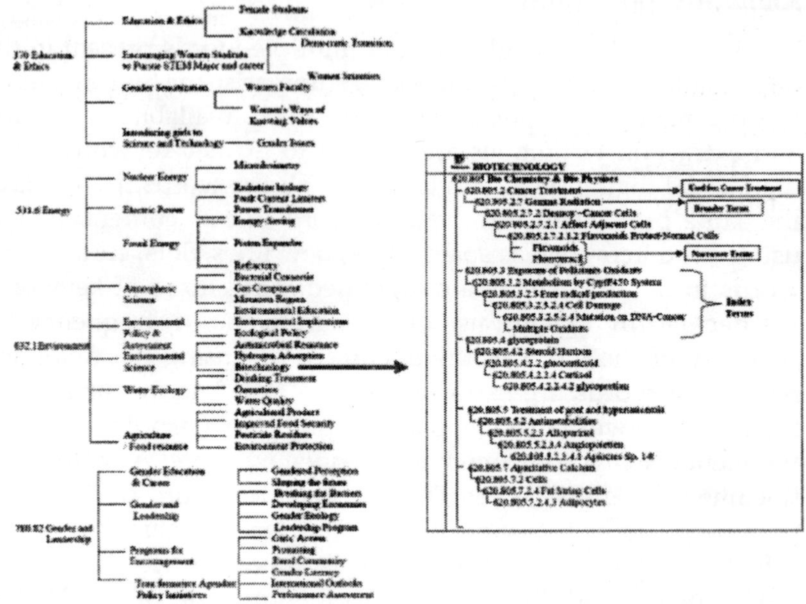

Fig. 2 : Semantic Mapping of Keywords Using DDC

Process of Aggregation

The process of aggregation refers to the linkage established between the metadata repository and the knowledge repository through the digital object descriptor. These two repositories are to be integrated for efficient search and retrieval. The following diagram explains the semantic based query handing system. For instance, when the user approaches the system with a query on 'flavonoids', the query handler will lead the user to entire spectrum of the given subject. He will be exposed to the documents not only on 'flavonoids' but also on the semantically related

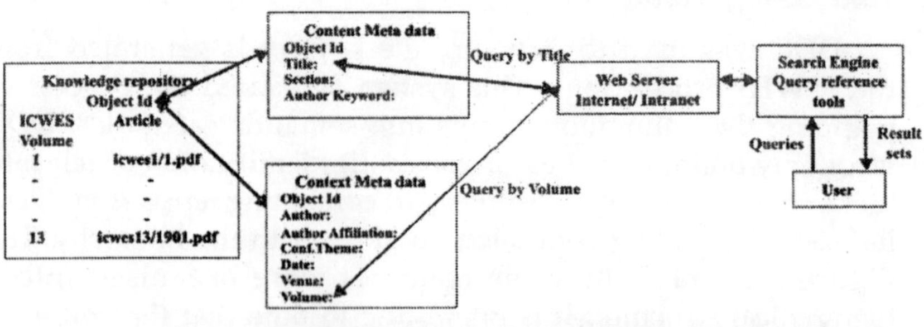

Fig. 3 : Ontology-based Information Retrieval Model

documents on 'flavonoids-protect-normal cells', 'affect adjacent cells' 'destroy cancer cells etc. In this way, the system will facilitate the user to broaden or narrow his search based on his requirement. The query optimisation is achieved in this semantic query handling method.

The digitisation project has brought to focus the fact that digital conversion of full text from printed documents seems to be simple compared to building a knowledge based ontology for the ICWES publications because the latter is an intellectually demanding activity. Though the existing classification schemes comes for rescue in concept categorisation and taxonomy building for the subjects in ICWES, it is not true for all the subjects covered by the entire set of papers . This situation has enforced a new knowledge organisation strategy. It also emphasizes the need for building subject specific taxonomy for the subject 'women in engineering and science'. The need for taxonomy based organisation of the publications on women in engineering and science is justified on the fact that search on a pile of randomly selected, unorganized content is time-consuming and costly.

FUTURE DEVELOPMENTS

Conclusion: There are many national and international conferences beyond ICWES viz: SWE, WEPAN, AWIS, GHC, **WIGSAT** etc. that have focused their attention on issues about women in engineering and science. The gender research publications from reputed organisations like the Anita Borg Institute of Women in Information Technology (ABIWT), CWTS are on the increase. It is the most appropriate time to build open access archives of all these publications to promote gender research in Women in Science and Engineering.

REFERENCES

- Koch, T. (1997). "The role of classification schemes in Internet resource description and discovery: DESIRE Project".
- Williamson, N.J. (1997). "Knowledge structures and the Internet". *Knowledge Organisation for Information Retrieval).* Proceedings of the 6th International Study Conference on the Classification Research. FID. The Hague. pp. 23-27.
- Saeed, H., Chaudhry, A.S. (2001). "Potential of bibliographic tools to organise knowledge on the Internet: a review of the use of Dewey decimal classification scheme for organising Web-based information resources". *Knowledge Organisation,* Vol. 28. No. 1.

23

Constrains in Building Domain-Specific Topic Maps for the Discipline "Gender Studies in Informatics (GSI)"

INTRODUCTION

The 21st century has witnessed an overwhelming research output on GSI but due to publication scattering and want of organised database, the outcome of these publications have not been visible to the policy-makers and gender scientists. Further, the traditional document management system put a heavy burden on the user in the process of information access, extraction and interpretation. Besides, the absence of domain-specific semantic index in the discipline GSI results in irrelevant retrieval of records resulting in high recall but low precision. In addition, the existing system makes the process of literature-search difficult and time consuming. The exponential growth of literature, the information overload, and the time wasted in searching and browsing in the field of GSI demanded a semantic information processing system. This situation calls for the development of Knowledge Management System (KMS) in GSI by building dynamic (i) knowledge repositories, (ii) semantic index and (iii) knowledge maps and thereby alleviates the problems encountered by the user in the traditional document management system.

NEED FOR KNOWLEDGE MANAGEMENT SYSTEM IN GSI

The gender problem received wider attention in the field of informatics across the globe in the recent years. While discussions about these gender issues are useful, there is no effort to consolidate these deliberations in an organised form. Similarly, research on GSI is gaining momentum in the last two decades but there is no knowledge management system (KMS) or subject portal in this area. Therefore, an attempt has been made in the direction of constructing a KMS on a sample database in the field of GSI. It further attempts to identify the modalities for organising knowledge in GSI, despite the fact that there is an absence of supporting tools like the semantic index or subject thesaurus in this field. It further identifies the appropriate tools and techniques to standardise the unstructured and complex data in order to represent the knowledge in an accurate and precise manner without time consumption. Attempts have also been made to capture the intellectual structure of the domain through concept maps/topic maps.

Focus of the study

The focus of study is to trace the evolution of the research literature on GSI since the conceptual contours and their evolution in the discipline GSI is lacking. A large number of publications from 1983-2003 are analysed to determine themes and trends in GSI.

1. The study also aims at creating different knowledge maps consisting of different types of objects like keywords, institutions and authors.
2. It further aims at designing efficient information retrieval tools in GSI using co-occurrence analysis.

BACKGROUNDS AND PREVIOUS WORK

Creation of knowledge database like CiteSeer Citation index that provides access to over 300,000 articles is a pre-requisite to promote research in GSI. Automatic indexing and categorisation of publication have become an integral part of establishing knowledge repositories in the recent years. The propagation of digital libraries has fuelled much work in the area of automatic categorisation and meta-data extraction. Topic maps for repositories and for knowledge organisation have been the trend in the last decade, which is a step forward in the area of KMS. It is interesting to note that the application of co-occurrences of the word have become a common phenomena in the area of concepts categorisation and formation of semantic maps. The technique of co-word analysis also has been used for building thematic maps in the last years Callon 86, Callon 91, Courtial 89, Law 92, and Whitaker 89. Based on these review of literature, the following research questions were generated pertaining to the present study:

(i) How to define organised knowledge structures in GSI in a principled way? (ii) How to deal with the heterogeneous subject data in GSI? Which semantic relation types should we use and standardise in organising the dataset in GSI? How to construct the knowledge maps and what could be inferred from the maps?

METHODOLOGY

Topic map creation is a multi-stage modularised process and the following steps are followed in designing the topic maps for GSI. They are (i) extraction of concepts from the keywords (ii) fixing their semantic relations and (iii) creation of topic maps. A concept, in its most generic sense, can be any "thing" whatsoever—a person, an entity, really anything—regardless of whether it

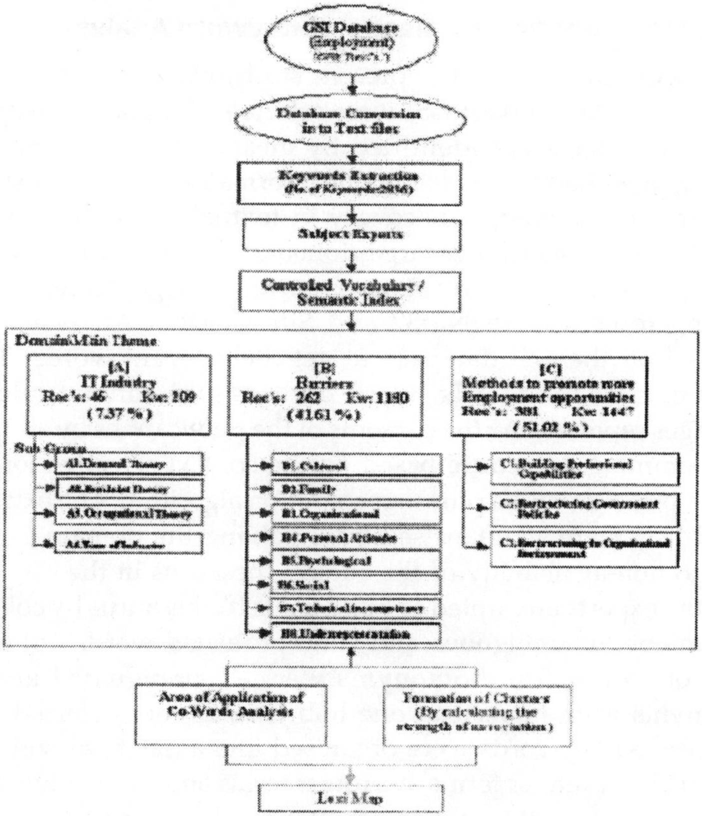

Fig. 1. Activities involved in building Topic Maps using Lexi maps & JCP techniques

exists or has an other specific characteristics, about which anything whatsoever may be asserted by any means whatsoever (H.H. Rath). Concept extractions are carried out by means of text mining. The process involved in the text mining are (a) segmentation; (b) phrase detection; (c) calculation of collocations and (d) integration of external knowledge. This process is carried out for all word types in the corpus. Semantic relation refers to the 'collocation of words' or the ' concept association between two words' and it is computed by joint occurrence of two given words A and B within a context. Creation of topic maps involves (i) formation of co-occurrence matrix, (ii) cluster formation and (iii) creation of maps. The following diagram represents the flow of activities in the formation of the topic maps.

Concept Extraction by Means of Keyword Analysis

For the purpose of the present study, about 689 documents dealing with the subject GSI were selected. The main concepts of these documents are identified by means of text mining. Text mining, also known as document information mining, text data mining, or knowledge discovery in textual database is an apt technology for analysing large domains of unstructured data in order to extract relevant patterns or knowledge. Here, the text mining tools like TexNet32 and Site Content Analyser were applied on the GSI database to get the relevant words. These tools extract the words, word-phrases and context-relevant passages representing the contents of the publications by adopting the stemming procedure based on the context sensitive longest-match principle and a phrase recognition algorithm. The extracted word lists were standardised by involving the domain-experts. Due to non-availability of the subject thesaurus in the discipline GSI, the experts attempted to build a macro-thesaurus by collating the unique, unambiguous and concept-related words out of the pool of words. The homonyms were disambiguated and the synonyms were hooked to one hub term as the preferred term. The filtered keywords were organised into a database with their appropriate broader terms, narrower terms and associative terms. Once extracted, the words are standardised and stored in a database (thesaurus) in order to be queried, data mined, summarised in natural language.

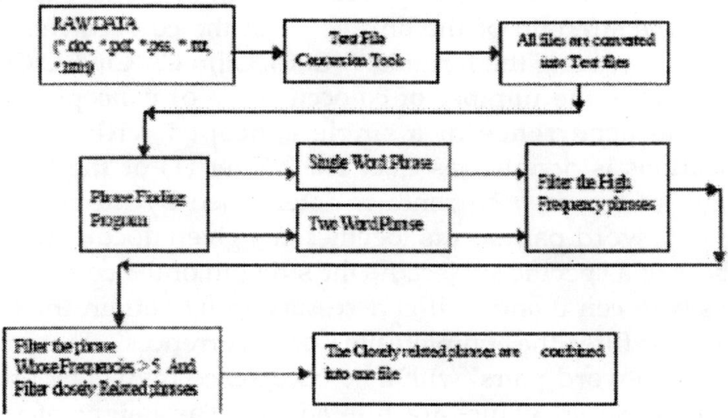

Fig. 2. Methods used for Extraction of Keywords from the Textile Corpus on GSI

Co-occurrence of Semantically Related Concepts

Since single concept does not convey meaningful connotations of a topic, associations of semantically related concepts are identified to form the domains and sub-domains of the subject GSI. The Salton's co-occurrence procedure is adopted to compute the cohesion between pairs of concepts in the given database and the results are presented in the co-occurrence matrix. Here, co-words are constructed by identifying the linkages or strength among the important concepts (keywords). The frequencies of the co-occurrences of concepts are ranked to form a matrix of co-word pairs. In this context, the occurrences of single concept in the whole sample were not taken into consideration for the formation of co-word matrix in order to avoid the spurious linkages. In the co-occurrence matrix, each cell in this symmetric matrix represents the number of times two concepts co-occur together (Cij). This method is followed by the 'co-word clustering method' and its purpose is to create groups or clusters of associated keywords (co-words) as a means to trace the numbers of research topics in the GSI database.

Building Lexi- Maps based on Co-occurrence Matrix

To understand the nature of relationship among the co-occurrence of concepts, lexi-map technique is adopted. In this method, each concept is considered as a node connected by the relation of co-occurrence to another node. Co-occurrences are the ties or links. The lexi-map is formed out of the co-occurrence matrix. The strength of the linkage 'S' of the co-occurrences are measured by using the formula: S(Ci,Cj, Cij)= Cij*Cij / CiCj 0 S 1 where 'Cij' is the number of co-occurrence of concepts i and j. Here, the occurrence of a single concept i within a set of publications is denoted as Ci.2. The higher (1) or the lower (0) strength of the co-occurrence is determined by the number of times a co-word pair occurs together in a given document or in a database of a specific subject. As the strength of the co-occurrence ranges between 0 and 1, it is necessary to fix certain thresholds in order to filter the 'uninteresting co-occurrences'. This implies that the 'co-word pairs' with a co-occurrence frequency under a certain threshold value, are filtered out. The height of such a 'noise' reduction threshold is determined in an ad hoc fashion and is usually set somewhere between 0.05 and 0.25 in this context in order to obtain a map representing the main linkages. The higher the occurrence of the co-word pair, the greater will be the strength of their association and vice-versa. From the strength of association one could identify the semantic relationship existing between the concepts. This also reflects the semantic structure of the existing subject.

Building Topic Maps of the Discipline GSI using JCP & Inclusion Index

Though 'Leximap' is a commonly used technique for the creation of topic maps, it has not given a methodology for positioning the neighboring concepts. Therefore, attempts have been made to adopt the 'Inclusion Index' and the 'Joint Conditional Probability Index' (JCP) to convert the co-occurrence data into a spatial configuration (or a map). While the Inclusion index determines the spatial occurrences of the concepts (distance) on the Topic maps, the JCP determines their strength of relations. Inclusion Index (I) is computed by using formula: (Cij/min(Ci, Cj)) where Cij is the count of all records in which the two concepts co-occur, and Ci and (Cj) are respectively counts of all records indexed. The degree of relatedness may vary between 0 to 1 where '0' indicates the state of no-co-occurrence; and '1' complete co-occurrence. The identification of relevant or master keywords can be fixed by setting a threshold value (5 occurrences). Only those nodes that have values between 0.25 and above are taken for analysis. The distances on the map, in this study are not an indication of the intensity of relationships. The strength of inclusion between concepts is determined by their co-occurrences. In this context, Joint Conditional Probability is used to measure the strength of relationship between a given pair of entities. The JCP of the co-occurrences of the concepts in a GSI database is calculated using the formula: ((Cij / Ci) + Cij /Cj)) /2 where Cij is the count of all records in which two concepts co-occur, and Ci (Cj) are the count of all records indexed. The JCP is 0 when the two concepts are never assigned to the same record, and approaches 1 as a joint assignment of that two concepts increase proportionately in comparison of that frequency of assignment in the database as a whole. The higher the JCP values, the stronger the links between the concepts. While the spatial distribution of the nodes are determined by the inclusion index, their strength of relations are fixed by the JCP index. It is the links between the concepts that are of interest, rather than the spatial arrangement; thus the structure of GSI has been arranged keeping in mind the better graphic display of the links.

ANALYSIS AND INTERPRETATION

Details of the Database Selected for the Present Study

The publication trend of the discipline 'Gender Studies in Informatics' has gained a momentum in the recent years. These publications have deliberated on a wide variety of topics viz. (i) gender situation in the IT labour market i.e. in the software, hardware, telecom, IT-enabled and business processing sectors; (ii) gender related barriers prevailing in IT related industries; (iii) and the strategies to maintain gender equity in the field of informatics etc. Parallel to the growth of publications on this discipline, there is a corresponding demand for literature on this area of research. This situation has demanded data consolidation and topic map generation to meet the user requirements. For the purpose of this study a sample database of 689 records covering 2836 keywords have been selected. Topic map techniques were applied on this basic data.

Outline of the Semantic Structure of the Discipline GSI

The 'knowledge management system (KMS)' of the discipline 'gender Studies in Informatics' is built on three major inter-related activities viz: (i) building a dynamic knowledge repository; (ii) developing a comprehensive and interactive semantic index or thesaurus and (iii) creating a knowledge or topic maps. The 'knowledge repository' component of the KMS involves in acquiring domain-specific knowledge in diverse forms (xml, html, doc, ps., etc) from heterogeneous sources like WWW, Journals, Conference Proceedings, Reports and Projects. The 'semantic index' component of the KMS involves in organising the heterogeneous knowledge on the basis of their epistemological and ontological structures. Such kind of organization results in dichotomous division of knowledge as 'conceptual model' and 'the representation paradigms' of the domain GSI. The following diagram explains the semantic structure of the discipline GSI. It is obtained by means of 'keyword extraction technique' and 'clustering technique' as suggested in the methodology part of this paper. It explains the organisational structure of the discipline GSI and enumerates the entities that form the domains, sub-domains, and facets.

Co-Occurrence Matrix

It is noticed that themes or topics are formed not by a single concept represented through a keyword but through a collection or combination of concepts (keywords). S.R. Ranganathan in his theory of 'Knowledge organisation' has discussed the various modes through which words would combine together and generate a new themes or topics. In this study, the co-word method is adopted to trace the formation of new themes. Table 3 depicts the number of times each concept (i) co-occurs with another concept (j) in the database taken for analysis. The cell value in the co-occurrence matrix represents the co-word pairs (Cij) selected for the current study. For instance, the theme 'C3' in Table-3 co-occurs with theme 'B3' 143 times & with 'C1' 172 times within a database of 689 documents having 2836 descriptors or keywords. In the same manner, the concept 'B3' co-occurs with concepts 'A1 & C1' 18 times and 110 times respectively. Similar is the case with concept 'A'. There is a closer correlation between the co-occurrence of the keywords and the formation of new themes. The more the co-occurrences of the keywords, the higher will be the emergence of new themes in any given subject. Though co-occurrence of themes is a meaningful measure to identify the cohesion existing between two thematic groups, it will not show the type and intensity of the relationship between the thematic pairs. In other words, it is observed that absolute frequencies of co-occurrences are a biased measure, which is otherwise known as "scale effect" in the raw co-occurrence data and therefore a further analysis like leximap techniques are applied on the co-occurrence data to identify the specific relations between the nodes. The procedure used for the computation of the leximap is given below:

(i) Compute pairwise co-occurrence for high-frequency words.

(ii) If this co-occurrence is lower than a threshold, then do not consider the pair any further.

(iii) For pairs that qualify, compute the cohesion value.

Cohesion(Ci, Cj)= co-occurrence-frequency/(sqrt (frequency (Ci)*frequency(Cj))) (1)

Leximap -Table Indicating the Strength of Relationship Between the Thematic Groups in GSI

Leximap table is based on the co-word pairs given in the co-word matrix (Table 1). The 15 thematic groups or sub-domains

Table 1. Co-Word Pairs Showing the Strength of Relationship Between the Thematic Groups in GSI

Ord.	*Node i(ci)*	*Node ii (<cj)*	*Co-oc (cij)*	*Stren-gth(s)*	*Range*
1	Building Professional Capabilities (C1)[291]	Restructuring the Organisational Environment (C3)[105]	172	0.2718	High
2	Organisational Bamers (B3) [232]	Restructuring the Organisational Environment (C3)[105]	143	0.2357	High
3	Organisational Barriers (B3) [232]	Building Professional Capabilities (C1)[291]	110	0.1792	High
4	Reconstructing Government Policies (C2) [721]	Restructuring the Organisational Environment (C3)[105]	105	0 1714	High

5	Organisational Barriers (B3) [232]	Underrepres entation (BS)[l 7Q]	SI	0 1654	High
6	Underrepres-entation (BS) [170]	Restructuring the Organisational Environment (C3)[105]	99	0.1542	High
7	Technical Incompetency (B7)[142]	Restructuring the Organisational Environment (C3)[10:5]	86	0.1393	High
8	Underrepres-entation (BS)[170]	Building Professional Capabilities (C1) [291]	80	0.1294	High
9	Building Professional Capabilities (C1) [291]	Reconstructing Government Policies (C2) [172]	79	0 1247	High
10	Organisational Barriers (C3) [232]	Technical Incompstiincy (B7) [421]	63	0.1205	High
11	Serial Banifi±s (B6) [133]	Restructuring the Organisational Enwon±nant (C3) [105]	7(5	0 11(51	High
12	Cultural Barriers (B3)[201]	Organisational Barriers (B3)[232]	56	0 112(5	Hi

derived out of the 2836 keywords representing the concept the GSI database have formed a 15 X 15 matrix. Out of the possible co-occurrences of themes formed from the above ma only 27 thematic pairs were chosen based on the threshold va prescribed (maximum>=5 co-occurences). Here, the wor representing each theme is considered as a node and t combination of these nodes with other nodes is measured b their strength value. Based on the calculated strength value (S) the type of relation existing between the thematic pairs viz: high, medium and low is determined. The following table illustrates the type of relationship exists between the co-word pairs.

The above table shows the linkages between the thematic pairs. For instance, the association of the node C3 is strong with a set of nodes as C1, B3, C2, B7 and B6; it is medium with another set of nodes such as A3 & A4 and it is weak with respect to B2 & B5. Similarly, the association of B3 is strong with respect to C1, B8, B7 &B1; and it is weak with respect to A1, A3 and B4. Same is the case with the other nodes. The association existing between the nodes given in table be represented in a more vivid manner through a diagram. The following diagram or map explains the assocition of the nodes in a better manner.

Leximap

The leximap shows the degrees of nodes on the map. The degree of a node 'X' is defined as a number of links incident with X and is denoted by d (X). The strong degree, medium degree and weak degree of a node 'X' is defined as number of strong, weak and medium links incident with it and it is denoted by $d_s(X)$, $d_m(X)$, $d_w(X)$ respectively. It is easy to verify that $d(X)=d_s(X)+d_m(X)+d_w(X)$. The above lexi-map indicates that $d(C3) = 10$, $d_s(C3)=6$, $d_m(C3)=2$, $d_w(C3)=2$; $d(B3) = 8$, $d_s(B3)=4$, $d_m(B3)=1$, $d_w(B3)=3$; $d(C1) = 8$, $d_s(C1)=4$, $d_m(C1)=3$, $d_w(C1)=1$; $d(B8) = 4$, $d_s(B8)=3$, $d_m(B8)=1$, $d_w(B8)=0$; $d(B1) = 3$, $d_s(B1)=0$, $d_m(B1)=2$, $d_w(B1)=1$; $d(C2) = 3$, $d_s(C2)=2$, $d_m(C2)=1$, $d_w(C2)=0$; $d(A4) = 3$, $d_s(A4)=0$, $d_m(A4)=2$, $d_w(A4)=1$; $d(A3) = 3$, $d_s(A3)=0$, $d_m(A3)=1$, $d_w(A3)=2$; We declare a node X as a, 'cluster' if $d_s(X) >= n$, for a given n. We take n =4 in the present context. Based on this criteria, it is observed that C1, C3 & B3 are clusters. Out of the 105 co-word combination for the 15 subject categories [n (n-1)/2], only 27 pairs have been taken for analysis filtering out the word-pairs fall below the threshold value (<5). It is observed from the Lexi-map that these 27 word pairs have lent themselves into three meaningful clusters. It is interesting to note that the subject C3 has linked with 9 other subject headings viz: A3, A4, B2, B3, B5, B6, B7, C1, C2 and formed the primary cluster. Similarly, the subject B3 has linked with 7 other subject headings viz; A1, A3, B1, B4, B7, B8, C1 and formed a secondary cluster. The tertiary cluster is formed by C1 in associated with other subject headings like A1, B1, B6, B8, C2. The following diagram illustrates the formation of the above mentioned clusters.

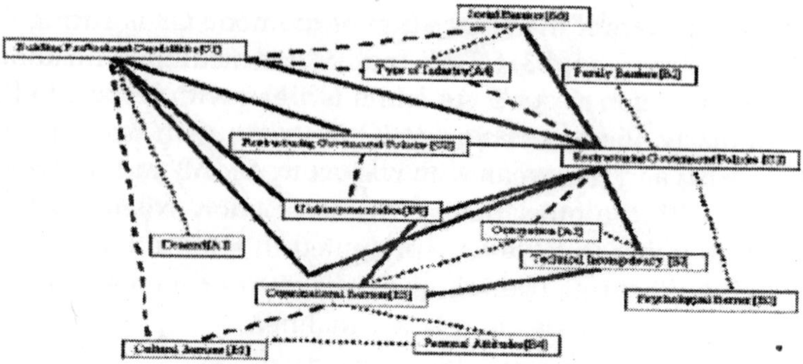

Fig. 3. Lexi-Map depicting the strength of relationship between the sub domain in the GSI

Core Theme Intermediate Theme Peripheral Theme

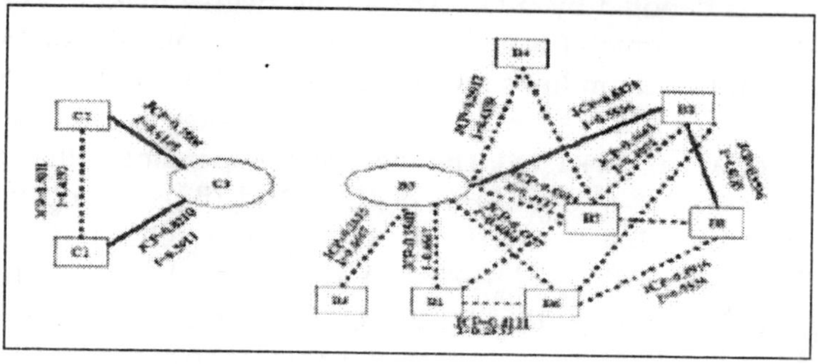

Fig. 4. Computation of Inter-relationship between the topics using JCP & Inclusion index

The inter and intra-relationship between the nodes have been calculated by using the clusion Index (I) and the Joint Conditional Probability Index (JCP). The inter-cluster relationships of the nodes A1-A4; B1-B8 and C1-C3 have been analysed. Based on the calculated values, the co-occurrence structure for the individual nodes are formed (Fig. 4). While considering the individual nodes in the group A, it is identified that none of the nodes in this group has any meaningful co-occurrence. On the other hand in group B, the node B3, form a cluster because of its strong and medium co-occurrence relationship with other nodes within their groups. For example d_s (B3)= 1 and d_m(B3) = 5. Similarly, in group C, the node C3 forms a cluster because of its stronger associat on with two other nodes C1 &C2. It is noted from the above analysis that the degree of potential nodes (d (X) = that form a cluster within groups are limited. Out of the 15 nodes taken for analysis only B3 &C3 have the potentiality to form a cluster.

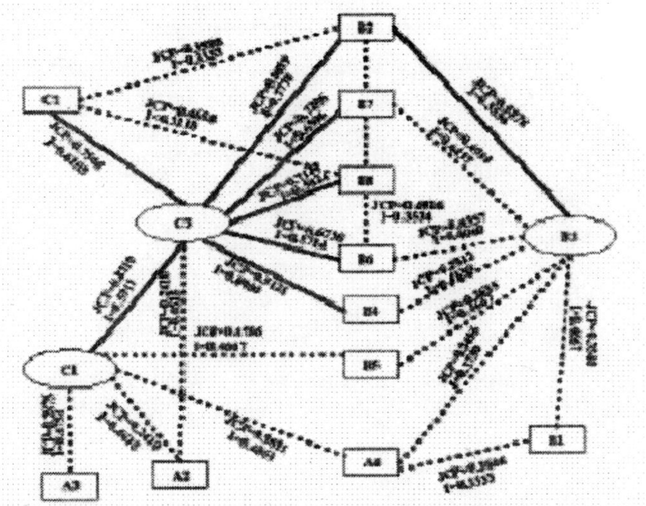

Fig. 5. Computation of Intra-relationship between the topics using JCP & Inclusion index

From figure 5, it is observed that out of the 15 nodes taken for analysis, only three nodes viz: C3, B3 & C1 forms the cluster because of their maximal degree. Out of these three clusters, the C3 has formed a larger cluster. For instance d (C3) = 8 where d_s (C3) =7, and d_m (C3) =1. In the same manner, d (B3) = 7; where d_s (B3) =1, and d_m (B3) =6. Similarly, d (C1) = 6 where d_s (C3) =1, and d_m (C3) =5. It is interesting to note that the intra relationship of the cluster C3 is stronger than the other clusters because of its stronger association both within (C1 & C2) and outside the clusters viz: B2, B4, B6, B7, B8 & A2.

CONCLUSION

In this paper an attempt has been made to map the structure of 'Gender Studies in Informatics' over a period of twenty years. This study has experimented with several techniques like the leximap, inclusion index, joint probability index etc in order to create topic maps of the given discipline. The inter and intra cluster maps applied here help to trace out the interactions among the sub-domains in the discipline GSI.

Index